A heart set free

The life of
Charles Wesley

Pre-eminent hymn-writer   **Fearless evangelist**

Powerful preacher

———

Arnold A. Dallimore

EVANGELICAL PRESS
12 Wooler Street, Darlington, Co. Durham, DL1 1RQ, England.

© Evangelical Press 1988
First published 1988
Second impression 1991

ISBN 0 85234 249 7

British Library Cataloguing-in-Publication data available

All Scripture references are taken from the Authorized
(King James) Version

This edition is not for sale in North America.

Typeset by Grassroots, London N3
Printed and bound in Great Britain by The Bath Press, Bath, Avon

The spirit of Charles Wesley's life

Oh, for a thousand tongues to sing
   My great Redeemer's praise!
The glories of my God and King,
   The triumphs of his grace!

My gracious Master, and my God,
   Assist me to proclaim,
To spread through all the earth abroad
   The honours of thy name.

Jesus! the name that charms our fears,
   That bids our sorrows cease;
'Tis music in the sinner's ears,
   'Tis life and health and peace.

He breaks the power of cancelled sin,
   He sets the prisoner free;
His blood can make the foulest clean
   His blood availed for me

Hear him, ye deaf; his praise, ye dumb,
   Your loosened tongues employ;
Ye blind, behold your Saviour come,
   And leap ye lame for joy.

               Charles Wesley (c. 1740).

Charles Wesley

Contents

Introduction

Charles Wesley and his brother John are widely known for their labours in the founding of Methodism. The year 1988 brings these men especially into the public mind again, for it marks the 200th anniversary of the death of Charles and the 250th of the conversion of each of them. These events are highly important to Christian men and women everywhere.

John Wesley has been kept before the public mind in numerous biographies, but the greatness and labours of Charles Wesley have been remembered only in part.

Charles is known for the quantity and quality of his hymns and many of them are still sung, Sunday by Sunday, in churches of all denominations. As a hymn-writer he can hardly be too highly esteemed. However, Charles Wesley was much more than a poet. During the first decade of Methodism's history its preachers were frequently confronted by vicious mobs, its congregations were attacked and several of its earliest meeting-houses were destroyed. Day after day, in the face of this situation, Charles proved himself a man of dauntless courage and his fearlessness served as an example to many others. Charles was also a fervent and powerful preacher and, as he declared the gospel, either in the meeting-house or on the street corner, his speech was 'in demonstration of the Spirit and of power'.

It is especially in these activities—as a pre-eminent writer of hymns, a fearless evangelist and a powerful preacher—that he is set forth in this book. I have not shunned to recognize his faults but, in keeping with the evidence, his abilities and accomplishments far outweigh any failings. I have endeavoured to understand his times and to enter into his thinking.

I express my thanks to Dr Frank Baker, the world's chief authority on the history of Methodism, for permission to quote from his works. I am also grateful to Mr D. W. Riley, F.L.A., Keeper of Printed Books at the John Rylands University, Manchester, for his help in providing photocopies of letters in the Methodist Archives.

I send this book forth with the prayer that some measure of the blessing that rested so bountifully on Charles Wesley's ministry may also rest on this effort to retell the story of his heroic life.

Arnold A. Dallimore
Cottam, Ontario, Canada.

Before I formed thee in the belly I knew thee;
and before thou camest forth out of the womb
I sanctified thee, and I ordained thee a prophet
unto the nations.

(Jeremiah 1 : 5).

When I call to remembrance the unfeigned faith
that is in thee, which dwelt first in thy grand-
mother Lois, and in thy mother Eunice; and I
am persuaded that in thee also.

(2 Timothy 1 : 5).

1.
Forebears of unyielding conviction

The year 1662 witnessed one of the darkest events in all English history. In an attempt to remove the remnants of Puritanism from the nation all ministers were ordered to conform to the doctrines and practices of the Church of England. Anyone who failed to do so was threatened with immediate dismissal from his living and, in what became known as 'The Great Ejection', nearly 2,000 men refused to conform and were thrust out from their churches and from their positions in the universities. They went forth with wives and families, many of them homeless and some into abject poverty. Some of England's most eminent scholars were among this noble company. The loss of the 2,000 men of conviction constituted a blow from which the Church of England failed to recover.

Moreover, further laws were enacted to prevent these 'nonconformists', or 'dissenters' as they were called, from continuing any ministry outside the church. They were forbidden to preach and any man who was found meeting in the company of more than five persons was liable to arrest. He might then suffer a ruinous fine, spend years in a filthy prison or even be banished to near slavery in a foreign land.

Two of the forebears of Charles and John Wesley were among these men of conviction and courage.

The first of these was their father's father. He was also named John Wesley and after graduating from Oxford University with the Master of Arts degree he conducted a vigorous ministry. But in 1662 he refused to conform and was ejected from his church in Devon. He had a wife and two young sons, but was now without a home and without an income. Nevertheless, he continued to preach. With the authorities hounding him, he fled from town to town, preaching daily in private houses. He was arrested more than once and spent years in prison, and during his final incarceration not only was he bereft of many of the necessities of life, but he had to sleep on the bare earth floor of the prison. Under the weight of his sufferings this good man's health gradually failed. His body grew steadily weaker, till he died at the age of forty-two.

The wife of this John Wesley also deserves our compassion. Throughout the greater part of her married life she lived without a regular home, saw her husband hunted and imprisoned and finally witnessed his passing at so early an age. And before her there now lay the lonely years of widowhood, without any definite means of support. She was left with four children to bring up, one of whom, Samuel Wesley, was to become the father of John and Charles.

Conditions were apparently somewhat better in the life of Susanna Annesley, the mother of the Wesleys. Samuel Annesley, Susanna's father, had graduated from Oxford with an M.A. and later was awarded the LL.D degree. His ministry in London proved exceptionally fruitful and he was known for his kindness to the sick and the poor.

In 1662, although he is said to have been receiving £700 a year, he refused to conform to the Church of England and was ejected from his living. He appears to have thereafter supported his family[1] by teaching. But he was not without difficulty, for 'The common informer sometimes tracked his steps with keen and malignant eye... "His nonconformity created him many outward troubles" and one magistrate was suddenly struck dead while signing the warrant for his apprehension.'[2]

After ten years of this persecution—in 1672—King Charles suspended certain of the laws prohibiting the Nonconformists' activities and they quickly sprang to life. Under this new measure of freedom Dr Annesley licensed a meeting-house and soon had a large congregation. 'During the next quarter of a century he was one of the most attractive, laborious and useful preachers of his day.' Various men of the nonconformist persuasion were frequent callers at his home and in their conversations the arguments against the Church of England were often presented and were made the subject of vigorous discussion.

Among the younger men who visited the Annesley home was Samuel Wesley. Following the death of his father, certain leaders among the nonconformists, regarding the young Samuel as a likely candidate for their ministry, had raised £40 a year towards his support and sent him to two excellent schools in London. Samuel later wrote an account which reported his life till he was twenty-six.[3] This document has often been overlooked in assessments of his personality and his activities, and we must consider it.

It is evident from Samuel's own statements that he was an intense personality, constantly industrious and capable in his studies. He had the gift of writing verse and frequently put it to use. He was in no way lacking in a sense of self-importance, and was, as he said, 'ambitious to be great and known in the world'. Among his young fellows he was pleasant and warm-hearted, but he also easily came into personal conflicts.

Samuel became acquainted with Susanna Annesley when he was twenty and she thirteen. But she was very mature for her age and possessed a strong and independent mind.

They may also have been attracted to each other by the fact that, although Samuel was the son of a man whose early death had been the result of his stand for nonconformity, and Susanna was the daughter of one who had suffered much for the same cause, both were now planning to leave the nonconformist ranks and to join the Church of England. It was not a matter of searching the Scriptures, for Samuel merely says he could see no reason for remaining outside of the church and Susanna, having often heard the subject discussed in her home, came to the same conclusion. They each withdrew from their nonconformist connection and became members of the Church of England. This action incensed Samuel's mother and strained relations between Susanna and her parents. But it revealed that, like their forebears, each of them possessed both the conviction and courage to take what they considered the necessary step, whatever sacrifice it might involve.

Samuel soon determined to enter the ministry of the Church of England. Knowing his decision would prove a further offence to his mother, he said nothing about it. But he got up very early one morning and set out, as he says, 'to foot it' to Oxford. He had very little money but was able to enter himself at Exeter College as a servitor. In this capacity he received free tuition and such money as the students he served chose to give him. He also received payment for assisting less capable students in their academic work and he wrote to friends and relatives seeking help, till he 'grew tired of asking and they of his doing so'.[4]

In addition, he gained royalties on a book of verse he published at this time. The oddity of some of the titles in this volume reveals something about his personal traits. He entitled the book *Maggots* and the frontispiece was a drawing of himself, wearing a crown of laurel and with a large maggot sitting on his head. Some of his titles were: 'The Tame Snake in a Box of Bran,' 'The Grunting of a Hog,' 'The Bear-Faced Lady,' 'A Cow's Tail,' 'To the Land of a Dog,' and 'A Box Like an Egg'.

Samuel was characterized by an exceptional determination. At one point his possessions were so few and his prospects so dark that he felt he must leave the university. Yet he struggled on and somehow constantly received just enough money to meet his immediate needs.

At one point, when his fortunes were at their lowest, on a winter morning he came upon an orphan boy lying under a hedge and weeping from cold and hunger. Samuel had only two pence at the time but he used one of them to buy a loaf of bread for the needy lad.

Despite his hardships Samuel remained at Oxford for four years and in 1688, at the age of twenty-six, he obtained the Bachelor of Arts degree and a few months later was awarded the M.A.

Matters now moved speedily for Samuel. He was ordained to the ministry of the Church of England and became the curate of a small church in London. The salary was merely £28,[5] but within two months he married Susanna Annesley. He says, 'I had no excuse in being married so hastily, before my fortunes were settled, unless a most passionate love be taken for one.'[6]

There was much reason, however, for Samuel's 'most passionate love'. No full description of Susanna has come down to us, but we have one of her sister, Elizabeth Dunton. It reads, 'Tall; of good aspect; hair of light chestnut colour; dark eyes; mouth small and sweet; air, somewhat melancholy, but agreeable; neck long and graceful; complexion fair; piety scarce paralleled, and wit solid. She is sweetly modest and has all kinds of virtues.'[7] Susanna was also tall and erect and she carried herself in a dignified and purposeful, yet graceful manner. Her two sisters are spoken of as beautiful women but she is said to have surpassed them both. She was steadfast in mind and spirit, strongly self-disciplined and constant in her devotion to God.

Samuel served his curacy for merely a few months. Wishing to advance himself he resigned and became chaplain on a naval vessel, where his salary was £70 a year. But he found this life sorely disagreeable, for he was frequently seasick and he also reported, 'I was very ill used, and nearly starved and poisoned ... nor had we either fish or butter in our ship and our beef stunk intolerably.'[8] Accordingly he soon gave up his chaplaincy and returned to London. But during his absence his wife had borne him a son, named like himself, Samuel.

After some months of difficulty Samuel accepted a curacy in the Lincolnshire village of South Ormsby. Here the salary was £50, and although he spoke of the parsonage as '... a mean cot, composed of reeds and clay', at least it was free. The Wesleys, however, were by now in debt. Samuel owed money for expenses incurred during his stay in London, and he now borrowed, he tells us, a further £20 to cover the expense of his removal to Lincolnshire. Moreover, he had as yet no furniture and expected that his father-in-law, Dr Annesley, would meet its costs but in this hope he was disappointed. So already at this early stage in their union the Wesleys were in debt and throughout their married lives they would never be free from the burden of owing money.

In addition to his ministry Samuel worked as an author. He assisted his brother-in-law, John Dunton, in editing a paper, the *Athenian Oracle*. Samuel wrote on several subjects but his chief contribution was in supplying answers to questions on a wide range of biblical and philosophical subjects. He also produced a work which greatly influenced the future course of his life. This was a *Life of Christ*, written in verse and illustrated with sixty copper plates. He asked for and received permission to dedicate this volume to Her Majesty, Queen Mary. In a bitter revolution the previous monarch, the Catholic King James II, had been exiled and William and Mary, strong Protestants, had been brought to the throne. Public opinion, however, was divided as to their reception and many people looked on them as usurpers.

Accordingly, in his *Introduction* Samuel declared his loyalty to the queen and praised her person. This was the first published declaration of allegiance to the new queen. As a result, the king[9] saw to it that Samuel was appointed to a much better living—that of St Andrew's parish, Epworth, with a salary of some £200 a year. Thus after six years at South Ormsby, where

six children had been born to them, in 1697 the Wesleys moved
to this second Lincolnshire curacy. They hoped that, with the
much larger income,[10] better times awaited them. But matters
did not go as well as they desired.

Many Anglican parishes in those days possessed a small
acreage known as 'glebe lands' and by farming this land the
incumbent could increase his income. Samuel therefore became
a part-time farmer, but the enterprise cost him more than he
made. A barn blew down and he had to have it rebuilt. He also
incurred unexpected expenses in entering his new parish, he was
making a small annual allowance to his mother and was seeking to pay off his past debts. After he had been in Epworth for
three years he was forced to admit that he had fallen far behind,
and he wrote to the Archbishop of York, stating, 'I [am]
ashamed... to confess that I [am] three hundred pounds in debt,
when I have a living of which I have made two hundred pounds
per annum...'[11] The archbishop, knowing Samuel's deep learning and force of character, and probably recognizing also that
he was not adept at business, came to his rescue and paid a considerable portion of what he owed.

Samuel was greatly disliked by several of his parishioners. We
shall pause to consider some of the reasons for this.

As a clergyman he possessed an authority which could extend
into certain legal matters. For example, it was his right to receive
a tithe of the crops produced by his people. One day he found
a man keeping a portion of the tithe for himself. Samuel seized
him, marched him into town and let the crowd that gathered
in the market-place know of the wrong deed the man had
committed.

But he was especially 'harsh and severe' with adulterers. We
are told that at times, 'The criminal was seen standing for three
successive Sabbaths, on the damp mud floor in the centre of the
church, without shoes or stockings; bareheaded; covered with
a white sheet; and shivering with cold. This was "doing
penance;" and the offender publicly stood forth as a warning
to others...'[12] There was one instance recorded in which, had
Samuel continued in his intention of forcing a guilty woman to
perform this public penance on three successive Sundays, she
would almost certainly have died, and he therefore called it off.

Samuel also exasperated people by a sudden change in his
stand on politics. At the time of a Parliamentary election he

declared he was in favour of the candidate for a certain party, but he suddenly changed his mind and declared himself for the man representing the opposite party. In their dislike, some men burned his crop of flax, and others seriously wounded his dog and stabbed his cattle.

One of Samuel's creditors, who was hostile towards him and to whom he owed £30, had him arrested and thrown into the debtor's prison at Lincoln. In a letter written in the jail he stated, 'My wife ... sent me her rings because she had nothing else to relieve me with; but I returned them...'[13] The rector was imprisoned for at least four months, and was finally rescued through the help once again of the archbishop and of other well-to-do persons.

During Samuel's time in jail his wife and family lived on bread and milk and following his release the archbishop wrote asking Susanna if she had ever been left hungry. She replied, 'My lord, I will freely own to your Grace that, strictly speaking, I never did want bread. But then I had so much care to get it before it was ate, and to pay for it after, as has often made it very unpleasant to me. And I think to have bread on such terms is the next degree of wretchedness to having none at all.'[14]

Samuel's imperious manner is evident also in the following episode. Although he had declared himself strongly in favour of King William and Queen Mary, Susanna was of a different opinion. She held to the doctrine of the divine right of kings and therefore she believed the exiled King James was still the rightful monarch. After they had been married fourteen years, Samuel, realizing that she did not say 'Amen' to his prayer for the king in the family devotions, vigorously asserted that he could no longer live with her. He left home[15] and as the weeks came and went she heard nothing from him. Susanna was left with six little ones to bring up but he had stated he would support them.

Samuel went to London and applied for a position as a naval chaplain. After an absence of five months he returned to Epworth, looked after certain items of business, and then, 'He left me,' wrote Susanna, 'with a resolution never to see me more.' He took what he thought was his final departure, but only reached the far end of Epworth when the rectory caught fire.[16] Being informed that his house was burning he hurried back and found two thirds of it destroyed. Recognizing that his responsibility to his wife and his little ones was increased, he decided to remain at Epworth and rebuild the house. However, he does not seem to have felt any remorse over his action. Not surprisingly, Susanna could no longer be her former self and she appears never to have regained her full respect for him.

Samuel's attitude towards Susanna is reflected in the following lines that he wrote:

> She graced my humble roof, and blest my life,
> Blessed me by a far greater name than wife;
> Yet still I bore an undisputed sway,
> Nor was't her task, but pleasure to obey;
> Scarce thought, much less could act, what I denied;
> In our low house there was no room for pride;
> Nor need I e'er direct what still was right,
> Still studied my convenience and delight.
> Nor did I for her care ungrateful prove,
> But only used my power to show my love;
> Whate'er she asked I gave, without reproach or grudge
> For still she reason asked, and I was judge;
> All my commands requests at her fair hands,
> And her requests to me, were all commands;
> To others' thresholds rarely she'd incline;
> Her house her pleasure was, and she was mine;
> Rarely abroad, or never, but with me,
> Or when by pity called, or charity.[17]

It is evident Samuel Wesley was something of a dual personality. On the one hand he was a true clergyman, a thorough scholar, highly industrious and he manifested an earnest spiritual concern for his flock and his family. But on the other hand he was a man of tremendous self-importance and felt himself to be in the right whatever he did. We must honour him for his deep learning and the steadiness with which he pursued his ministry, but also regret the weak spots in his behaviour.

Nevertheless, both Samuel and Susanna were characterized by extraordinary strength of will. He proved indomitable, as we shall see, in the nearly twenty-five years that he devoted to writing a commentary in Latin on the book of Job, and she was to prove equally strong in the manner in which she educated her family and in the patience with which she bore her numerous trials.

Charles Wesley's two grandfathers had been men who were

willing to sacrifice their comforts and even life itself for the sake of what they deemed divine truth and this same unyielding conviction was manifest also in their children, Samuel and Susanna Wesley.

It has been recorded that Mrs Wesley, when she resumed her educational duties in the new rectory-house, added to her programme the singing of one or more of the psalms. The voice of melody is seldom lost on the mind of the young, and how much that new duty contributed to produce the love of poetry and psalmody which in so marked a manner characterized both John and Charles Wesley in after years, it would be impossible to tell.

(George J. Stevenson, 1876).

2.
The boy at home and at school

Charles Wesley was a premature baby. He was born on 18 December 1707, '... several weeks before his time; he appeared dead rather than alive... He did not cry, nor open his eyes, and was kept wrapped up in soft wool until the time when he should have been born according to the usual course of nature, and then he opened his eyes and cried.'[1]

There were then seven children at home: six girls and John. An elder son, Samuel junior, was now nearly eighteen, but he had left Epworth some years earlier to attend the Westminster School in London.

The house in which Charles began to grow up in the company of his parents, his six sisters and John, is described as '... built all of timber and plaister, and covered with thatche, the whole building being contrived into three stories, and disposed in seven chief rooms—a kitchinge, a hall, a parlour, a butterie, and three large upper rooms, and some others of common use'.[2]

Yet before long this house was to be swept away in flames. On a winter night, at a time when Charles was fourteen months old, the roof caught fire. Samuel hurriedly awakened his family, but the flames, blown by a strong wind, raced rapidly through the building. A nurse picked up Charles and quickly carried him to safety. With some difficulty the girls made their way down the stairs and some of them found it necessary to climb out through a window. Susanna, who was pregnant at the time, moved more slowly and was burned about the legs as she waded through a wall of flame.

Of course, a crowd gathered immediately, and Samuel made his way among them, anxiously searching for his children and rejoicing when he found them safe. Suddenly a cry was heard from an upstairs window. It was John, a boy of five, and he was surrounded by flames. Many onlookers felt there was no way he could be rescued and Samuel, thinking him lost, solemnly commended his soul to God. But despite the danger a man took his stand beneath the window and another climbed to his shoulders. John came immediately to his arms and was lowered to the ground. That moment the roof fell in and the flames consumed the spot where he had been standing only seconds earlier. John never forgot the event and throughout his life he frequently referred to himself as 'a brand snatched out of the burning'.

While the house was being rebuilt the children were lodged with friends and relatives. Two of the girls went to Gainsborough and two others to the home of Samuel's brother Matthew, a well-to-do surgeon in London. Charles was at this time only just beginning to take his first steps, and his parents, who remained at Epworth, kept him with them. Susanna soon had another little one to look after as well, for less than a month after the fire Kezia, the last of her nineteen children, was born.

The Wesley children had never been allowed any close association with other families in Epworth. But now they came into contact with various people, many of whom had standards much lower than those of the Wesley rectory. At the end of a year, although the rebuilding was not entirely finished, the family returned. It was soon evident that the children had picked up words and manners they had not known before.

Mrs Wesley acted without delay to deal with this situation. For one thing, she had the children come to her, one at a time, in the evenings, for instruction in the Scriptures and in righteous living, and she considered the saving of their souls her paramount responsibility. She also continued this instruction in their daily schooling, for she taught them at home and their lives were conducted according to a definite method.

This had been true from the start and she stated, 'When turned a year old they were taught to fear the rod and to cry softly.'[3] As they made progress the rod was used following any infringement of the stated will of either parent, while all acts of obedience were commended and encouraged. The school was composed of two periods of three hours each, and it began and closed with prayer and the singing of psalms. 'There was no such thing as loud talking, or playing allowed,' she stated, 'but everyone kept close to business for the six hours.'[4] She also enunciated the principle that in training children, 'The first thing to be done is to conquer their will and bring them into an obedient temper,'[5] and she worked hard to inculcate the need for honesty, industry and reliability.

We read of the Wesley girls playing cards, but in general toys were unknown in the family and the children grew up recognizing the seriousness of life. There were books and singing in the home but the girls also fed chickens and ducks and worked in the garden. Despite his considerable salary[6] Samuel constantly struggled to meet his debts and Susanna and her daughters lived almost in penury. Samuel was clearly impractical in the affairs of daily life and, after visiting the Epworth rectory, his brother Matthew wrote severely upbraiding him for having his house only half-furnished and his daughters very poorly dressed.

Regrettably, little about the boyhood of Charles Wesley has come down to us. We know, however, that he learned the alphabet in one day, that he continued to make good progress and before long was able to express himself correctly in speech and in writing. His father also took part in his education and it was from him that Charles acquired the foundation of knowledge of the Greek and Latin authors on which he would later build a deep classical knowledge.

Charles must undoubtedly have been writing verse during his boyhood. Although none of his early compositions have been preserved, we must assume that the man who later proved so capable in the writing of poetry could not but have written it from the time his education began. Moreover, the deep sensitivity, the tendency to high excitement, followed often by deep depression—the emotions that characterized much of his later life—must also have already been manifest in the boy.

Before long, however, Charles was robbed of John's strong company. Despite the struggle with debt, Samuel Wesley was determined to give his boys the best education England could provide and he placed John, at the age of eleven, in the Charterhouse School in London. Accordingly, during the next year Charles was left much in the company of his sisters and his mother.

But when Charles was only eight years old he too left Epworth to attend school in London. His older brother Samuel was serving as an usher (a teaching assistant) at the Westminster School, which was attached to the famous Westminster Abbey. This

brother, knowing his father's wishes for his sons, arranged that
Charles should live at his home, which was adjacent to the abbey,
and consented to pay the costs of his training, leaving his father
responsible only for his clothing.

The course of study in an English school of those days was
especially planned to instil a knowledge of the classical
languages—their grammar, history and literature. Discipline was
severe at Westminster and the cane was used with frequency.
Charles, possessing as he did a mercurial personality, apparently
found it difficult at first to maintain a long concentrated study.
But it is evident that under the watchful care of Samuel he
increasingly disciplined himself till he worked with steady
diligence.

Although he was still so young, Charles was kept from indulg-
ing in the evil ways of the world around him. Samuel guided
his life during these days at school and saw to it that he lived
according to the principles he had learned at home. He also
inculcated a still firmer adherence to the Church of England,
confirming his belief in her doctrines and increasing his reverence
for her sacraments.

Charles had been at Westminster only a few months when
he heard some very strange news from Epworth. Beginning about
1 December 1716, several weird noises were heard in the rectory, and the Wesleys immediately concluded the house was
haunted. In fact the girls soon named the 'ghost' after a former
inhabitant of the rectory, terming it 'Old Jeffrey'. There were
numerous reports of knockings in the walls, of an animal 'like
a badger' running in the house, of door-latches lifted by an
unseen hand, and of a bed being elevated repeatedly while one
of the girls was sitting on it. In order to test 'Old Jeffrey' Samuel
sometimes omitted saying the prayer for the king at the family
devotions, and each time he did so the 'ghost' was silent. The
noises continued for two months and then ceased as suddenly
as they had begun.

Inexplicable as this phenomenon may be, we do well to notice
some possible explanations which have been put forward and
which may help towards understanding it.

In the first place, just before it all started the rector had for
some weeks been preaching against the practice of witchcraft.
The noises may have been a series of mischievous pranks by
certain of his parishioners, by way of response. Or perhaps some

of the parishioners who worked on the rebuilding of the rectory following the fire may have installed some kind of knocker attached to a hidden cord, which could be pulled from outside and which they now decided to use, to torment the rector.

The suggestion was made at the time that one of the girls—probably Hetty—stayed up late entertaining a boy-friend. There was also a rumour that a man was seen escaping through the sink stone—a wide stone drain that projected through the kitchen wall.

In those days many people in England believed in ghosts and on hearing some sound at night (made perhaps by a bird in the eaves or by rats) the Wesleys may therefore have jumped to the conclusion that the house was haunted.[7] It is also probable that they imagined many of the details they afterwards spoke about. The suddenness with which the phenomenon started and stopped strongly suggests a human agent.

The readiness of the Wesleys to believe that this was in fact a ghost is an indication of how easily all the family accepted the idea of the preternatural. Susanna thought for a time that the presence of 'Old Jeffrey' might indicate that one of their sons—either Samuel, John or Charles, all of whom were in London—had died. And John later suggested that it might have been the judgement of God upon his father for having left Susanna fourteen years earlier over her refusal to respond to his prayer for the king.

At the Westminster School, among its more than 400 boys, there was much rough play and many an attempt at bullying, which often led to fist-fighting. But although Charles was of smaller than average build, he proved himself exceptionally capable in this activity. At times he also defended others who needed help, and among these was a Scottish boy named James Murray. Because Murray's father was believed to favour the exiled King James, he was ill treated by some of the Westminster lads, and more than once Charles came to his aid. In later life James Murray became England's Chief Justice and was created Lord Mansfield. In adult life the paths of Charles Wesley and Lord Mansfield sometimes crossed and on such occasions there was evidence of warm mutual respect, in remembrance of their former friendship.

During his years at Westminster Charles was offered the possibility of becoming the heir of a relative—a wealthy Irish

gentleman named Garett Wesley. Charles's father allowed him
to choose for himself, and since to accept would have meant a
rather worldly life, Charles gave evidence of already possessing
high principles by refusing. The offer was then made to another
relative, Richard Colley. Colley accepted and changed his name
to 'Wesley', and in later years was made Lord Mornington. One
of his grandsons, Arthur Wellesley (another spelling of the name
'Wesley') rose to lasting fame: he is best known by his title 'the
Duke of Wellington' and is remembered as the commander of
the English armies in the defeat of Napoleon at Waterloo.

When Charles was still only thirteen he had the opportunity
of being selected to become what was known as 'a King's
Scholar'. It was also termed 'being elected into college', for those
who gained this standing would undoubtedly also be granted
an entrance into either Oxford or Cambridge. Each candidate
first chose a 'help'—an older boy who was to be his tutor through
this time of particular testing. We are told, 'Soon after Christmas
preparation began. This consisted of some months' severe work,
under the most enthusiastic tuition. At half past six or a quarter
to seven every morning the candidate came ''up college'' to the
bedside of his help with his Latin and Greek grammars. Hundreds of questions and answers upon these were gradually
mastered...

'As the time drew near, preparation filled every leisure
moment. The help caned his man if he was idle or did not attend
at the appointed time. At last, on the first Monday in Lent, the
''Challenges'' began.'[8]

The headmaster took his chair, with the two candidates standing in front of him, and the helps with their grammar and
epigram books on either side. The boys then put questions to
each other, using every possible device for puzzling the opponent.
'For eight or ten weeks the struggle lasted, both morning and
afternoon, on three or four days a week. A hundred Greek
epigrams and a book of selections from Ovid's *Metamorphoses* were
the only books, but the questions on grammar were such that
a challenge between two boys has been known to last from early
in the morning till nine at night.'[9]

Charles succeeded in this gruelling test. He became a King's
Scholar—a standing which absolved him from all further tuition
fees and allowed him to live in the school's dormitory and to
have his meals in the dining hall without charge. It also raised

him to the position of 'Captain of the School', and in this role he served as a liaison between the masters and the boys.

Charles's time at Westminster was well spent. It must be realized that during much of that period he had been a guest in the home of his brother, that this brother was a clergyman and that he lived virtually in the shadow of Westminster Abbey. In later pages we shall see Charles vigorously contending for the Church of England and willing to part with anyone in his unyielding allegiance to her. We therefore do well to recognize the strong influence he was under throughout these formative years of his life.

During these years Charles became well learned in classical studies. He developed a wide knowledge of Latin and Greek, their grammar, their history and their chief authors. He proved to possess a native affinity for the classics and they became so much a part of his being that they came to mould his thinking and were manifest in his speech and writing.

The picture we have of Charles Wesley at this period of his life is of someone who was exceptionally sprightly and abounding in activity. His mind was quick and he would make sudden decisions and respond to a challenge with vehemence. His spirit was basically warm and friendly, but he could prove the avowed enemy of anything he considered wrong or unfair.

Above all, his nature was essentially that of the born poet. We have no knowledge as to what extent he actually wrote verse during these years, but we know that throughout this time he constantly revealed the poet's emotions. He was deeply sensitive and although he could be in rapturous joy in one hour, in the next he could be deeply despondent. Not so much by definite intention as by native inclination, he expressed his thoughts in sentences that were marked by the harmony of his words, and in phrases characterized by rhythm and balance.

As we have seen, however, any boy who became a King's Scholar, 'could, by ordinary application, make sure of a scholarship at Christ Church, Oxford'.[10] This sequence proved true for Charles Wesley and, having succeeded so well in his studies at Westminster, after eleven years there he prepared to leave it and follow his grandfathers, his father and his brothers in becoming a student at that great English seat of learning, Oxford University.

Charles Wesley was a man made for friendship; who, by his cheerfulness and vivacity, would refresh his friend's heart; with attentive consideration, would enter into and settle all his concerns; so far as he was able, would do anything for him, great or small; and, by a habit of openness and freedom, leave no room for misunderstanding.

(John Gambold, a university associate).

3.
The youth at Oxford

Charles Wesley entered Oxford University in 1726 at the age of nineteen.

During his years at Westminster he had been under the watchful eye of his brother, Samuel. But now he was free from this oversight, and around him there lay many moral dangers. These were the days in which the standards of the nation had been grievously lowered. Drunkenness, gambling, stealing and immorality were common, and Deism—the belief that God is merely an impersonal 'First Cause'—was widely accepted.

In later years Charles described the university as a place

> Where learning keeps its loftiest seat,
> And hell its firmest throne.

He also testified,

> Bolder I with my fellows grew,
>   Nor yet to evil ran,
> But envied those who dared break through,
>   And copy lawless man;
> From parents' eye far off removed,
>   I still was under thine,
> And found, for secret sin reproved,
>   The government divine.[1]

But at first Charles was not a good student. Though he refrained from seeking 'the pleasures of sin', he also admitted, 'My first year at college I lost in diversions.'[2]

At Oxford Charles was frequently in the company of his brother John. For almost a year John had been a Fellow of

Lincoln College—a position that provided him with a set of rooms
at the college and an income of £40 a year. He was soon to earn
the degree of Master of Arts and to be elected Greek Lecturer
and Moderator of the Classes.

Not far from Oxford there lay a magnificent rural area, the
Vale of Evesham. For some time John had been friendly with
a circle of refined young ladies who lived in the villages of
Buckland, Broadway and Stanton, and Charles now joined him
in this association. With their beautiful stone houses and Gothic
churches, set in delightful surroundings, these places could not
have failed to awaken romantic feelings in the hearts of the
Wesleys. They undoubtedly also were aware of the difference
between the calm and dignified life of their acquaintances in these
villages and the life of purposefulness and intensity to which they
had been accustomed in Epworth.

With these young ladies the Wesleys sang, danced and played
cards. Their conversation chiefly concerned polite literature and
formal religion, and they referred to one another by pseudo-
classical names: John Wesley was 'Cyrus'; Charles 'Araspes';
Mrs Pendarves (a young widow) 'Aspasia'; Ann Granville
'Selima'; Sally Kirkham (Mrs Capone) 'Varanese'; and others
of their circle were known as 'Sappho' and 'Serena'. The Wesleys
flirted innocently with this pleasant company and both came close
to falling in love.

But from 1726 onwards John's reading tended to centre his
thoughts more on religious matters than on social pleasures. He
read Thomas à Kempis' *Christian Pattern*, Jeremy Taylor's *Holy
Living* and *Holy Dying* and a little later, William Law's *Serious
Call* and *Christian Perfection*.[3] 'These convinced me, he wrote,
more than ever of the absolute impossibility of being half a Christian. And I determined through his grace ... to be all devoted
to God, to give him all my soul, my body and my substance.'[4]

With this new determination John now largely gave up his
friendship with the young ladies and laboured in his efforts to
serve God. He also decided to enter Holy Orders and in August
1727 (eight months after Charles had arrived at Oxford) he was
ordained a deacon.[5] Shortly afterwards he temporarily left
Oxford to become curate to his father at Epworth and Wroote.

Charles had undoubtedly benefited from John's influence, yet
John said of him, 'He pursued his studies diligently, and led
a regular harmless life: but if I spoke to him about religion, he

would warmly answer, "What, would you have me to be a saint all at once?" and would hear no more.'[6]

During his second year at Oxford, however, Charles also experienced a reformation. He too read Jeremy Taylor and Thomas à Kempis and he gave up his diversions. In order to judge himself as to the use of his time and the nature of his thoughts he determined to keep a diary, and he wrote to John asking his advice as to what matters he should record. He then went on to report the change he was experiencing, stating, 'God has thought fit... to deny me at present your company and assistance. It is through him strengthening me, I trust to maintain my ground till we meet. And I hope that neither before nor after that time, I shall relapse into my former state of insensibility ... 'tis owing, in great measure, to somebody's prayers (my mother's most likely) that I am come to think as I do; for I cannot tell myself how or when I awoke out of my lethargy—only that it was not long after you went away.'[7]

Several authors have assumed that these experiences of improvement in the lives of the Wesleys were their conversions. But we must recognize that they as yet had no true knowledge of the way of salvation—justification by faith—which they were to experience with life-transforming power some ten years later. We may best look upon these earlier events as humanly-effected change.

This alteration led Charles into what was to prove a historic development. He wrote, 'Diligence led me into serious thinking: I went to the weekly sacrament, and persuaded two or three other students to accompany me, and to observe the method of study prescribed by the statutes of the university. This gained me the harmless name of Methodist.'[8]

Two of these students, William Morgan and Robert Kirkham, began to meet regularly with Charles to read the Greek New Testament and certain favourite authors, and to assist one another in maintaining a fervently religious life. It was a special joy to these men when in November 1729, after an absence of more than two years, John Wesley returned to Oxford. Since he was not only older than the others, but was also superior in learning and possessed a native gift of taking charge, the leadership of the little group was immediately accorded to him. Other students became attracted to this activity, including Benjamin Ingham, John Gambold, John Clayton, Thomas Broughton,

James Hervey, John Hutchings, Charles Kinchin and George Whitefield, who were all added to this fellowship by 1733.

The practices of this company were mocked by other students and won for them such names as 'Bible Bigots', 'Sacramentarians' and 'Methodists'. They were also known as 'the Holy Club', and we may best refer to them by this title.[9]

These men lived according to rule. They rose early, spent time in devotions and then set about fulfilling their plan of the day's activities. At nightfall each wrote a diary entry, examining his use of time and judging himself for any wasted moment. They attended the sacrament each Sunday, fasted on Wednesdays and Fridays, regularly visited Oxford's two prisons—the Bocardo and the Castle—and contributed to a fund by which they aided the prisoners' children. They were certain that these good works were somehow effective towards the saving of their souls.

George Whiteheld said of the Holy Club men, 'Never did persons strive more earnestly to enter in at the strait gate. They kept their bodies under, even to an extreme. They were dead to the world, and willing to be accounted as the dung and offscouring of all things, so that they might win Christ. Their hearts glowed with the love of God and they never prospered so much in the inner man as when they had all manner of evil spoken against them falsely from without.'[10]

The Wesleys were encouraged in these activities by their father. To John he wrote, 'Go on, then, in God's name, in the path to which your Saviour has directed you, and that track wherein your father has gone before you. For when I was an undergraduate at Oxford, I visited those in the castle there, and reflect on it with great satisfaction to this day. Walk as prudently as you can, though not fearfully, and my heart and prayers are with you.'[11]

In 1730 Charles informed his father that he was now tutoring a few pupils and was thus earning something towards his own support. His father replied, 'You may easily guess whether I were not pleased... both on your account and on my own. You have a double advantage by your pupils, which will soon bring you more if you will improve it, as I firmly hope you will, in taking the utmost care to form their minds to piety, as well as learning.'[12]

By 1734 Samuel had suffered three accidents. The most severe occurred when he was suddenly jolted out of a wagon and fell directly on his head, after which he remained in a dazed condition for some hours. He had spent more than twenty years in writing a commentary in Latin on the book of Job and by 1735 he had it almost finished. But he no longer had the normal use of his right hand, having suffered a partial paralysis, and was making great efforts to write with his left.

Samuel now recognized that his life was drawing towards its close. He knew that when he died Susanna would be left without an income or a home unless one of his sons could be persuaded to take the Epworth living. But Samuel junior had recently left Westminster and was now the head master of a school at Tiverton in Devon, and therefore could not consider it. Charles was not a possibility for he was not yet ordained. Accordingly he wrote to John, urging him to apply for the living and presenting several reasons why he should do so.

At first John disagreed. He told his father he wanted to remain at Oxford and there continue his efforts to increase in knowledge and piety. But under further persuasion he submitted to his father's idea. He wrote to Thomas Broughton, who, as a curate at the Tower of London, was in touch with men of influence, and asked that he make application on his behalf. Broughton replied, telling him the application was too late, as the living had already been given to another man.[13]

Both Charles and John held before them the prospect of spending their lives as tutors at Oxford. They had not the least idea of the careers of fiery evangelism on which they would later embark. Charles had obtained his Bachelor's degree in 1730 and proceeded to his Master's, which he received in 1733, and both he and John were well suited to a lifetime in the university.

Their father, meanwhile, was failing rapidly. In July 1734 Charles wrote to his brother Samuel, 'My father declines so fast, that before next year he will, in all probability, be at his journey's end; so that I must see him now, or never more with my bodily eyes. My mother seems more cast down at the apprehension of his death than I thought she could have been; and what is still worse, he seems so too.'[14]

The rector grew steadily weaker till, on 25 April 1735, he passed away. Charles, again writing to his brother Samuel, stated, 'The fear of death he had entirely conquered, and at last gave up his latest human desires of finishing Job, paying his debts, and seeing you.

'He often laid his hand upon my head, and said, ''Be steady. The Christian faith shall surely revive in this kingdom; you shall see it, though I shall not.'' '[15]

Samuel Wesley was a thorough scholar, deeply learned in several of the languages of the ancients. He spoke of himself as 'beating rhyme' and was gifted to some extent in the writing of verse. He had been rector at Epworth for nearly thirty-nine years and despite certain evident failings, he was a man of un-flinching principle and pious purpose. But above all, he was the father of two sons who were to prove special instruments in the hands of God in that 'reviving of the Christian faith' which he foresaw upon his deathbed.

In a letter to brother Samuel, Charles said, 'His passage was so smooth and insensible that, notwithstanding the stopping of his pulse, and the ceasing of all signs of life and motion, we con-tinued over him a good while, in doubt whether the soul was departed or no ... We have computed the debts and find they amount to £100, exclusive of cousin Richardson's. Mrs Knight, the landlady, seized all the quick stock, valued at above £40, for £15 my father owed her... And my brother this afternoon gives a note for the money, in order to get the stock at liberty to sell... and will be paid as it can be sold. My father was buried very frugally, yet decently, in the churchyard, according to his desire ... bring all accounts of what he owed you, that you may mark all goods in the house as principal creditor, and thereby secure to my mother time and liberty to sell them to the best advan-tage ... If you take London in your way, my mother desires you will remember that she is a clergyman's widow. Let the society give her what they please, she must be in some degree burden-some to you...'[16]

So ended the Wesleys' relationship with Epworth. The household goods were sold and the living passed into the hands of another man. John completed his father's Latin commentary on Job, had it printed without delay and personally placed a copy in the hands of the queen.

It has been stated that Susanna received the interest on £1000 left by a sister-in-law[17] but there is no evidence that this was so. Nor is there any record of her receiving anything from the Lon-don society of which Charles spoke.

From now on, Susanna was dependent on her children. She went first to live with her daughter Emilia, who conducted a school for girls at Gainsborough. It was undoubtedly a place of noise and bustle, but despite the fact that she was now elderly she remained there for more than a year.

She then moved to the home of her son Samuel at Tiverton in Devon. Although he could by no means be regarded as well-to-do, he was the best-off of all her children and he proved very good-hearted to her.

But Samuel's wife had a very sharp tongue,[18] and after only ten months in their home Susanna went to live with her daughter Martha in the Wiltshire village of Wooton. Martha's husband, the Rev. Westley Hall, had been a member of the Holy Club and, although in a few years' time he was to become a profligate sinner, during the time she was staying in his home, Susanna wrote of him: 'He behaves like a gentleman and a Christian, and my daughter with as much duty and tenderness as can be expected; so that on this account I am easy.'[19]

Then in 1739, after nearly two years with the Halls, Mrs Wesley moved to London. As we shall see, her son John had by that time acquired a building there called the Foundery which he used as a meeting-house and where he also lived. She went to live with him and was there till her death in 1742 at the age of seventy-three. These years with John were undoubtedly among her happiest and we shall consider later the few events from that period which have come down to us.

Shortly after his father's death Charles made two decisions which fundamentally altered the course of his entire later life. Firstly, following again in the footsteps of his grandfathers, his father and his brothers, he decided to enter the ministry of the Church of England. Secondly, under the influence of a Dr Burton, a teacher at Oxford, and of his brother John, he decided to accompany John as a missionary to the newest of England's colonies, Georgia, a wilderness state and the southern British outpost in America.

There is a widespread theory to the effect that Charles and John Wesley spent much time in America and that they established Methodism on that continent. It is also assumed by some that they made several visits to the colonies.

The truth of the matter is that they came to America but once, and they ministered only in Georgia—a wilderness state of less than one thousand settlers. Charles remained for less than six months and John for a year and ten months. Charles stayed for a month in Boston on his return voyage to England but was sick and bedridden most of that time.

During these days in America the Wesleys were not converted and since they knew only the idea of 'salvation by works' they had as yet nothing of the essential message of Methodism, 'justification by faith'. This they were to experience and then to declare soon after their arrival in England.

4.
The missionary to Georgia

The colony of Georgia had been founded in 1732 under the leadership of a Parliamentarian, Colonel James Oglethorpe. Having headed a commission concerning conditions in England's prisons Oglethorpe realized that there were hundreds of people rotting away their lives in debtors' prisons and he determined it would be better to give them an opportunity to make a new life for themselves by emigrating to America. Moreover, during those years numerous people in Europe were suffering papal persecution and Oglethorpe intended to offer to them too the opportunity of a new start in the transatlantic colony.

Oglethorpe realized that such a venture called for clergymen of heroic mould and on meeting John Wesley he challenged him to undertake the task. By taking a leave of absence John was able to retain his fellowship at Oxford and, feeling that life in the primitive land would enable him to subdue his nature and come nearer to attaining the salvation of his soul, he accepted the challenge.

Charles Wesley stated, 'I only thought of spending all my days in Oxford. But my brother, who always had the ascendant over me, persuaded me to accompany him and Mr Oglethorpe to Georgia.'[1] Undoubtedly, both the brothers felt the thrill of entering the New World and rejoiced in the hope of ministering to the Indians. But like John, Charles also hoped to save his own soul.

The news that her two sons intended to leave England and become missionaries to a far-off colony must have come as a distinct shock to Mrs Wesley, especially since she was now so dependent on them. None the less, she declared her willingness that they fulfil their plan and even stated, 'Had I twenty sons I would rejoice that they were so employed.'[2]

General Oglethorpe

In preparation for his clerical duties Charles was ordained, first as a deacon, and then, a week later, as a priest of the Church of England.

The brothers sailed on the *Simmonds* on 22 October 1735. With them sailed two friends: Benjamin Ingham, who had been a member of the Holy Club, and Charles Delamotte, the son of a wealthy London sugar merchant. The vessel put in for a few days at Cowes on the Isle of Wight, an island on the south coast of England. The four men went ashore and Charles preached for the first time, entirely reading his sermon, as was the custom of most clergymen at that time.

There were 120 passengers aboard the *Simmonds* and they were largely of two distinct kinds. The first were of an unsavoury sort and several of them had been released from prison. The others belonged to a religious group known as Moravians. They were characterized by their unworldly nature and by their willingness to serve others, and they were on their way to America not only to become settlers but also to serve as missionaries.

The Wesleys and their two associates began living by rule. Each evening they planned their duties for the following day and the time to be given to each activity. They got up at four in the morning and devoted the first hour to private prayer. Then for two hours the four met together to read the Bible and study certain of the church fathers. They had breakfast and then assembled all the passengers who were willing to come for public prayers. From nine o'clock till twelve John Wesley studied German, Charles wrote sermons, Delamotte read Greek and Ingham taught the children. During the afternoon the four of them went among the people, warning those they felt particularly needed it and seeking to establish a witness for righteousness.

Two of the women passengers, however, showed a particular interest in John and Charles. One was a Mrs Welch and the other a Mrs Hawkins. Their husbands were on board but the two wives very frequently visited the attractive young clergymen, claiming to be coming for spiritual advice. Charles felt their purpose was mischievous, but John, apparently more susceptible to female company, gave no evidence of suspecting their motives. He assumed their concern was genuine, reporting on one occasion, 'Mrs Hawkins expressed a desire of receiving the Holy Communion. Several being informed of it, warned me of her insincerity, and laid many crimes to her charge, of which I

informed her. In the evening she replied clearly and calmly to
every article of the charge, and with such an appearance of
innocence ... that I could no longer doubt of her desire to be
not only almost but altogether a Christian.'³ Charles expressed
his definite opposition to allowing her to partake of the Communion and he soon came to the belief that the two women were
definitely out to cause trouble.

This voyage witnessed an event which proved of tremendous
significance in John's life. The *Simmonds* encountered a most
violent storm. 'A great sea broke in upon us, which split the
main-sail, carried away the companion ... and rushed into the
great cabin.'⁴ Most of the passengers were overcome by fear,
but while they screamed in terror, the Moravians, who were in
the midst of a hymn while the storm was at its worst, calmly
continued to sing and pray. John Wesley was deeply moved as
he witnessed their quietness even though they faced the danger
of any moment being thrust beneath the waves. He reported,
'I asked one of them afterwards, "Was you not afraid?" He
answered, "I thank God, no." I asked, "But were your women
and children not afraid?" He replied mildly, "No; our women
and children are not afraid to die." '⁵ John admits that amidst
the furious winds, the raging seas and the terrible shaking of
the little vessel he himself was filled with fear and he recognized
that, scholar and clergyman though he was, he knew nothing
of the peace these people possessed. This was the first experience
the Wesleys had ever had of evangelical Christianity and it left
a mark which would not be erased.

They encountered further storms but these proved less violent.
Finally, on 5 February the vessel reached the coast of Georgia and
the next day the four men went on shore, cautious and cour-
ageous, but not anticipating the trials that lay before them.⁶

John Wesley had hoped to preach to the Indians but since
he lacked any knowledge of their language he began his work
instead as parish priest at the colony's only settlement, Savannah.
Charles and Ingham travelled about 100 miles to the south, where
Colonel Oglethorpe now began to establish another settlement.
It was called Frederica and was intended to serve as a military
outpost to guard against the attacks of the Spaniards from
Florida. Although he was officially Secretary for Indian Affairs
and secretary to Colonel Oglethorpe, Charles also undertook his
duties as the local parish priest.

Despite his university experience and his basically friendly nature, Charles found himself almost immediately at odds with the people. Evidently he made the mistake of believing that as a clergyman he possessed a measure of legal authority over his parishioners. His father had held to this belief and such a power had indeed been exercised by rectors in England, but Charles was to find the idea was not well accepted in America.

Moreover, Charles thought that all Christians ought to follow certain rules of life and he hoped to impose on his parishioners a system something like that practised by the Holy Club. He therefore lost no time in having a drum sounded four times a day, to call them to assemble for prayers, but he found almost everyone rejected the idea. Likewise, he refused to baptize infants by sprinkling and insisted that they be immersed, not once, but three times in succession. On his second day in Frederica he wrote, 'I began talking to M. Germain, about baptizing her child by immersion. She was much averse to it, though she owned it a strong healthy child. I then spoke to her husband, who was soon satisfied, and brought his wife to be so too.'[7]

But within four more days he added, 'M. Germain now retracted her consent for having her child baptized: however, M. Colwell's I did baptize by trine immersion...'[8]

Mrs Welch and Mrs Hawkins, together with their husbands, were living at Frederica, and on his third day in the settlement, Charles attempted to reconcile differences that had sprung up between the two women. He assured Mrs Welch that Mrs Hawkins bore her no ill will, only to be told, 'Mrs H[awkins] is a very subtle woman.'

Indeed, it was quickly evident he could expect nothing but trouble from this pair of termagants. Knowing that Charles had manifested opposition to their intrigues while on board ship, they now regarded him with hostility. For instance, he says that on his second Sunday in the colony, Mrs Hawkins, in a fit of temper, '... charged and fired a gun ... She cursed and swore in the utmost transport of passion, threatening to kill the first man who should come near her.' Referring to John's attitude, he asked, 'Alas, my brother! what has become of thy hopeful convert?'[9] He continued, '[She] said she would blow me up, and my brother, whom she once thought honest, but was now undeceived: ... but she would be revenged, and expose my d----d hypocrisy, my prayers four times a day by beat of drum, and abundance more, which I cannot write, and thought no woman, though taken from Drury Lane, could have spoken. I only said I pitied her, but defied all she and the devil could do.'[10]

Difficulty now arose from an unexpected source—from Colonel Oglethorpe. In fact, on only his third day in the Colony Charles stated, 'I heard my first harsh word from Mr Oglethorpe.'[11] And before another week had passed he declared, 'I was enabled to pray earnestly for my enemies, particularly for Mr Oglethorpe, whom I now looked upon as the chief of them.'[12]

The colonel's hostility was fully manifest. For instance, he had provided Charles with nowhere to sleep except on the ground in another man's hut. But during this first week Charles wrote, 'I was forced to exchange my usual bed, the ground, for a chest, being almost speechless through a violent cold.'[13] While he was still in this condition Oglethorpe called him out of the hut at 7.30 one morning, told him there had been a meeting on the previous evening and that several of the men had charged him with stirring up the people to mutiny and to leave the colony. He declared that since those who complained were chiefly men who came to the religious services Charles was to blame for their attitude. To this he could only reply, 'I seldom have above six at the public service.'

By the time he had been in the colony three weeks Charles was so distraught that he sent Ingham to Savannah to ask John and Delamotte to come to him.

While he waited for them to arrive matters became still worse. Up to this point, some in the settlement had at least not shown any opposition, but now he wrote, 'My few well-wishers are afraid to speak to me. Some have turned out of the way to avoid me ... The servant who used to wash my linen sent it back to me unwashed.'[14] Charles learned of some boards that were to be destroyed and he endeavoured to obtain a few so that he might use them to lie on and thus avoid the necessity of sleeping on the ground. But his request was refused. Then a man died in Frederica and Charles obtained his bed, but was only able to use it for one night. 'Mr Oglethorpe,' he wrote, 'gave away my bedstead from under me, and refused to spare one of the carpenters to mend me up another.'[15]

On learning of Charles's situation John and Delamotte hastened to Frederica—a trip of 100 miles by open canoe along

the coast. When they arrived—on Saturday, 10 April—Charles
stated he was so exhausted he could not have read prayers once
more. Because of the danger of having their conversations
overheard, distorted and spread abroad, the brothers found it
necessary to speak in Latin, even when in the woods. Charles
proved too weak to conduct his Sunday services himself and
therefore this duty fell upon John.

While John was in Frederica the cause of Oglethorpe's hostility
became evident. It had stemmed from the evil tongues of Mrs
Hawkins and Mrs Welch. Perhaps out of a mischievous love of
scandal, or perhaps motivated by a desire to turn the settlement
into a place of unbridled licentiousness, the two of them had
spread the tale that they had committed adultery with Colonel
Oglethorpe. But they also informed Oglethorpe that Charles had
concocted the story and had told it to everyone he met. Through
his conversations with the two women John learned of their evil
scheme and how it had developed, and he informed both
Oglethorpe and Charles of what the women had done.
Oglethorpe then confronted Charles and Charles asserted, 'I
absolutely deny the whole charge. I have neither raised nor spread
this report, but whenever I heard it, checked it immediately.'[16]
Influenced by each of the brothers, Oglethorpe accepted Charles's
denial, so that the latter recorded: 'When I had finished this relation he seemed entirely changed, full of his old love and confidence in me.'[17] 'He condemned himself for his anger, (God
forgive those who made me the object of it!) which he imputed
to his want of time for consideration.'[18] 'He ordered me
whatever he could think I wanted; [and] promised to have me
an house built immediately.'[19]

Notwithstanding the reconciliation with Oglethorpe, Charles
felt doubly alone when, after a stay of two weeks, John and
Delamotte returned to Savannah. He was still unwell and also
very unhappy in performing his work as a secretary. Indeed,
before he had been in the colony a week he had declared, 'I was
wholly spent in writing letters for Mr Oglethorpe. I would not
spend six days more in the same manner for all Georgia.'[20]

Accordingly, Charles arranged that as soon as possible he and
John would exchange places for a time. In all, he had been in
Frederica something less than three months when he left it. 'I
was overjoyed at my deliverance out of this furnace,' he declared
as he bade the settlement goodbye.[21]

At Savannah he carried on John's work of expounding the morning and evening lessons on the Sunday and visiting the parishioners during the week. He also fulfilled his duties as secretary, especially that of writing licences for the men who traded with the Indians.

To Charles's relief, however, these labours were soon interrupted. Colonel Oglethorpe came to Savannah and stated that Charles must shortly return to England. It was believed by many people in the homeland that Georgia was on the verge of failure and Oglethorpe wanted Charles to testify on the colony's behalf before its board of trustees. With this prospect of leaving America before him Charles at first resigned his secretaryship but under Oglethorpe's persuasion eventually agreed to retain the position for a while longer.

He needed no time to prepare for the journey and his *Journal* entry for the following day, 26 July 1736, reads, 'The words which concluded the lesson, and my stay in Georgia, were, "Arise, let us go hence." ... When the boat put off I was surprised that I felt no more joy in leaving such a scene of sorrows.'[22]

Charles embarked for England from Charleston, South Carolina, on 11 August. But the full voyage was not to be made as expected. The captain of the vessel was a vile man, who was drunk much of the time and incapable of carrying his responsibility. His ship was also sadly in need of repair and seemed so likely to sink that his sailors constantly urged him to put in at one of the ports along the Atlantic coast. After more than a month of dangerous sailing he anchored at Boston, Massachusetts.

Charles remained at Boston for a month and was so weak that for much of this time he was confined to bed. But several ministers welcomed him and he proved well enough to preach on the Sundays. He was urged to undertake a ministry in the area and was offered his choice of a church in the city or in the country, but he refused to consider remaining in America.

He was struck by the orderliness of Boston and after visiting Harvard University he remarked, 'I had only time to observe the civility of the Fellows, the regularity of the buildings and the pleasantness of the situation.'[23] Everything he saw 'seemed to present the very reverse of Georgia'. Despite his enjoyment of Boston at the end of a month he took passage, on a different vessel, for England. He was never again to set foot in America.

Yet still there were trials. The third day out of port he recorded, 'There was so prodigious a sea that it washed away our sheep, and half our hogs, and drowned most of our fowl.'[24] Storm followed storm and although the sailors manned the pumps continually the ship was hourly in danger of being lost. But calms followed storms until, finally, five-and-a-half weeks after leaving Boston the vessel reached land at Deal in England. The date was 3 December 1736 and Charles was within two weeks of his twenty-sixth birthday.

Of course the question arises, why Charles Wesley had failed so seriously in his first attempts to perform the work of the ministry. Undoubtedly, he was basically too much of the autocrat and people rejected his efforts to set rules for their lives. It is also true that because of his intense and poetic nature he had proved exceptionally sensitive to the attitudes and the opposition of men and women around him. But, above all, he was not yet converted. His only message at this time was one of works, and he was still unaware of the great, fundamental truth that he was soon to experience, and that he would thereafter declare to the multitude—the truth of 'justification by faith'!

Long my imprisoned spirit lay
  Fast bound in sin and nature's night;
Thine eye diffused a quickening ray;
  I woke! The dungeon flamed with light!
My chains fell off, my heart was free,
  I rose, went forth, and followed thee.

(Charles Wesley).

Therefore being justified by faith, we have peace
with God through our Lord Jesus Christ.

(Romans 5:1).

5
'I woke! The dungeon flamed with light!'

Charles Wesley returned to England unwell in body and dejected in spirit. Nevertheless, he immediately began calling on several friends. Since there had been a report that he had drowned at sea they were delighted to see him alive and welcomed him joyfully. In view of the rumour that Georgia was about to fail many wanted news of conditions in the colony and especially information about relatives who had emigrated there. He said nothing about the troubles he had experienced, but constantly reported the areas of success and stated, 'I sent them away advocates for the colony.'[1]

He called on the Bishop of London, who had ecclesiastical authority over the colony, and was well received. At the express wish of Colonel Oglethorpe he visited several of the trustees individually and he also appeared before the entire board of twenty-one members, but proved too weak to make them all hear adequately, so one of them read the documents for him.

Charles also appeared for the colony before England's Board of Trade. A strong disagreement had developed between South Carolina and Georgia, in which Carolina had alleged that, although Georgia collected a licence fee from men who traded with the Indians, several of these men frequently crossed the unmarked border and did their trading in Carolina. But Charles had become familiar with the activities of the traders and he proved an important witness on Georgia's behalf.

Charles had at this time been sorely deceived by a Dutchman named Apee. This man had lived for some months in Georgia and had associated himself with Charles in Savannah. He had sailed on the vessel that carried Charles to Boston, had remained

there till Charles boarded the one that was to take him to England
and had then obtained passage in that vessel too. On first meeting
Charles he had expressed his desire to be baptized and thereafter
had professed to be a most sincere seeker after righteousness.
He also claimed to have a fortune waiting for him in Holland
and on this basis he borrowed £24 from Charles. But it soon
became evident that he already owed money to several men, and
on reaching England he attempted to go his way without paying for his passage across the ocean. He proved a forger, a thief
and a liar and was imprisoned forthwith in London. However,
he managed to secure his release and the last Charles mentions
of him is that he stole a valuable watch and escaped with it to
Paris. Apee had forced Charles to recognize that he must not
accept every professed spiritual seeker as real.

By the time Charles had completed his appearances before
the trustees and the Board of Trade, Colonel Oglethorpe had
returned to England. Charles once more endeavoured to resign
as secretary, but Oglethorpe again pleaded with him not to do
so and Charles agreed to remain temporarily in the office.
Oglethorpe also urged him to return to his work in the colony,
but he replied that he would consider going again solely as a
clergyman, but never as a secretary. At least, while he remained
in his position as secretary he received a salary from the trustees.

Having met his responsibilities in London, Charles was free
to visit elsewhere. He went to Oxford, called on certain acquaintances there and visited the prisoners. From there he journeyed
to Wooton and stayed at the home of his sister Martha and her
husband, Westley Hall. Then he went on to Tiverton in Devon,
where his brother Samuel was now the headmaster of a boys'
school. His mother was staying with Samuel, but was unwell
at the time and he found her 'indisposed in her chamber'. She
forbade Charles ever to return to Georgia and ordered him 'to
accept the first preferment offered'. [2]

For the next three months or so he repeated this circuit—
London, Oxford and Tiverton and back to London—often calling
also at other places on the way.

In all these contacts Charles maintained a definite religious
purpose. There was a marked earnestness about him and he
urged everyone he conversed with to undertake a strongly
disciplined life and to perform good works. For instance, on
meeting some Holy Club friends at Oxford he exhorted them

'to resume all their rules of holy living', and he says of a student, Richard Graves, 'I encouraged him to go on in the narrow way; and strongly recommended stated hours of retirement.'[3]

Nevertheless, although he continued to deliver this message, another element soon began to come into his conversations. Of his visit to a man in London he says, 'We had some close talk about the new birth ... I took the opportunity of recommending regular retirement and religious acquaintance.'[4] He called at the Delamotte mansion, Blendon Hall, near Bexley, a few miles east of London, and says that 'We soon fell into talk about the new birth.'[5] Of a later visit there he reports, 'I spent an hour... in discoursing of the inward change and reading [William] Law.'[6]

His sister Kezia told him 'She believed now there was such a thing as a new creature... that she was not, but longed to be converted.' He says, 'I prayed over her... then used Pascal's prayer for conversion.'[7] He tells of a conversation with a friend at Oxford and states, 'I... had some close talk with him on the new birth, self-renunciation etc. ... He seemed on the brink of the new birth.'[8]

These are the first evidences in Charles's *Journal* that he had become aware that there is such an experience as 'the new birth'. But although he manifestly longed to experience it himself his only thought as to how to do so was by continuing in good works and increased self-denial.

However, two new influences now came into Charles's life. One was the ministry of the twenty-two-year-old preacher, George Whitefield. A warm friendship had sprung up between Charles and George during their days at Oxford. But in the spring of 1735 Whitefield had been converted[9] and had quickly become an exceptionally earnest Christian. After a further period at Oxford he had been ordained and by the time with which we are now dealing, November 1737, he was preaching in London twice daily to tremendous congregations. Charles records attending his ministry, saying of one such occasion, 'I met and turned back with Betty [Delamotte] to hear Mr Whitefield preach, not with persuasive words of man's wisdom, but with the demonstration of the Spirit and with power. The churches will not contain the multitudes that throng to hear him.'[10]

Whitefield was not yet as informed on evangelical matters as he would become in a year's time. Nevertheless, he constantly declared the necessity of the new birth and his sermon on 'Ye must be born again' was in print and was widely read. His ministry could not have failed to instil this truth all the more deeply in Charles's mind.

A second influence on Charles was the testimony of a Moravian, Peter Böhler. Böhler, a German and a former professor at the University of Jena, intended to emigrate to America and Charles began to teach him the English language.

Late in January 1738 Whitefield sailed out of Deal on his way to Georgia. The day he left John Wesley sailed in. John returned in a very downcast mood and in answer to his own question as to what he had learned during his days in Georgia, he replied, 'Why, what I the least of all expected, that I, who went to America to convert others, was never myself converted to God.'[11] The information that he now received of the tremendous ministry Whitefield had exercised and of his constantly overflowing congregations could not but have intrigued him deeply and have filled him with a determination that some measure of such tremendous success would one day be his.

In view of the wealth of biography that has since been accorded to John Wesley it is easy to assume, as many have done, that he was gifted with great wisdom and glowing success from the very first of his ministry. Accordingly, it is necessary to recognize that in his mission to Georgia he had failed miserably.[12] Like Charles he was not yet converted and his only message was that of self effort and the attempt to perform good works.

When he arrived in London John frequently joined Charles in attending a society in Fetter Lane. This was one of several small bodies known as 'religious societies' which were nominally in association with the Church of England. Despite his broken English Peter Böhler had begun to teach at this society and his Moravian beliefs and practices were being accepted by several of the members.

Charles and John were in almost daily contact with Böhler and the relation worked to their advantage. For instance, recognizing Charles's extraordinary earnestness Böhler asked him, 'Do you hope to be saved?' He replied, 'I do!' 'For what reason do you hope it?' 'Because I have used my best endeavours to serve God.' Charles reports, 'He shook his head, and said no more. I thought him very uncharitable, saying in my heart, "What, are not my endeavours sufficient ground of hope? Would he rob me of my endeavours? I have nothing else to trust to.'''[13]

In a conversation John held with Böhler around this time John projected his own ideas of being saved by his works. 'My brother, my brother,' declared Böhler, 'that philosophy of yours must be purged away!'[14] In answer to John's question as to whether, since he did not yet possess faith, he should leave off preaching, Böhler replied, 'Preach faith *till* you have it, and then, *because* you have it, you will preach faith.'[15]

There now began for the Wesleys a search for this faith, which they knew they needed and of which they had been informed by Böhler. Yet 'faith' had become in their thinking a sort of entity on its own and they were virtually seeking 'faith' and 'an experience' rather than seeking Christ. This concept was to colour their theology and ministries for much of the rest of their lives.

With a burning earnestness they both longed to receive this 'faith'. But Böhler said of Charles, 'He does not know how he shall begin to be acquainted with the Saviour,' and his words were true of both of the brothers. Their lack of knowledge on the subject is manifest in Charles's report of a visit he and John made at this time to the Delamotte home. He says, 'We sang and fell into a dispute whether conversion was gradual or instantaneous. My brother was very positive for the latter, and very shocking; mentioned some late instances of gross sinners believing in a moment. I was much offended at his worse than edifying discourse. Mrs Delamotte left us abruptly. I stayed and insisted a man need not know when first he had faith. His obstinacy in favouring the contrary opinion drove me at last out of the room.'[16]

During a period of sickness Charles was visited by Böhler. Following the visit he reported, 'I immediately thought it might be that I should again consider Böhler's doctrine of faith; examine myself whether I was in the faith; and if not, never cease seeking after it, till I obtained it.'[17]

Charles was then living in the home of James Hutton, a Christian book-dealer, but because of the intensity of his search he moved and went to live with a man who he thought could help him. This was John Bray, a brazier in Little Britain, and Charles spoke of him as 'a poor ignorant mechanic, who knows nothing but Christ; yet by knowing him, knows and discerns

all things'.[18] Charles was still so weak that he had himself
carried there in a chair.

The following entries in his *Journal* were written at this time:

'*May 12*.... This day (and indeed my whole time) I spent
in discoursing on faith, either with those that had it, or those
that sought it; in reading the Scripture, and in prayer.

'*May 13*. I waked without Christ; yet still desirous of finding him ...At night my brother came, exceeding heavy. I forced
him (as he had often forced me) to sing an hymn to Christ, and
almost thought he would come while we were singing...

'*May 14*. The beginning of the day I was very heavy, weary,
and unable to pray; but the desire soon returned ... I longed
to find Christ, that I might show him to all mankind; that I might
praise, that I might love him.'[19]

Charles now learned that the idea of 'justification by faith'
was not something new in church history but that it had been
the chief teaching of the great Reformer, Martin Luther.

'*May 17*.... To-day I first saw Luther on the Galatians,
which Mr Holland had accidentally lit upon. We began and
found him nobly full of faith. My friend, in hearing him, was
so affected as to breathe out sighs and groans unutterable.'[20]

But Holland, a commercial painter 'in rather a large way of
business', had a still more triumphant testimony regarding the
experience. He wrote, 'Mr Charles Wesley read the Preface
aloud. At the words, "What, have we then nothing to do? No!
nothing! but only to accept of him 'who of God is made unto
us wisdom and righteousness and sanctification and redemption,' " there came such a power over me as I cannot well
describe; my great burden fell off in an instant; my heart was
so filled with peace and love that I burst into tears. I almost
thought I saw our Saviour! My companions, perceiving me so
affected, fell on their knees and prayed. When I afterwards went
into the street, I could scarce feel the ground I trod upon.'[21]

Charles went on to report, 'I spent some hours this evening
with Martin Luther, who was greatly blessed to me, especially
his conclusion of the second chapter. I laboured, waited, and
prayed to feel "who loved *me*, and gave himself for *me*".'

He also tells of a woman at Bray's house who testified to having received faith. Charles questioned her as to whether she
possessed perfect peace and loved Christ above all things, and
when she replied assuredly, 'I do!' he asked if she was afraid

to die. She responded, 'I would be willing to die this moment; for I know my sins are blotted out ... He has saved me by his death.'[22]

The statements of Martin Luther and the testimony of Holland and of this woman served to increase Charles's desire that he too might receive this faith. He thought Christ might appear to him in a physical manifestation and stated, 'I looked for him all night with prayers and sighs and unceasing desires.'

But the next day, 20 May, he reported, 'I waked much disappointed, and continued all day in great dejection, which the sacrament did not in the least abate.'[23] That evening, as Bray read to him the narrative of Christ's healing of the paralysed man, with its assurance that 'The Son of Man hath power on earth to forgive sins,' Charles said, 'It was a long while before he could read this through for tears of joy; and I saw herein and firmly believed, that his faith would be available for the healing of me.'[24]

21 May was Pentecost Sunday in the Church of England. It was also to be the day of Charles Wesley's conversion.

'I waked,' he wrote, 'in hope and expectation of his coming.' He heard someone speaking downstairs, and said, 'I hoped it might be Christ indeed.' Bray then read to him from Psalm 32: 'Blessed is the man to whom the Lord imputeth no sin,' and although he says that at first, 'I felt a violent opposition and reluctance to believe,' he goes on to report, 'yet still the Spirit of God strove with my own and evil spirit, till by degrees he chased away the darkness of my unbelief. I found myself convinced, I knew not how nor when; and immediately fell to intercession.'[25]

That evening he wrote, 'I now found myself at peace with God, and rejoiced in hope of loving Christ. My temper for the rest of the day was mistrust of my own great, but before unknown weakness. I saw that by faith I stood; by the continual support of faith, which kept me from falling, though of myself I am ever sinking into sin. I want to be still sensible of my own weakness... yet confident of Christ's protection.'[26]

Two days later he said, 'I began an hymn upon my conversion.' It may have been at this time that he wrote the hymn that begins,

> Where shall my wondering soul begin?
>   How shall I all to heaven aspire?
> A slave redeemed from death and sin,
>   A brand plucked from eternal fire,
> How shall I equal triumphs raise,
> Or sing my great Deliverer's praise?

But it is more likely that the hymn he wrote then was one that emphasizes the truth he had learned through reading Luther. In strong reference to Luther's comment on the 'conclusion of the second chapter of Galatians' he had said, 'I laboured, waited and prayed to feel "who loved *me* and gave himself for *me*." ' His conversion hymn may, then, well have been one which also emphasizes these pronouns and which there is reason to believe he wrote, if not at this very time, at least very shortly afterwards. Its opening lines read:

> And can it be that I should gain
>   An interest in the Saviour's blood?
> Died he for me, who caused his pain?
>   For me, who him to death pursued?
> Amazing love! how can it be
> That thou, my God, should'st die for me?

The hymn goes on, like Luther's *Commentary*, to emphasize the personal pronouns and is indeed a testimony to having received the experience of conversion.

It it not important whether it was either of these or some other hymn that Charles Wesley wrote to commemorate that momentous day, Sunday, 21 May 1738. He exclaimed, 'I was in a new heaven and a new earth!' and those words sum up the new life that now flooded his soul.

That evening John wrote, 'I received the surprising news that my brother had found rest to his soul.' But he himself continued seeking till, three days later, in a meeting in Aldersgate Street, he heard a man read from Martin Luther. Undoubtedly the reader was William Holland, and John made the report that has since become known to thousands: 'I felt my heart strangely warmed. I felt I did trust in Christ, Christ alone for salvation: and an assurance was given me that he had taken away *my* sins, even *mine*, and saved *me* from the law of sin and death.'[27]

Charles Wesley's *Journal* also tells of this historic event. He writes, 'Towards ten, my brother was brought in triumph by a troop of our friends, and declared, "I believe." We sang the hymn with great joy, and parted with prayer. At midnight I gave myself up to Christ; assured I was safe, sleeping or waking.'[28]

Forth in thy name, O Lord, I go,
  My daily labour to pursue;
Thee, only thee, resolved to know,
  In all I think, or speak, or do.

The task thy wisdom hath assigned,
  Oh, let me cheerfully fulfil!
In all my works thy presence find,
  And prove thine acceptable will.

Thee may I set at my right hand,
  Whose eyes my inmost substance see;
And labour on at thy command,
  And offer all my works to thee.

Give me to bear thy easy yoke,
  And every moment watch and pray;
And still to things eternal look,
  And hasten to the glorious day.

For thee delightfully employ
  Whate'er thy bounteous grace hath given;
And run my course with even joy,
  And closely walk with thee to heaven.

(Charles Wesley).

6.
Learning to preach the gospel

When Susanna Wesley learned that her two sons had professed to be converted she knew not what to say. Charles wrote to her reporting his experience and, in keeping with her long-standing beliefs, she replied, 'I think you are fallen into an odd way of thinking. You say that till within a few months you had no spiritual life, nor any justifying faith. Now this is as if a man should affirm he was not alive in his infancy, because when an infant he did not know he was alive. All, then, that I can gather from your letter is that till a little while ago you were not so well satisfied of your being a Christian as you are now. I heartily rejoice that you have now attained to a strong and lively hope in God's mercy through Christ. Not that I can think that you were totally without saving faith before: but it is one thing to have faith, and another thing to be sensible we have it.'[1]

Notwithstanding our appreciation of Susanna's intellect, we must recognize that in facing this question of 'the new birth' she did not turn to the Scripture to discover its teaching and thereby to form her conviction. Rather, as the letter shows, she relied on human reason, tradition and experience and it was by these that she came to her conclusion. In certain other doctrinal matters we shall later see her sons adopting the same procedure. Charles immediately demonstrated, by a new assurance and a new strength in his daily living, that he had received new life.

Despite his mother's frequent admonitions to 'stop at the second glass', he had in the past sometimes been drunk. Now, however, he reported, 'I [was] amazed to find my old enemy, intemperance, so suddenly subdued, that I almost forgot I was ever in bondage to him.'[2] Whereas he had previously been subject to sudden bursts of temper, now he began to control his temper and six days after his conversion we find him writing,

'I felt a motion of anger, from a trifling disappointment; but it was no sooner felt than conquered.'[3]

He could still experience periods of deep depression, yet these inevitably gave way to joy, which was often of a rich and abounding nature. This is evident in the following reports:

'*June 1st, 1738*. I was troubled today, that I could not pray, being utterly dead at the sacrament.'

'*June 2d*. I was still unable to pray; still dead in communicating; full of cowardly desire for death.'

'*June 3d*. My deadness continued, and the next day increased. I rose exceeding heavy and averse to prayer; so that I almost resolved not to go to church ... When I did go, the prayers and sacrament were exceeding grievous to me...'[4]

He states that Ingham, William Holland and a Mr Brown called and they all joined in singing and in prayer, and gradually his spirits revived. Charles prayed especially for Brown and declared the good news of the gospel, and while he was speaking 'Mr Brown found power to believe.' In the experience Charles learned a lesson and he defined it, saying, 'I ... rejoiced in my trials having continued so long, to show me that it is then the best time to labour for our neighbour, when we are most cast down, and most unable to help ourselves.'[5]

Charles's daily witnessing was new also. He continued the activity he had practised before his conversion, but now, as he spoke to men and women about 'justification by faith', he did so on the basis of personal experience. He was not theorizing but was speaking that which he knew and felt, and he now could assure everyone he met:

> He breaks the power of cancelled sin,
>   He sets the prisoner free;
> His blood can make the vilest clean,
>   His blood availed for me.

He went out with a strong sense of a God-given authority. At times his manner appears tinged with severity, yet we cannot but rejoice in his fervour as we notice the following reports made within a few weeks after his conversion: 'In the coach to London I preached faith in Christ. A lady was extremely offended; avowed her own merits in plain terms; asked if I was not a Methodist; threatened to beat me. I declared I deserved nothing but hell; so did she; and must confess it, before she could have a title to heaven. This was most intolerable to her. The others were less offended...'[6]

'A gentlewoman, who has long been under the law, calling to see me, I thought as she lived in the midst of opposers, no good could be done by speaking. Yet was I overruled to preach the gospel. She seemed convinced and comforted ... Two or three others calling were reproved of sin by the Holy Spirit of God. Miss Claggetts seemed on the very border of Canaan ...'

'My inward temptations are, in a manner, uninterrupted. I never knew the energy of sin, till now that I experience the superior strength of Christ.'

'I took coach for Blendon with Mr Bray; and had much talk with a lady about the fall, and faith in Christ. She openly maintained the merit of good works. I would that all who oppose the righteousness of faith were so ingenuous: then would they no longer seek it as it were by the works of the law.'

'In riding ... to Blendon, I was full of delight, and seemed in new heavens and new earth. We prayed and sang, and shouted all the way. We found Miss Betsy and Hetty [Delamotte sisters] at home, and prayed that this day salvation might come to this house.'[7]

Charles stayed at the Delamottes' for three weeks. He tells of 'Mr Bray relating the inward workings of God upon his soul, and I the great things he had lately done for me.'[8] He reports also his labouring in prayer on behalf of the family, their maids, their gardener and their minister. Concerning these efforts he stated, 'I returned to town, rejoicing that God had added to his living church seven more souls through my ministry.'[9]

Despite his zeal, however, Charles still manifested certain immature features. He frequently reported 'consulting the oracle', by which he meant opening the Bible at random and accepting the first verse his eye lighted upon as being the direct message of God to him in the circumstances he was then experiencing. Similarly, in seeking to come to a decision concerning a course of action both he and John practised the casting of lots: they wrote each of the various possible courses of action on a separate slip of paper, put them face down and they took it that the first one they picked up revealed God's mind in the matter. Charles also tells of a man who 'declared ... he had seen as it were a whole army rushing by him, and bearing the broken body of Christ,' and apparently accepting the vision as real, he says of this man, 'My heart bore witness to the work of God in his.'[10] He saw evidences of the activity of God in all manner of the details of daily life. For instance, on one occasion, he says, 'At this instant came a flash of lightning, then thunder, then violent rain. I accepted it as a sign that the skies would soon pour down righteousness.'[11] Charles and John later overcame these superstitious tendencies, but for some months immediately following their conversion both were prone to them.

During these post-conversion weeks John Wesley recognized his need of further spiritual instruction. He made such statements as: 'I received a letter from Oxford which threw me into much perplexity,'[12] and '...I felt a kind of soreness in my heart, so that I found my wound was not fully healed.'[13] Accordingly, he determined to visit the Moravians at their headquarters, Herrnhut in Germany, so that from these men who had been his first teachers concerning 'the new birth' he might now receive 'the full assurance of faith'. He sailed on 14 June, three weeks after his momentous experience of 24 May.

Charles was the same in his public ministry as in his private witnessing. He preached in religious societies, in the few churches that allowed him their pulpit, in private homes and once in Westminster Abbey. We see his fervour and boldness in the following statements: 'At the society I read my sermon, "The Scripture hath concluded all under sin" and urged upon all my usual question, "Do you deserve to be damned?" Mrs Platt, with the utmost vehemence, cried out, "Yes; I do, I do!" '[14]

'I was so faint and full of pain, that I had not power to speak: but I had no sooner begun my sermon than all weakness vanished. God gave me strength and boldness: and after an hour's speaking, I found myself perfectly well. I went and accosted Mrs Delamotte in her pew ... she just spake to me: Betsy wondered she could bring herself to it.'[15]

'I read prayers in Islington Church, and preached with boldness. There was a vast audience, and better disposed than usual. None went out, as they had threatened, and frequently done heretofore; especially the well-dressed hearers, "whenever I mentioned hell to ears polite" and urged that rude question, "Do you deserve to be damned?" '[16]

At this period Charles read his sermons, virtually word for word, from a manuscript. While such a method was the common practice of ministers in his day it robbed him of freedom of expression and prevented him from using any unprepared-for opportunities that might arise. It was manifestly not a practice he enjoyed and five months after his conversion he thrust it off. He wrote, 'Seeing so few present at St Antholin's, I thought of preaching extempore: afraid; yet ventured on the promise, "Lo, I am with you always;" and spake on justification from Romans 3, for three quarters of an hour, without hesitation. Glory be to God, who keepeth his promises for ever.'[17] Although he did not know it, he was thus being prepared for the years of open-air preaching that lay before him.

Charles witnessed magnificent evidence of the power of the gospel as he ministered to the condemned men in London's Newgate prison. Being asked to do so by a fellow minister he reported, 'I went with him ... and preached to the ten mal-efactors, under sentence of death; but with a heavy heart. My old prejudices against the possibility of a death-bed repentance still hung upon me; and I could hardly hope there was mercy for those whose time was so short. But in the midst of my languid discourse a sudden spirit of faith came upon me, and I promised them all pardon, in the name of Jesus Christ, if they would then, as at the last hour, repent and believe the gospel.'[18]

His report continues: 'I visited one of them in his cell, sick of a fever; a poor black that had robbed his master. I told him of one who came down from heaven to save lost sinners, and him in particular; described the sufferings of the Son of God, his sorrows, agony, and death. He listened with all the signs of eager astonishment; the tears trickled down his cheeks while he cried, "What? Was it for me? Did he suffer all this for so poor a creature as me?"'[19]

When he visited the prison again three days later Charles said, 'I rejoiced with my poor happy black; who now *believes* the Son of God loved him and gave himself for him.' As Charles declared the gospel's good news to the felons, even in what he called 'the condemned hole', he saw its effect on them, one by one. But he also experienced its effect afresh within his own heart as, dealing with these pitiable individuals in this wretched place, he declared, 'I had great help and power in prayer ... I found myself overwhelmed with the love of Christ to sinners.'[20]

As the day of execution approached Charles increased his efforts. He and Bray allowed themselves to be locked in with the condemned men throughout the night; they 'wrestled in mighty prayer' and saw fear and despair give way to peace and joy on one countenance after another.

On the morning of the hanging a boisterous crowd, intent on making sport of the event, gathered as usual at Tyburn, the place of execution. As the death cart drew onto the field, Charles and a few friends were there to meet it. 'The black spied me, coming out of the coach,' says Charles, 'and saluted me with his looks. As often as his eyes met mine, he smiled the most composed, delightful countenance I ever saw.'[21]

Charles made his way through the crowd and climbed into the cart, but when the official chaplain tried to do the same 'The prisoners begged he might not come; and the mob kept him down.' There, in the death cart, disdainful of the jeers of the crowd, Charles again spoke words of scriptural comfort to the poor victims. He and his companions sang for all to hear a hymn that had been written by his father:

> Behold the Saviour of mankind
>   Nailed to the shameful tree!
> How vast the love that him inclined
>   To bleed and die for thee!
>
> 'Tis done! the precious ransom's paid;
>   'Receive my soul!' he cries;
> See where he bows his sacred head!
>   He bows his head, and dies!

A rope from an overhead scaffold was placed around the neck of each prisoner. Charles continued his ministrations, praying, giving encouragement and kissing whom he could. As the final moment approached he again broke into song:

> To the dear fountain of thy blood,
>   Incarnate God, I fly;
> Here let me wash my spotted soul,
>   From sins of deepest dye.
>
> A guilty, weak and helpless worm,
>   Into thy hands I fall;
> Be thou my life, my righteousness,
>   My Jesus and my all.

'When the cart drew off,' says Charles, 'not one struggled for life. We left them going to meet their Lord, ready for the Bridegroom... I spoke a few suitable words to the crowd, and returned full of peace in our friends' happiness. That hour under the gallows was the most blessed hour of my life.'[22]

Charles expressed his new life also in the writing of poetry. As we have seen, he had inherited this gift from his father and although it had undoubtedly been resident in him since childhood, his conversion unlocked it and set it free. During this early ministry he says little in his journal about his composing hymns and, indeed, this is true throughout his life. But he had within him virtually a treasury of poetry. He constantly experienced the emotions of the true poet, his mind instinctively invested words with harmony, and hymn after hymn flowed from his pen. Many of his productions possess a combination of tenderness and strength, of beauty and biblical truth, that has given them, from that day to this, a unique place in Christian singing. We shall later give attention to this rich gift and to Charles Wesley's position as undoubtedly the greatest of all Christian hymn composers, but in the meantime we must constantly bear in mind this extraordinary ability and the fact that he was daily and spontaneously writing verse.

John Wesley's visit to Germany kept him out of England for three months. He found among the Moravians a disciplined community life and a warm and zealous spirituality. But he had gone to Herrnhut seeking an answer to the question as to how to obtain 'the full assurance of faith', and although the Moravians gave him several answers, none was definite or clear. Count Zinzendorf, their leader, was not entirely a believer in the inspiration of the Scriptures and he held that the *Augsburg Confession* was more inspired than certain parts of the Bible. He practised the opening of the Bible at random to find direction and 'he carried his lot-casting apparatus in his pocket... It was a little green book with detachable leaves; each leaf contained some motto or text, and when the count was in difficulty he pulled out one of the leaves.'[23]

Accordingly the Moravians failed to be the teachers Wesley had expected. But they did affect his mind in two important regards. He was convinced, in the first place, that he should look for experience as a basis on which to formulate doctrine, and, secondly, that he could receive a second Christian experience which would add to the blessing already effected in his conversion.

On his return from Germany John was something of a Moravian himself. A letter he wrote to the church at Herrnhut revealed this tendency and also describes the work being done at that time in England by Charles and himself.

'We are endeavouring...,' he wrote, 'to be followers of you, as ye are of Christ. Fourteen were added to us since our return, so that we now have eight bands of men, consisting of fifty-six persons... As yet we have only two small bands of women—the one of three and the other of five persons ... Though my brother and I are not permitted to preach in most of the churches in London, yet (thanks be to God) there are others left wherein we have liberty to speak the truth as it is in Jesus. Likewise every evening... we publish the word of reconciliation, sometimes to twenty or thirty, sometimes to fifty or sixty, sometimes to three of four hundred persons, met together to hear it.'[24]

This is John Wesley's own picture of the size of the congregations to which he and Charles ministered at this stage in their careers. They preached in only a few churches and in certain religious societies, and this was the kind of life they expected to lead for the rest of their days. Nevertheless, a great change was in store for them.

In December 1738 George Whitefield returned from his first visit to America. His ministry in Georgia had been highly successful and his return brought four former Holy Club men, Ingham, Kinchin, Hutchings and Hall, hastening to London. There they joined with the Wesleys and Whitefield in a week of prayer and of consultation concerning their future labours. Charles Wesley stated, 'The whole week was a festival indeed; a joyful season, holy unto the Lord,'[25] and Whitefield manifested the enthusiasm that characterized them all in his report: 'Sometimes whole nights were spent in prayer. Often have we been filled as with new wine. And often have we seen them overwhelmed with the divine presence and crying out, "Will God indeed dwell with men upon earth? How dreadful is this place! This is none other than the house of God and the gate of heaven!" '[26]

On the New Year's Eve, as 1738 was closing and 1739 was opening, these men met with 'about sixty brethren' for the

Moravian love feast. John Wesley made a striking account of the event, saying, 'About three in the morning, as we were continuing instant in prayer, the power of God came mightily upon us, insomuch that many cried out for exceeding joy, and many fell to the ground. As soon as we were recovered a little from that awe and amazement at the presence of his majesty, we broke out with one voice, "We praise thee, O God; we acknowledge thee to be the Lord!" '[27]

As we read these statements we cannot fail to recognize that here were men filled with a mighty zeal, a torrent of enthusiasm—men ready 'to spend and be spent' for God. However, their fervour needed a channel in which to flow, in which its force could be harnessed. And it shortly found just such a channel. George Whitefield began preaching in the open air, and soon he led John and Charles Wesley into undertaking the same ministry. They could each now gather an audience in any town or city in England and their congregations would often be greater than even the largest churches could hold.

This difficult but glorious ministry constituted Charles Wesley's chief activity throughout the following sixteen years, and the experiences he had just been through had served to prepare him for this labour. He was gradually gaining victory in matters in his personal life; he preached with a strong realization of God-given authority; he witnessed the divine power in operation in the saving of various men and women under his ministry; he had overcome the need to use a manuscript in preaching and had begun to speak extempore; and in his experiences among the prisoners he had become convinced that the worst of men may be saved, even at the eleventh hour. Having been taught these lessons, he was ready now to put them into effect in the mighty undertaking of the open-air ministry.

A strong necessity was laid upon me, that I could not rest, but must go to the utmost of my ability to exhort. I could not meet or travel with anybody, rich or poor, young or old, without speaking to them concerning their souls ... I was absolutely dark and ignorant with regard to the reasons of religion; I was drawn onwards by the love I had experienced, as a blind man is led, and therefore I could not take notice of anything in the way.

My food and drink was praising my God. A fire was kindled in my soul, and I was clothed with power, and made altogether dead to earthly things ... I lifted up my voice with authority, and fear and terror would be seen on all faces ... I was given a commission to rend and break sinners in the most dreadful manner. I thundered greatly, denouncing the gentry, the carnal clergy and everybody.

(Howell Harris)[1].

7.
The gospel in the open air

Whitefield was himself led into the open-air ministry by the example of a tireless, fearless, dynamic Welshman, Howell Harris.

Harris, a schoolteacher living at Talgarth in South Wales, had been converted in the spring of 1735, without the aid of any human instrument. Overflowing with joy and moved by a burning desire to win men and women to Christ, he began to gather the neighbours into his mother's kitchen to tell them what God had done for his soul.

Then he took to the outdoors. He attended various events that drew crowds together—such things as sports matches, wakes, agricultural fairs and the like and, taking his stand on anything that served as a platform—a wagon, a stone wall or a pile of turf—he there declared the gospel with fervency and power. Numerous hearers were brought to deep repentance and the lives of many were remarkably transformed by the grace of God.

On his return to England Whitefield opened correspondence with Harris. As a result, although he knew it would be considered utterly fanatical for a Church of England clergyman to preach out of doors, he recognized the practice could open the way to reach thousands of men and women with the gospel and he determined to undertake it. He set out for Wales, intending to meet Harris and observe him as he preached to some of his great open-air gatherings. But he paused on reaching Bristol to minister in some of the religious societies, in the prison and in the few churches that invited him, and he found himself fully employed.

Adjacent to Bristol, however, there was a coal-mining district known as Kingswood. It was populated by some hundreds of miners and their families, and no school or church had ever been built for them. They toiled for long hours amid the grime of

the coal dust for low wages, and they were a sullen and sometimes
a vicious people. Despite these uninviting conditions Whitefield
went out to Kingswood. It was a Saturday in an exceptionally
cold February, but 200 people gathered to hear him. 'Blessed
be God,' he said, 'I have now broken the ice. I believe I was
never more acceptable to my Master than when I stood to teach
those hearers in the open fields.'

Having thus begun the great task of preaching in the out-of-
doors, Whitefield continued to perform it. He returned to
Kingswood on the Tuesday and this time his audience numbered
'nearly two thousand' and repeating the effort on the Friday he
found 'four or five thousand' there. On the Sunday he preached
there again and now his hearers were estimated at 'ten thousand'.

After continuing this activity for some weeks Whitefield wrote,
'Having no righteousness of their own to renounce, they were
glad to hear of a *Jesus* who... came not to call the righteous, but
sinners to repentance. The first discovery of their being affected
was to see the white gutters made by their tears, which fell plen-
tifully down their black cheeks... Hundreds and hundreds of them
were soon brought into deep convictions which... happily ended
in a sound and thorough conversion.'[2]

Whitefield expanded this work, holding meetings all around
the area and preaching two and three times a day. He went into
Wales and met Howell Harris, and the two of them undertook
an evangelistic tour, with Whitefield preaching in English and
Harris in Welsh.

Because of his responsibilities to America, however, Whitefield
could give a mere six weeks to his labours in the Bristol area.
He therefore needed to find someone to carry on the work he
had begun, but since he was conducting more than twenty services a week, there were few men able or willing to undertake
it. He considered two or three friends but finally settled on John
Wesley and wrote, asking him to come and take over this work.

The task of preaching to such vast companies of people was
something entirely new in Wesley's experience and ministering
in the fields was directly contrary to his ecclesiastical principles.
Indeed Whitefield's request sorely disturbed both John and
Charles and also the members of the Fetter Lane Society. They
sought directions by opening the Bible at random, but the result
was very disappointing, for each time they tried, the verse they
came upon spoke of either trouble or death. After some days

'of extreme emotion and anxiety' John wrote, 'I go,' and Charles stated, 'We dissuaded my brother from going to Bristol, from an unaccountable fear that it would prove fatal to him... He offered himself willingly to whatever the Lord should appoint. The next day he set out... I desired to die with him.'[3]

After reaching Bristol Wesley stood with Whitefield as the latter preached to a congregation estimated as 30,000. Whitefield also arranged that John would preach in the open air to a week-day meeting he had announced, and, despite his reluctance, John did so. Whitefield left for London, but John remained behind and undertook the heavy activity Whitefield had commenced. Thus, far from going to his death, John Wesley had entered upon the major work of his life.

In London Whitefield's ministry drew tremendous congregations. Although he was only twenty-three he preached twice and three times a day, and his evening audiences, on both Sundays and weekdays, were estimated as seldom less than 25,000.

Whitefield also took steps to thrust Charles Wesley out into the open-air ministry. In order to accustom him to the sight of so many people, he had Charles stand with him as he ministered to some of his huge London crowds. 'I stood by G. Whitefield,' said Charles, 'while he preached on the mount in Blackheath. The cries of the wounded were heard on every side. What has Satan gained by turning him out of the churches?'[4]

It is evident that Charles experienced a strong desire to enter upon this labour too. He knew that John had undertaken it at Bristol and when John made a temporary visit to London he saw Whitefield influence him to preach out-of-doors there as well. Despite his Church of England principles and his personal sensitivity, Charles longed to begin the great task himself.

Charles made his first attempt at outdoor preaching while visiting in a country place outside of London. 'Franklyn, a farmer,' he wrote, 'invited me to preach in his field. I did so to about five hundred... I returned to the house rejoicing.'[5]

Yet on his return to London he was not ready to undertake this activity there. Accordingly, Whitefield continued his persuasions and Charles wrote, 'My inward conflict continued. I perceived it was the fear of man; and that, by preaching in the field next Sunday, as George Whitefield urges me, I shall break down the bridge and become desperate. I retired and prayed for particular direction; offering up my friends, my liberty, my life, for Christ's sake and the gospel's. I was somewhat less burdened, yet could not be quite easy till I gave up all.'⁶

At this point Whitefield put a special pressure on Charles. Whitefield had preached each Sunday morning in a kind of park named Moorfields and had drawn a regular congregation of some 10,000. But on the following Sunday he had arranged to minister elsewhere and he therefore informed Charles that this congregation would be waiting for him to preach to them! Confronted by the challenge, Charles could not fail to accept it.

'I prayed,' he wrote, 'and went forth in the name of Jesus Christ. I found near ten thousand helpless sinners waiting for the word in Moorfields. I invited them, in my Master's words, as well as name: ''Come unto me, all ye that travail and are heavy laden, and I will give you rest.'' The Lord was with me, even me, his meanest messenger, according to his promise ... My load was gone, and all my doubts and scruples. God shone upon my path; and I knew this was his will concerning me.'⁷

On the following Sunday a very different form of ministry awaited Charles: it was his turn to preach before the University of Oxford. This was a prestigious opportunity and he performed the task, he says, 'with great boldness'. Moreover, in an interview with the vice-chancellor he 'gave him a full account of the Methodists; which he approved; but objected the irregularity of our doing good in other men's parishes ...All were against my sermon, as liable to be misunderstood.'⁸

Back in London Charles preached on the next two Sundays, following the pattern Whitefield had set: in the morning to 'near ten thousand' at Moorfields and in the evening to 'double that number' on Kennington Common. It was evident that he could go on in this manner, undoubtedly with such vast numbers before him each Sunday and with tremendous crowds on weeknights also.

At the prospect of this heavy responsibility Charles's mercurial nature began to beset him. He was a man of strong emotions and a poet's sensibilities, and although these qualities gave force to his preaching, they also made him desire at times to live a more meditative life. He also recognized the danger of pride in ministering to such large congregations and the trials he experienced are manifest in the following statements.

'*Sunday, July 22d*. [1739] I never knew till now the strength of temptation and the energy of sin. Who, that conferred with flesh and blood, would covet great success? I live in a continual storm. My soul is always in my hand. The enemy thrusts sore at me, that I may fall; and a worse enemy than the devil is in my own heart.'[9]

'*Tuesday, August 7th*. Too well pleased with my own success, which brought upon me the buffetings of Satan.'[10]

At this point in their lives both Charles and John looked upon Whitefield as the leader, the general superintendent, of the work they were doing. Charles now felt that he should inform Whitefield that he was not prepared to carry on the open-air ministry permanently. Accordingly, he wrote to him, first reporting on his preaching at certain towns on his return journey from Oxford, and then stating, 'I am continually tempted to leave off preaching, and hide myself like J. Hutchins. I should then be freer from temptation and at leisure to attend my own improvement. God continues to work *by* me, but not *in* me, that I can perceive. Do not reckon upon me, my brother, in the work God is doing: for I cannot expect he should long employ one who is ever longing and murmuring to be discharged. I rejoice in your success, and pray for its increase a thousand fold.'[11]

During the days that followed, although Charles frequently made statements of this nature, he did not 'leave off preaching'. It was manifestly a tremendous labour to preach so often and to such large numbers without our modern electrical amplification of sound, and we may well understand Charles's desire to 'be discharged'. But he had inherited much of the unyielding tenacity of his parents and, despite his frequent reluctance, he continued to preach in the open air. Indeed, he persevered in the mighty task and it was to be the chief activity of the next sixteen years of his life.

Charles also assisted various people in a personal way. One of these was William Seward, a young widower who had attained financial success in the stock market. On meeting Seward Charles spoke of him as 'a zealous soul, knowing only the baptism of John',[12] but a week later he said, 'W. Seward testified faith.' Seward proved very zealous for the Lord and consecrated his time and his possessions to furthering the spread of the gospel. He became particularly devoted to Whitefield and expressed a desire to follow him wherever he might go. He went with Whitefield on his next trip to America, but despite his eagerness his company was not entirely propitious for his zeal showed

increasing signs of fanaticism. However, he lived little more than
a year after this, dying as a result of an attack upon Howell Harris
and himself during an open-air meeting in Wales. He was at
his best while under Whitefield's direct influence.

After merely two months of preaching outdoors in London,
Charles Wesley set out for Bristol. But he stopped on the way
to preach at Evesham, the home of Seward's brothers and their
families. He wrote, 'I preached from George Whitefield's pulpit,
the wall ... Many, I am persuaded, found themselves stripped,
wounded, and half-dead; and are therefore ready for the oil and
the wine.'[13] He also gave evidence of the first signs of a coming
theological controversy, for he was opposed by some of the
Sewards who professed to hold to the Calvinistic doctrines, but
who showed few signs of spiritual life. We shall hear more of
this issue later.

Seeking a man to take over the work he had commenced at
Gloucester, Whitefield asked Charles to preach there and also
asked a friend to 'arrange places' at which he might speak.
Charles reveals some of both the trials and joys of his labour
in his report of this visit to Gloucester, the town in which
Whitefield had been born.

He writes, 'By ten last night the Lord brought us hither
through many dangers and difficulties. In mounting, I fell over
my horse, and sprained my hand. Riding in the dark, I bruised
my foot. We lost our way as often as we *could*. Two horses we
had between three...'[14]

'Before I went forth into the streets and highways, I sent, after
my custom, to borrow the church. The minister (one of the better disposed) sent back a civil message, that he would be glad
to drink a glass of wine with me, but durst not lend me his pulpit
for fifty guineas.

'Mr Whitefield [a brother of George] durst lend me his field...
For near an hour and a half God gave me voice and strength
to exhort about two thousand sinners to repent and believe the
gospel.

'My voice and strength failed together; neither do I want them
when my work is done.'[15]

But besides the difficulty of travel and the heavy burden of
the work, the open-air ministry required also a great measure
of self-renunciation. The sacrifice is manifest in an event that
took place at this time. During their days at the university the

Wesleys had frequently been guests at the home of a family named Kirkham, who lived at Stanton near Oxford. They were people of cultivated taste and the father was the rector of the local Church of England.

Charles reports that, as he went to preach at one of his open-air meetings at Gloucester, 'An old intimate acquaintance (Mrs Kirkham) stood in my way, and challenged me, "What, Mr Wesley, is it you I see? Is it possible that you who can preach at Christchurch, St Mary's etc., should come hither after a mob?" I cut her short with, "The work which my Master giveth me, must I not do it?" and went to my mob, or (to put it in the Pharisees' phrase) this people which is accursed. Thousands heard me gladly, while I told them of their privilege of the Holy Ghost, the Comforter, and exhorted them to come for him to Christ as poor lost sinners. I continued my discourse till night.'[16] That he had indeed 'offered up friends, liberty and life, for Christ's sake and the gospel's,' is well illustrated by this incident.

At Bristol Charles temporarily took over the work that had been conducted by John. He stayed, as John had done, at the home of Mrs Grevil, Whitefield's sister, a widow who operated a grocery business. She attended the gospel preaching of her brother and of the Wesleys.

Charles began to minister, as Whitefield had done, at six o'clock on Sunday mornings on the Bowling Green. He likewise followed Whitefield in preaching at Rose Green, Hanham Mount, the Brick Yard, Baptist Mills, Weaver's Hall and the two main societies: Gloucester Lane and St Nicholas Street. These places, at which Whitefield had first preached and where John and Charles followed him, proved the cradle of Methodism in Bristol.

Throughout his ministry Charles preached with the authority of 'a man sent from God'. But during these early months this quality lent a seeming severity to his utterance. This is manifest in the following entries that he made in his *Journal* during these weeks in Bristol.

'*September 8th* ... I prayed God to direct me what to preach upon, and opened on Ezekiel's vision of dry bones. "So I prophesied as I was commanded; and as I prophesied, there was a noise, and, behold a shaking!" The breath of God attended his word. A man sunk down under it. A woman screamed for mercy, so as to drown my voice. Never did I see the like power among us.'[17]

'*September 9th* ... I preached on "When he is come he shall convince the world of sin, and of righteousness," etc. ...I never spoke more searchingly... some Pharisees quitted the field, feeling the sharpness of the two-edged sword.'[18]

'*September 10th* ...I discoursed two hours on John 3. A notorious drunkard gave glory to God, declaring he had found mercy last night... This stirred the Pharisee in a woman's soul, and she cried out against him most vehemently. I took and turned her inside out, and showed her her spirit in those who murmured at Christ for receiving sinners.'[19]

Several further such statements could be quoted from his records of these days.

Yet, together with this measure of severity, there was an extraordinary earnestness, and God used his ministry in the salvation of numerous men and women. Hard hearts were broken and stubborn wills were subdued under his preaching, and almost every day's entry in his *Journal* tells of someone who entered a new life through Charles's declaration of the gospel.

For instance, he reports, 'After sermon a poor collier afforded me matter of rejoicing... He... owned he was the wickedest fellow alive a month ago; but now finds no rest in his flesh by reason of his sin. Observing him much dejected ... I asked him if he was sick. "No, no," he answered, "my sickness is of my soul." Here he informed me that he had come home with such a weight upon him, that he was ready to sink. It continued all night; but joy and deliverance came in the morning.'[20]

Or again, '...while I was expounding Isaiah 4, a man perceived his filth purged away by the Spirit of judgement and burning.'[21]

'While I was repeating..., "Is not my word like a fire saith the Lord, and like a hammer that breaketh the rock to pieces?" a woman fell down under the stroke of it. I found afterwards, that the Good Samaritan had poured in his oil, and made her whole. Another declared he had bound up her wounds also. I heard on all sides the sighing of them that were in captivity, and trust [that] more than I know were set at liberty...'[22]

'They come to me daily, who have found Christ, or rather are found by him, so that I lose count of them.'[23]

We learn something more about Charles's ministry from the

statements of one who heard him during these days—Joseph Williams, a layman from Kidderminster. He tells of visiting Bristol and going to hear Charles: 'I found him standing on a table-board, in an erect posture, with his hands and eyes lifted up to heaven in prayer, surrounded by, I guess, more than a thousand people, some few of them fashionable persons... but most of them of the lower rank of mankind ... he prayed with uncommon fervency, fluency and variety of proper expression.

'He then preached about an hour in such a manner as I have scarce ever heard any man preach: i.e. though I have heard many a finer sermon, according to the common taste, or acceptation, of sermons, yet I think I never heard any man discover such evident signs of a vehement desire, or labour so earnestly to convince his hearers that they were all by nature in a sinful, lost, undone, damnable state; that, notwithstanding, there was a possibility of their salvation, through faith in Christ; that for this end our sins were imputed to him, or he was made sin for us... in order that his righteousness might be imputed... to as many as believe on him ...

'All this he backed with many texts of Scripture, which he explained and illustrated, and then by a variety of the most forcible motives, arguments and expostulations, did he invite, allure, quicken and labour, if it were possible, to compel all, and every of his hearers, to believe in Christ for salvation.'

Williams goes on to tell of accompanying Charles to a society meeting that evening. He says, 'We found them singing an hymn... He first prayed; then expounded part of the 12th chapter of John, in a most sweet, savoury, spiritual manner; then sung an hymn, then proceeded a while further in the exposition, then sung again; then prayed over a great number of bills... and then concluded with a blessing; in all of which he took up near two hours.

'But never, sure, did I hear such praying. Never did I see or hear such evident marks of fervency in the service of God. At the close of every petition a serious "Amen," like a gentle, rushing sound of waters ran through the whole audience, with such a solemn air as quite distinguished it from whatever of that nature I have heard attending the responses in the church service...

'If there be such a thing as heavenly music upon earth, I heard it there; if there be such an enjoyment, such an attainment, as

heaven upon earth, numbers in that society seemed to possess
it. As for my own part I do not remember my heart to have been
so elevated in divine love and praise... and an affecting sense
and savour thereof abode in my mind many weeks after.'[24]

The task Charles was performing was an exacting one. It
required an unusual power of voice, great clarity of enunciation
and the expenditure of tremendous physical energy. He reports
the sense of weakness with which it often left him: 'I always find
strength for the work of the ministry, but when my work is over,
my strength, both bodily and spiritual, leaves me. I can pray
for others, not for myself. God by me strengthens the weak hands,
and confirms the feeble knees; yet I am myself as a man in whom
is no strength. I am weary and faint in my mind, longing continually to be discharged.'[25]

Nevertheless, notwithstanding the enervation his preaching
so often produced and his frequently expressed desire 'to be
discharged', Charles persevered in the task for which God had
so manifestly gifted him. He daily, and even twice or three times
a day, preached the gospel and as he laboured thus was able
to say, 'I knew this was his will concerning me.'

And after some days Paul said unto Barnabas, Let us go again and visit our brethren in every city where we have preached the word of the Lord, and see how they do.

And Barnabas determined to take with them John, whose surname was Mark.

But Paul thought it not good to take him with them, who departed from them from Pamphylia, and went not with them to the work.

And the contention was so sharp between them, that they departed asunder one from the other; and so Barnabas took Mark, and sailed unto Cyprus.

And Paul chose Silas, and departed, being recommended by the brethren unto the grace of God.

(Acts 15: 36—40).

8.
Doctrinal differences and sad divisions

The point we have now reached in the life of Charles Wesley is one at which doctrinal divisions arose in the work. The year was 1739 and he had reached the age of thirty.

In these conflicts each of the Wesleys acted not only with firm conviction but also with militant assertiveness. In turn, if we are truly to know Charles we have no choice but to consider his words and manner in this strife. We do so, however, with the knowledge that in a few years' time his opinion would be to a large extent altered and he would again become friendly with those from whom he now parted.

Of course, numerous reports of this affair have been published. But much of the evidence has been allowed to remain hidden and the story has been presented almost solely from John Wesley's side. Accordingly, to look on it now more objectively will undoubtedly seem biased to many readers.

The Wesleys separated first from the Moravians. Peter Böhler, whose influence in the lives of Charles and John we have already seen, became the teacher of the Fetter Lane Society. Whenever the brothers were in London they attended the meetings of this society and John assisted Böhler in drawing up new rules by which it could be governed. Under Böhler's influence the society began to follow certain Moravian customs and the majority of the members concurred with this trend.

Böhler, however, soon left for America and his place was taken by another German, Philip Henry Molther. Molther immediately expressed his dislike of the noisiness of the meetings. He said he was 'almost terror-stricken at hearing their sighing and groaning, their whining and howling, which strange proceeding they call the demonstration of the Spirit and power'.[1] Mistakenly assuming that the faith of many of these people could not be real, he attempted to institute certain of the practices of a German movement known as Quietism. He advocated 'the stillness teaching', urging his hearers to become utterly passive in religious matters and to wait before God in 'stillness' till true faith should be born within them. He taught that they would do well to abstain from all outward religious acts, especially from attending the sacraments of the Church of England, lest they regard such acts as 'means of grace' and trust in them for salvation.

The Wesleys looked upon this teaching as a direct denial of the authority and the function of the church and they vigorously opposed it. A conflict ensued and Charles reports his estranged relations with several of those who had formerly been his close friends.

In his *Journal* he makes, for example, the following statements: 'James Hutton came to fetch me to Molther, at J. Bray's. I chose rather to fast than to eat; and to pray in God's house, than dispute in another's. I called with Maxfield on Molther in the afternoon. He did not much open himself; only talked in general against running after ordinances. We parted as we met, without either prayer or singing.'[2]

'I spent an hour with Charles Delamotte. The Philistines have been upon him and prevailed. He has given up the ordinances, as their being matter of duty.'[3]

'I disturbed Mr Stonehouse[4] before his time. It was but eight o'clock. However, he rose and came with me ... He is now taught to teach, that there are no degrees of faith; no forgiveness or faith, where any unbelief remains; any doubt, or fear, or sorrow.'[5]

'Simpson took upon him next to reprove me for mentioning myself in preaching, and showing such vehemence, which, [he asserted], was all animal spirits. I took him up short, that I should not ask him, or any of the brethren how an ambassador of Christ should speak ... Simpson spoiled all again, by accusing me with "preaching up the ordinances". I got home, weary, wounded, and bruised, and faint, through the contradiction of sinners; *poor* sinners, as they call themselves, these heady, violent, fierce contenders for stillness. I could not bear the thought of meeting them again.'[6]

'Simpson and the rest have dissuaded them, and indeed all our friends, from ever hearing my brother or me, or using any of the means. They condemn all doing good, whether to soul or body. "For unless you trust in them," say they, "you would not do good works, so called."'[7]

'Only Almighty God can root out those cursed tares of pride, contempt and self-sufficiency, with which our Moravianized brethren are overrun.'[8]

'I found Bell, Bray, Hutton, Holland, Ridley, and others of the same class. I withstood them to the face, and appealed to the God that answereth by fire, for the truth of my doctrine, that the ordinances bind all, both justified and unjustified.'[9]

'I went straight to Blendon [the home of the Delamotte family]; no longer Blendon to me. They could hardly force themselves to be barely civil. I took an hasty leave, and with an heavy heart, weighed down by their ingratitude, returned to Bexley.'[10]

This strife went on for six months. John Wesley then brought it to an end by declaring his separation from the Moravians in one of the society meetings. Nineteen members followed him as he strode out and he joined them to his own society which by that time he had founded in London.

Charles Wesley felt that in standing against what he considered the erroneous practices of the Moravians he was also standing for the true customs of the Church of England. But it is difficult not to feel that he was exaggerating in applying such terms as 'those cursed tares of pride, contempt and self-sufficiency' to these warm-hearted people. He gave up his association with several men who had formerly been his warm friends, but we shall rejoice to see him, later in life, admitting his error and renewing fellowship with many of those from whom he now separated.

The second conflict was aroused by an action on John Wesley's part. In order to understand the matter we need to familiarize ourselves with his position at this time.

Although John Wesley later came into great prominence, at this point (the summer of 1739) he was but little known. The leader of the revival was George Whitefield; Whitefield's name was virtually a household word, and he had congregations of 10,000 in Bristol, and similar numbers in London and Gloucester. As we have seen, he had led Wesley into undertaking the open-air preaching in Bristol and had followed this up by introducing him to his congregations in London and Gloucester. Wesley manifestly wanted a share of the great success, too, and Whitefield assured him, 'Indeed, I wish you all the success you could desire,' and said, 'May you increase, though I decrease,' and 'Though you come after me, may you be preferred before me.'

Around this time John Wesley began to witness some extraordinary accompaniments of his ministry in Bristol. In his services several persons fell into convulsion-like experiences. He reports, for instance, 'Many of those that heard began to call upon God with strong cries and tears. Some sunk down, and there remained no strength in them; others exceedingly trembled and quaked; some were torn with a kind of convulsive motion in every part of their bodies, and that so violently that often four or five persons could not hold one of them. I have seen many hysterical and many epileptic fits; but none of them were like these in many respects.'[11]

In some instances the affected persons came out of the experience in a short time, but others remained subject to it for some hours. 'While I was speaking, says Wesley, 'one before me dropped down as dead, and presently a second and a third. Five others sunk down in half an hour, most of whom were in violent agonies ... In their trouble we called upon the Lord, and he gave us an answer of peace. One indeed continued an hour in strong pain, and one or two more for three days; but the rest were greatly comforted in that hour, and went away rejoicing and praising God.'[12]

Whitefield, however, was opposed to John Wesley's practice of encouraging these experiences and Charles Wesley termed them 'the fits' and virtually made fun of them. But John believed they were directly given by God and since they occurred under the ministry of no other man,[13] he assumed that God had particularly chosen him and was thus approving his labours.

In placing his Bristol work in John's hands, Whitefield, together with several of the London brethren, 'had conjured me,' says Wesley, 'to enter into no disputes—least of all concerning "Predestination," because his people were so deeply prejudiced for it'.[14] None the less, four weeks later, after casting a lot, Wesley preached a most vehement sermon 'Against Predestination.' He made no attempt to expound any Scripture on the subject, but, dealing with predestination only in an extreme form, and speaking on the basis, not of searching the Scriptures, but merely of human reason, he derided it.

For instance, John asserted, 'It is a doctrine full of blasphemy; of such blasphemy as I should dread to mention, but that the honour of our gracious God, and the cause of truth, will not suffer me to be silent ... This doctrine represents our blessed Lord, Jesus Christ the righteous, ... as a hypocrite, a deceiver of the people, a man void of common sincerity ... This is the blasphemy clearly contained in *the horrible decree* of predestination! And here I fix my foot. On this I join issue with every assertor of it.'[15]

Having made these and several similar assertions, Wesley imagined for the moment that the doctrine of predestination were true and on that basis he addressed the devil. He asserted that if this were the case God would be 'the devouring lion, the destroyer of souls', and he closed his sermon by declaring, 'Sing O hell, and rejoice, ye that are under the earth! For God, even the mighty God, hath spoken, and devoted to death thousands of souls, from the rising of the sun to the going down thereof! Here, O death, is thy sting! Here, O grave, is thy victory! ... Let all the sons of hell shout for joy! For the decree is past, and who shall disannul it?'[16]

John Wesley assumed that in these severe words he was belittling the system of doctrine commonly known as Calvinism. And this was the system held to by Whitefield, the friend who only four weeks earlier had set him before the very congregation to which he was now preaching against these beliefs.

Like the Wesleys, Whitefield had been brought up in the Church of England and he had known nothing of 'justification by faith'. While he was at Oxford, however, he read Henry Scougal's *The Life of God in the Soul of Man* and he had then learned that there is an experience known as 'the new birth', that in this God puts his very life into the believing soul and that this life is both divine and eternal. A year later he came into this experience himself and received this new life. He went on to seek ordination, and in preparation, together with his study of the Scriptures, he studied also the Articles of the Church of England, the seventeenth of which enlarges magnificently on the church's teaching concerning predestination. At his ordination, he declared, as did all other ordinands, the Wesleys included, that he believed this article.

Whitefield believed that natural man is 'dead in trespasses and sins', and can do nothing towards saving himself. He held that salvation begins with God and that God commences it in the soul, placing therein faith to believe, giving a desire after holy things and granting eternal life. Whitefield preached the gospel freely to all, and assured every coming soul of a hearty welcome in Christ, yet he believed that all who came had been predestinated by God and that Christ had died for such ones in particular.

At times he used the word 'Calvinism' but more often he termed this system of theology 'the doctrines of grace'. By no means was he following John Calvin but he declared, 'My doctrines I had from Jesus Christ and his apostles.' His belief was in no sense mere fatalism and he did not mention predestination when preaching to the unsaved. The saved, however, found the doctrine a great cause for joy and praise.

The Wesleys, on the other hand, held to the system known as 'Arminianism'. In this they had been instructed in their boyhood home, and during their days at Oxford Susanna, in her letters, reinforced the idea. But on this subject, as we have seen in other matters, she did not base her arguments on a full study of the Scriptures, but her statements were based on human reason and on tradition. As John did in his sermon, she argued against what she supposed was Calvinism, but in fact what she condemned was an extreme form of it which was held by only very few.

Charles and John believed that, despite man's fall, he retained a free will which he could employ in choosing to reject or receive Christ. If he received Christ the action was the result of his own decision, and although he was then saved, if he turned back from following Christ he would be lost again. They spoke of 'assurance of salvation', but it was not an assurance of eternal life, but rather an assurance that applied only to the present moment.

When Whitefield learned that, despite his having 'conjured' Wesley not to do so, John had preached against predestination and had falsely portrayed Calvinism, he was much distressed. He wrote to John, urging him not to publish this discourse, but as soon as Whitefield sailed on his next visit to America (August 1739) Wesley gave it a wide distribution.

While Whitefield was in America throughout 1740 both John and Charles preached against the Calvinistic doctrines. One of

Howell Harris's correspondents reported, 'Mr Charles goes on in the most strong manner, constantly railing at either the Predestinarians or the Moravians'.[17]

Likewise, John Cennick, a fervent but inoffensive man, stated that as he 'happened to dine with Charles', the latter 'began to dispute about election. He fell into a violent passion and affrighted all at the table, and rising from the table, he said he would go directly and preach against me, and accordingly did. He called Calvin the first-born son of the devil and set all his people into a bitter hatred of me.'[18]

After he had introduced John to his Bristol congregation, Whitefield had laid the first stone of a school he intended to have built at Kingswood. He had also begun, in his ministry at London and elsewhere, to raise money for its construction and undoubtedly had collected sufficient money to meet its full costs.[19] Wesley wished to see the two leading Bristol societies joined together and Whitefield used his influence to accomplish this union.

During Whitefield's absence John laid hold of the two buildings that had been constructed in the Bristol area—the school at Kingswood and the New Room in which the two Societies, now united into one, held their meetings.

When Whitefield returned from America in March 1741, having led the work of the Great Awakening there, he found that back at home the Wesleys had largely succeeded in turning his people against him. However, a large wooden tabernacle was built for him and he began to gather back his congregation. He also published a reply[20] to Wesley's sermon and while he makes his arguments distinctly this reply is remarkable for the respect and good will that he displays in it.

At this point, however, Whitefield made his one mistake in these dealings with Charles and John. In publishing his sermon John had intimated that he had been especially directed by God to 'preach and print' against predestination and, although he did not say so, he was referring to the lot he had cast. But the inference of being divinely authorized to act in this matter implied that his sermon must be correct as to its doctrinal statements. Therefore the issue was one of doctrine and not of personalities, and Whitefield pointed out that Wesley was referring to the casting of a lot, and not to some special authorization given by God.

Moreover, some few months after Whitefield's return John

began to soften in his attitude towards Whitefield, and this
Charles did not like. Charles wrote to John and his letter reveals
how militant he could be: 'O thou eternal Phrygian! I am too
full to write or speak! Do you know the value of souls! precious,
immortal souls! yet trust them within the sound of predestination?
This is outdoing your own outdoings. Stop the plague *just now*,
or it will be too late. Send me word, first post, that you have
warned our flock from going to hear the other's gospel ...

'Send me word, I say, by next post, that you have restrained
the unwary, or I shall, on the first preaching night, renounce
George Whitefield from the house-top.'[21]

Other instances of Charles's polemic actions could be cited
but the extracts quoted above are sufficient to reveal how convinced he was of the correctness of his own opinions and how
ready to contend against anyone who disagreed.

The Wesleys also began to assert another teaching in which
they differed from virtually all other Christians of that time. This
was the teaching that John termed 'Christian perfection'.

However, John did not clearly define his meaning. Rather
he left the concept with two very different meanings. It could
mean merely Christian maturity, and with this, of course, no
one disagreed. But it could also mean a state of sinlessness, the
rooting out of the entire old nature, and to this numerous Christians took exception. Yet it was this latter view that John stressed
and this was the teaching's only *raison d'être*. The Wesleys
assumed it gave their doctrinal position a superiority over the
views of all others round about. It became for John, however,
a means of separating his followers from other Christians, giving them a particular identity and making them exclusively his
own.

In this concept of perfection Charles was in agreement with
John, as we see in the following statements from his *Journal:* 'I
asked her, "Do you know Christ died for you?" "Yes" she
answered joyfully, "for me, and for the whole world. He has
begun, and he will finish, his work in my soul." "But will he
save you," I said, "from *all* sin?" She replied, "I know he will.
There shall no sin remain in me."'[22]

'Mr Wynn of Painswick. He ... had received remission of sins.
He had heard of nothing farther and yet wanted something more,
he knew not what, till God sent him hither. Now he rejoiced
in hope of redemption from all iniquity.'[23]

'I prayed by a dying woman, who waits for redemption from *all* iniquity *here*: otherwise she knows she can never see God. About noon I applied ... ''But ye are washed, but ye are sanctified,'' etc. Never have I spoke more closely to those who rest in the first gift.'[24]

George Whitefield, Howell Harris, Lady Huntingdon and many others totally disagreed with the Wesleys in this concept of a person being instantaneously made perfect, and in his later years we shall rejoice to see Charles himself largely departing from this view.

Although Whitefield had done everything possible to prevent strife with the Wesleys, John finally wrote him a very severe letter and blamed him for beginning the dispute. Whitefield said no more. He allowed John to retain both the New Room and the Kingswood School and, assisted by John Cennick, he built another school in Kingswood and, later, a large tabernacle in Bristol. After ten years had passed he said in reference to the treatment he had suffered at this earlier date: 'It is good for me that I have been maligned, judged by and separated from my nearest, dearest friends. By this I have found the faithfulness of him who is the friend of friends...'[25]

It is evident the Wesleys had a strong polemic element in their natures. We have seen that during his days at Westminster School Charles frequently engaged in fist-fights and throughout life he fought his theological battles with the same fervour. Nevertheless, if this trait seems a weakness, it was also a strength. It reveals that Charles was characterized by unmovable convictions and undaunted courage—qualities in which he was like his grandfathers and his father, all of whom had earlier exhibited just such features.

Moreover, in Charles Wesley, together with this controversial faculty there also dwelt a rich tenderness, a fellow feeling with men and women in any need, and we follow him as he manifested both of these characteristics in the ministry now before him.

The mere enumeration of his services gives no adequate idea of the strain upon Charles Wesley. His preaching was so tender, so pathetic, so full of convincing power that it made heavy demands upon his physical strength.

At times he was so drawn out in his zeal for souls that he continued speaking for three hours. Once he notes that he began again and again after he thought that he had concluded. The sight of the multitude thirsting for the Word of God, in days when the Methodist preacher was often their only guide and helper, made Charles Wesley eager to declare to them all the counsel of God.

(John Telford,
The Life of Charles Wesley, M.A., 1900).

9.
Preacher and pastor

As has already been mentioned, during 1738 John Wesley led in the construction of the New Room in Bristol, and in this he held the meetings of the two religious societies that Whitefield and he had united into one. He also acquired a building in London—a former factory which to some extent he now repaired, which he named the Foundery. It contained a large assembly hall and also his own living apartment. Here, in 1739, he had his mother come to live with him.

In November of this year, however, the Wesleys learned some very sad news. Their elder brother Samuel, who was a schoolmaster at Tiverton in Devon, suddenly died. 'He had gone to bed, seemingly as well as usual, was taken ill about three o'clock in the morning, and died at seven.' He had been an able schoolteacher, possessed considerable poetic gifts and, as we have seen, had been of true assistance to Charles during the latter's days at Westminster. Immediately upon hearing of his passing Charles and John set out for Tiverton, to be of what help they could to Samuel's widow and children. It was the first time either of them had been to Devon, and this visit to the south-west of England soon led to their travelling further west still, into Cornwall—an activity we shall see in due course.

Upon his opening of the Foundery in 1739, this building became John's headquarters and the centre of Wesleyan Methodism. And it continued to serve these purposes until it was replaced by a new chapel nearly forty years later.

Bristol and London now became the chief scene of the labours of the two brothers. While John took charge of the work in London Charles did the same in Bristol, and at the end of a month or two they alternated. But they not only preached in the New Room and the Foundery—they also launched out into

The Foundery, London

the areas round about and formed new Methodist societies in London and in the region adjacent to Bristol.

During November 1740, at the invitation of three Church of England clergymen, Charles made his first visit to Wales. He preached daily for two weeks near Cardiff and his emotional nature made a profound appeal to the Welsh people.

Here, however, he met his first experience of violence. A physician, after attending a service, angrily confronted him, demanding he apologize for terming him 'a Pharisee'.

Charles replied, ' "I still insist you are a Pharisee, and cannot endure sound doctrine. My commission is, to show you your sins; and I shall make no apology for so doing, to you or any man living. You are a damned sinner by nature, and a Pharisee, like me ... You are a rebel against God, and must bow your stiff neck to him before you can be forgiven ... You are no Christian at all, unless you have received the Holy Ghost."

'Here he lifted up his cane and struck me. Mrs Philips intercepted and broke the blow; F. Farley tripped up his heels; and the company rushed in between ... There was a great outcry among the women. Several of them he struck, and hurt, and raged like one possessed, till the men forced him out.'[1]

A bailiff[2] arrived. Addressing him directly, Charles asserted, 'Mr Bailiff, I honour you for your office' sake; but was you yourself, or His Majesty King George, among my hearers, I should tell you both that you are by nature damned sinners. In the church, while preaching, I have no superior but God; and shall not ask man leave to show him his sins.'[3]

Meanwhile a company of actors, armed with pistols, surrounded the building and threatened to burn it down. They were militant against Charles because many of the people who usually attended their plays had chosen instead to come to his services, and they were left temporarily unemployed. Nevertheless, despite the threats, Charles and his people 'prayed and sang' and they did so 'with great tranquillity till one in the morning'.[4]

But at three o'clock an actor broke in secretly. He was discovered, carrying a sword, and appeared about to attack Charles. Certain of the men seized him and Charles reports, 'The spirit of faith was kindled among us, at the sight of danger. Great was our rejoicing within, and the uproar of the players without, who strove to force their way after their companion. My female advisers were by no means for my venturing out, but [for] deferring my journey.'⁵ Charles had arranged, however, to be back in England very shortly. Therefore, accompanied by a friend, he went out and walked, he says, 'through the midst of our enemies'.

As the Wesleys ministered in any town they always sought to enlist all interested persons into attending a regular society. By the time 1740 closed they had several small bodies, some in London and some in and near Bristol and others at various locations between these two cities. In performing these tasks Charles had not the slightest intention of forming a new denomination, but his purpose was that of strengthening the Church of England. Each society was nominally part of that national body and he regarded himself as its faithful servant, seeking only its welfare.

As we survey Charles Wesley's labours during 1741—he was then thirty-three—it is evident he was not only a mighty evangelist but he had also become an exceptionally helpful pastor. He daily ministered to the people of his societies and entered feelingly into the joys and sorrows of their lives. His care for men and women is particularly evident in his visits to those who were drawing near to the close of life's journey and, although during this year he seems not to have performed any marriages, he did conduct several funerals. We feel something of his large heart, his deep emotions and his burning sincerity as we read the following statements from his *Journal.*

'*April 9th [1741].* I got some hours for visiting our numerous sick, most of whom I found in a good way; only one backslider... was in the depth of despair.'

'*April 11th.* Today he called forth another of his dying witnesses; the young woman whom, at my last visit, I left in utter despair. This morning she broke out into, "I see, I see it now, that Jesus died for me, and for all the world." ...Some of her words to me were, "Death stares me in the face; but I fear him not. He cannot hurt me..." '

'*April 13th.* While I was in great love, warning the bands, the Spirit of power came down, the fountain was set open, my mouth and heart enlarged, and I spoke such words as I cannot repeat. Many sunk under the love of Christ crucified, and were constrained to break out, "Christ died for all." '

'*April 19th* ...I heard that our sister Richardson had finished her course. My soul was filled with strong consolation, and struggled, as it were, to go after her...'

'*April 21st*. I hastened to the joyful funeral of our sister Richardson. The room was crowded within and without. My subject was "I know that my Redeemer liveth" etc. (Job 19: 25). I spoke searchingly to the hearsay-believers; and then largely of her, whose faith they might safely follow. Great was my glory and rejoicing over her ...

'The whole Society followed her to her grave. Through all the city Satan raged exceedingly in his children, who threw stones and dirt at us.'

'*April 22nd*. I sharply reproved three or four inflexible Pharisees; then prayed the Lord to give me words of consolation, and immediately I was filled with power, which broke out as a mighty torrent. All our hearts caught fire in a moment, and such tears and strong cryings followed, as quite drowned my voice. I sat still while the prayer of the humble pierced the clouds, and entered into the ears of the Lord of Sabaoth.'

'*April 24th* ... I rode to Kingswood, where many were come from far, to spend the night in watching and prayer. We had much of the divine presence; but remained myself like Gideon's fleece; till, at midnight, a cry, "Behold, the Bridegroom cometh!" The flame was kindled, and the Lord our God was among us as in the holy place of Sinai.'

'*Sun., May 3rd*. At Kingswood as soon as I had named my text, "It is finished!" the love of Christ crucified so constrained me, that I burst into tears, and felt strong sympathy with him in his sufferings. In like manner, the whole congregation looked upon him whom they had pierced, and mourned.'

'*May 4th*. I saw my dear friend again, in great bodily weakness, but strong in the Lord... I spoke with her physician, who said he had little hope of her recovery; "Only," added he, "she has no dread upon her spirits, which is generally the worst symptom. Most people die for fear of dying; but I never met with such people as yours. They are none of them afraid of death." '

'*May 5th* ...A wild collier brought me four of his children, and threw the youngest on the table before me, crying, "You have got the mother, take the bairns too."'

'*May 6th*. I found our sister Hooper just at the haven. She expressed, while able to speak, her fulness of confidence and love; her desire to be with Christ ...

'At my next visit, I saw her in her latest conflict. The angel of death was come, and but a few minutes between her and a

blessed eternity ... My soul was tenderly affected for her sufferings, yet the joy swallowed up the sorrow ...I asked her whether
she was not in great pain. ''Yes,'' she answered, ''but in greater
joy. I would not be without either.'' ...

'When I saw the breathless temple of the Holy Ghost my heart
was still... We knelt down and gave God thanks from the ground
of our heart. We then had recourse to the book of comfort, and
found it written... ''Let us labour therefore to enter into that
rest.'' '

'*May 14th* ...I saw two more of our sick sisters; then two of
the brethren in Kingswood, who were all rejoicing in hope of
a speedy dissolution ...I prayed by a seventh in Bristol, who
laughed at the king of terrors. If God be not with us, who hath
begotten us these?'

'*May 22nd*. I preached a funeral sermon over sister Lillington,
and attended her to her grave ... I gave an exhortation to repentance, though Satan greatly withstood me; thereby teaching me
never to let go unwarned the poor sinners that come on such
occasions.'

'*Sunday, May 31st* ...I read in the society my account of H.
Richardson's death. She, being dead, yet spoke so powerfully
to our hearts, that my voice was lost in the sorrowful sighing
of such as be in captivity. To several God showed himself the
God of consolation also: particularly to two young Welshmen...
They had heard most dreadful stories of us Arminians,
freewillers, perfectionists, papists; which all vanished like smoke
when they came to hear with their own ears.'

'*June 5th*. The morning word was a sharp, two-edged sword
... the poor self-deceiver I spoke with yesterday, could not bear
it, but cried out, ''You are a child of the devil, and your society
are all accursed.'' ... See the false assurance of unbelief, and
tremble! One, in the gall of bitterness, the bond of iniquity, per-
suades herself that she is in the glorious liberty of the sons of
God.'

'*July 11th*. I preached at Bristol, then among the colliers, a
third time at Bath, a fourth at Sawford, and yet again in the
Wood ... Preaching five times a day when [God] calls me to it,
no more wearies the flesh than preaching once.'

'*Sunday, August 2nd* ... I preached a funeral sermon over Rachel
Peacock, who died in the Lord most triumphantly. She had continual joy in the Lord, which made her cry out, ''Though I groan,

I feel no pain at all; Christ so rejoices and fills my heart.'' Her mouth also was filled with laughter, and her tongue with joy. She sang hymns incessantly.

'At the sight of her coffin my soul was moved within me, and struggled as a bird to break its cage. Some relief I found in tears, but still was so overpowered, that, unless God had abated the vehemence of my desires, I could have had no utterance. The whole congregation partook with me of the blessedness of mourning.'

'*August 5th* ... Coming to pray by a poor Welsh-woman, she began with me, ''Blessed be God that I ever heard you! Jesus, *my* Jesus, has visited me on a bed of sickness. He is my heart. He is my strength. None shall pluck me out of his hand. I cannot leave him, and he will not leave me.'''

'*August 17th*. I visited one who was forsaking the fellowship, whom God had arrested in her flight by sickness, convinced, condemned and justified her again.'

'*August 22nd* ... At Sawford, ... the enemy stirred up his servants to fierceness of opposition. But we defied them in the name of the Lord, who first restrained and then stilled, the madness of the people.'[6]

While on a further mission to Wales during the same year (1741) Charles was asked to call on a country squire, Robert Jones. Jones was a man of possessions and position and had been awakened under the ministry of Howell Harris. He revealed a spiritual hunger as Charles talked with him, and he arranged to have him preach at a local Church of England.

'God was amongst us,' reported Charles, 'and a mighty tempest was stirred up around him. He shook many souls out of their carnal security. Never hath he given me more convincing words. The poor simple souls fell down at the feet of Jesus. Their shepherd, also, was deeply affected, and hid his face, and wept ... God had spoken to his heart, and the hearts of his people; for, when we were gone out of the church, it was still filled with the cries of the wounded.'[7]

Robert Jones also was deeply moved and he urged Charles to delay his return to Bristol so that he might hear him once more. Charles preached again in a nearby church and also 'to some hundreds in the courtyard' of Jones's home, Fonmon Castle. Before leaving he wrote, 'I took sweet counsel with Mr Jones alone. The seed is sown in his heart, and shall bring forth fruit unto perfection.'[8]

At Charles's request Jones accompanied him to Bristol and to Kingswood. He heard several of the colliers testify concerning their experience of the saving grace of God and of their transformed lives, and he joyfully acknowledged, says Charles, 'that God was with us of a truth'. Upon Jones's return to Wales so zealous did he prove that his friends asserted he must be beside himself. But he did not have long to serve God upon earth, for in less than a year, although he was only thirty-six, he died. The Wesleys were deeply saddened by the loss of this man who could have proved of great value in their work.

Thus we have seen Charles Wesley during his first year as an itinerant preacher. He now lived virtually a homeless life, spent much of his time on the road, ate what he might and slept in whatever homes were offered. He daily went out with zeal, earnestly declared the gospel and met frequent violence with undaunted courage. He was used of God in leading souls to Christ and, in dealing with men and women, especially as they drew near to death, he proved himself a wise and tender pastor.

Moreover, the hostility he met had served to prepare him for the abundance of such treatment he was to meet during the ensuing years of open-air ministry. Similarly, the work of a pastor that he so ably performed made him the more ready to extend understanding and help to souls in need throughout the rest of his life.

If Methodism had not come into contact with the mob it would never have reached the section of the English people which most needed salvation. The 'Religious Societies', shut up in their rooms, would never have reformed the country.

It was necessary that a race of heroic men should arise, who would dare to confront the wildest and most brutal men, and tell them the meaning of sin, and show them the Christ of the Cross and of the Judgement Throne.

The incessant assaults of the mob on the Methodist preachers showed they had reached the masses. With a superb courage ... the Methodist preachers went again and again, to the places from which they had been driven by violence, until their persistence wore down the antagonism of their assailants. Then, out of the once furious crowd, men and women were gathered whose hearts the Lord had touched.

(John S. Simon,
The Revival of Religion in the Eighteenth Century).

10.
Into darkest England

By 1742, the period we have now reached, Susanna Wesley, Charles's mother, was 'a lone widow, aged and infirm, eyesight dim, and frame tottering on the verge of the grave'.[1] 'For years she had suffered great debility and much sickness, which one of her daughters declares was "often occasioned by want of clothes or convenient meat ".'[2] During the time she lived with John she was in comfortable surroundings and, of course, had no monetary needs. Above all, she witnessed the growth of his work and rejoiced in his ministry and these months were undoubtedly some of the most contented she had known.

Moreover, despite the attitude she had manifested towards her sons' profession of conversion, she herself seems in her last years to have entered into such an experience. On an occasion when her son-in-law Westley Hall was officiating at the communion service at the Foundery, she stated, 'While my son Hall was pronouncing the words in delivering the cup to me, "The blood of our Lord Jesus Christ which was shed for thee," the words struck through my heart, and I knew that God, for Christ's sake, had forgiven all my sins.'[3]

Before long, however, it was evident that Mrs Wesley was failing rapidly. As the end drew near Charles was out of town, but John and his five sisters were gathered in her bedroom. John read the solemn commendatory prayer. Her look was calm and serene and a little before she lost her speech she said, 'Children, as soon as I am released, sing a psalm of praise to God.'[4] Thus died Susanna Wesley, on 23 July 1742.

Charles wrote a verse that was engraved upon her tombstone[5] which contained the lines:

> True daughter of affliction, she,
> Inured to pain and misery,
> Mourned a long night of grief and tears,
> A legal night of seventy years.

Of course, he was implying that until her experience in receiving the cup from Westley Hall she had remained in the darkness.
Numerous evangelical authors have soundly rejected this statement and, although throughout previous days she seemed not
to have understood the nature of the 'new birth', there are many
passages in her letters which manifest her assurance that salvation
was to be gained through faith in Christ.

To Charles she wrote in 1738, 'It is not in wealth, or honour,
or sensual pleasure to relieve a spirit heavy laden and weary of
the burden of sin. These things have power to increase our guilt
... but none to make our peace with him, to reconcile God to
man and man to God ...

'No, there is none but Christ, none but Christ, who is sufficient for these things. But, blessed be God, he is an all-sufficient
Saviour; and blessed be his holy name that thou hast found him
a Saviour to thee, my son!'[6]

Here, undoubtedly, was a woman who long had known Christ
and had walked with him and while we cannot but regret her
years of looking to her works to save her, we may well rejoice
in the final clarity of her vision and the assurance it afforded.

During 1742 both Charles and John Wesley went into parts
of England in which they had not formerly laboured. These were
especially the Midlands and the north of England. In several
towns, after some days of preaching, they left behind an infant
society—a company of people who manifested a strong spiritual
interest and whom they counselled to meet together regularly
to strengthen one another in their new desires.

In the following year, 1743, Charles returned to the same parts
of the country and he found that in many places the seed they
had sown the previous year was now bringing forth fruit. He
learned that several of the societies that he and John had founded
were still in existence and some of them were flourishing. For
instance, in the Staffordshire town of Wednesbury he remarked
that the society they had left with a handful now numbered above
three hundred.[7]

At the nearby town of Walsall, however, Charles met nothing

but opposition. He stood on the steps of the market-house and began to preach, but he later reported, 'The street was full of fierce Ephesian beasts... who roared, and shouted, and threw stones incessantly. Many struck, without hurting me. I besought them in calm love, to be reconciled to God in Christ. While I was departing, a stream of ruffians was suffered to bear me from the steps. I rose, and, having given the blessing, was beat down again. So [the same thing] the third time, when we had returned thanks to the God of our salvation, I then, from the steps, bade them depart in peace, and walked quietly back through the thickest of the rioters.'[8]

Charles moved on to Sheffield. After speaking of the society there as 'sheep in the midst of wolves', he stated,

'At six I went to the society-house... Hell from beneath was moved to oppose us. As soon as I was in the desk [the pulpit] ... the floods began to lift up their voice. An officer ... contradicted and blasphemed. I took no notice of him and sung on. The stones flew thick, hitting the desk and people. To save them and the house, I gave notice I should preach out, and look the enemy in the face.

'The whole army of the aliens followed me. The captain laid hold on me and began reviling. I ... preached the gospel with much contention. The stones often struck me in the face. After sermon I prayed for sinners, as servants of their master, the devil; upon which the captain ran at me with great fury... He forced his way through the brethren, drew his sword and presented it to my breast. My breast was immediately steeled. I threw it open, and, fixing my eye on his, smiled in his face, and calmly said, "I fear God and honour the King." His countenance fell in a moment, he fetched a deep sigh, put up his sword, and quietly left the place.

'...We returned to our brother Bennet's, and gave ourselves unto prayer. The rioters followed, and exceeded in their outrage all I have seen before. Those of Moorfields, Cardiff, and Walsall, were lambs to these. ... Satan now put it into their hearts to pull down the society-house, and they set to their work while we were praying and praising God. It was a glorious time with us ...

'One sent for the constable, who came up, and desired me to leave the town, "since I was the cause of all this disturbance". I thanked him for his advice, withal assuring him, "I should not go a moment the sooner for this uproar; was sorry for *their* sakes that they had no law or justice among them: as for myself, I had my protection, and knew my business, as I supposed he did his.'' In proof whereof, he went from us, and encouraged the mob.

'They pressed hard to break open the door. I would have gone out to them, but the brethren would not suffer me. They laboured all night for their master, and by morning had pulled down one end of the house.'[9]

On the following day Charles wrote, 'It being agreed that I should preach in the heart of the town, I went forth nothing doubting. We heard our enemies shouting from afar. I stood up in the midst of them and read the first words that offered ...

'I... walked through the open street... with the multitude at my heels. We passed by the spot where the house [had] stood: they had not left one stone upon another ...The mob attended me to my lodgings... but as soon as I entered the house they renewed their threatenings to pull it down. The windows were smashed in an instant; and my poor host was so frightened, that he was ready to give up his shield...

'The house was now on the point of being taken by storm. I was writing within, when the cry of my poor friend and his family, I thought, called me out to those sons of Belial.'[10]

Charles slept that night in the room that the rioters had largely dismantled. At five the next morning he addressed the believers from 'those comfortable words, ''Confirming the souls,'' ' and experienced, he says, 'the extraordinary blessing I expected'. He left the people rejoicing in God 'who had delivered us out of the mouth of the lions'.

After entering the town of Thorpe he sought to reach Barley Hall, the building in which the Methodist society met. But he found that the people 'were exceeding mad against us'. He and a companion, David Taylor, 'one of Lord Huntingdon's servants', made their way towards the hall, when, '... the ambush rose, and assaulted us with stones, eggs and dirt. My horse flew from side to side, till he forced his way through them. David Taylor they wounded in his forehead, which bled much: his hat he lost in the fray.

'I returned and asked what was the reason a clergyman could not pass without such treatment. At first the rioters scattered; but their captain, rallying, answered with horrible imprecations, and stones that would have killed both man and beast... My horse took fright, and hurried away with me down a steep hill, till we came to a lane, which I turned up... The enemy spied me from afar, and followed, shouting. Blessed be God, I got no hurt, but only the eggs and dirt. My clothes indeed abhorred me, and my arm pained me a little by a blow I received at Sheffield ...

'I met many sincere souls assembled in Barley Hall to hear the Word of God. Never have I known a greater power of love. All were drowned in tears; yet very happy.'[11]

After preaching amid more peaceful conditions at Leeds and Birstall Charles journeyed towards Newcastle. But, 'Near Ripley my horse threw, and fell upon, me. My companion thought I had broken my neck; but my leg only was bruised, my hand sprained, and my head stunned; which spoiled my making hymns, or thinking at all, till the next day ...'[12]

Charles's fall from his horse reminds us that he suffered trials other than those of facing the mobs. In our present day of comfortable cars and excellent roads we do well to realize that he travelled from town to town on horseback. And in those days many English roads were little more than trails, very dusty in summer and either deep in mud or frozen into ruts in winter. Charles was manifestly an able rider, but he sometimes suffered falls and these occasionally left him injured. We also need to remember that he was living a homeless life and, although he sometimes stayed with Christian friends, there were many occasions on which he spent the night in a lodging-house or in some wayside inn, and more than once the bed he slept in was full of fleas.

During 1743 and 1744 certain of Charles's views and practices were beginning to change. For one thing, he came to recognize that everyone who professed faith in Christ was not necessarily converted.

He stated, 'We have certainly been too rash and easy in allowing persons for believers on their own testimony; nay, and even persuading them into a false opinion of themselves.'[13]

And to 'a young son in the gospel', he declared, 'Be not oversure that so many are justified. By their fruits ye shall know them. You will see reason to be more and more deliberate in the judgement you pass on souls. Wait for their conversation. I do not know whether we can infallibly pronounce *at the time* that anyone is justified. I once thought several in that state, who, I am now convinced, were only under the drawings of the Father. Try the spirits, therefore, lest you should lay the stumbling-block of pride in their way, and by allowing them to have faith too soon, keep them out of it for ever.'[14]

At about the same time Charles reports the case of a woman who, although she declared she was converted, told him she had never been proud in all her life. 'Now what madness,' he wrote, 'to tell this soul, so utterly ignorant of herself, that she is justified! She may be so, for what I know; but for me positively to determine it, would be the way, I think, to stop the work in its beginning.'[15]

The practice Charles thus adopted was a wise one and many of today would do well to copy it.

The violence continued during this 1743 trip to the Midlands and the north of England. But it was manifested in perhaps an increased measure when, after preaching in Epworth, London and Bristol and other places along the route, he travelled on to the most westerly county of England, Cornwall. One of the chief industries of Cornwall was the mining and smelting of tin. But the county was also infamous for the practice of smuggling in which a number of its inhabitants frequently indulged. Many were ignorant and vicious and of one of his first services there Charles reports, 'I had just named my text at St Ives ... when an army of rebels broke in upon us ... They began in an outrageous manner, threatening to murder the people if they did not go out that moment. They broke the sconces, dashed the windows in pieces, tore away the shutters, benches, poorbox, and all but the stone walls ... Several times they lifted up their hands and clubs to strike me ... they beat and dragged the women about, particularly one of great age, and trampled on them without mercy. The longer they stayed, and the more they raged, the more power I found from above. I bade the people stand still and see the salvation of God; resolving to continue with them, and see the end ... The ruffians fell to quarrelling among themselves, broke the town clerk's (their captain's) head, and drove one another out of the room.

'Having kept the field, we gave thanks for the victory; and in prayer the Spirit of glory rested upon us.'[16]

Despite this treatment received on a Friday, Charles preached at St Ives again on the Saturday, using as his text, 'No weapon

that is formed against thee shall prosper.' Also the same day
he declared the Word at Gwennap 'to near two thousand hungry
souls'. Here he found the attitude of the hearers very different.
He stated concerning the people of Gwennap and those of a
neighbouring town, Redruth,'If any man speak against us, say
they, he deserves to be stoned.'[17]

Nevertheless, the violence still met him in other places in
Cornwall. Concerning the Sunday he says, 'At Wednock many
listened to my description of our Lord's sufferings from Isaiah
53. After evening service I would have finished my discourse;
but the minister's mob fell upon us, threatening and striking
all they came near. They swore horribly they would be avenged
upon us, *for our making such a disturbance on the Sabbath-day*... They
assaulted us with sticks and stones, and endeavoured to pull me
down. I bade them strike me, and spare the people...

'We were now encompassed with a host of men, bent on
mischief, with no visible way of escape; but the Lord hath many
ways. He touched the heart of one of our persecutors, who came
up to me, took me by the hand, and besought me to depart in
peace, assuring me he would preserve me from all violence.
Another gentleman did the same. I told them I had an unseen
Protector...

'I stayed some time to make my observation. Ten cowardly
ruffians I saw upon an unarmed man, beating him with their
clubs, till they felled him to the ground. Another escaped by the
swiftness of his horse. My convoy they set upon for dissuading
them, and forced him to fly for his life.

'I walked on slowly with all the rabble behind. One of the
brethren attended me ...About six we rested at brother Nance's.
The enemy still pursued. I went out and looked them in the face,
and they pulled off their hats, and slunk away.'[18]

The Mayor of St Ives, however, was openly opposed to this
behaviour against the Methodists. He was a Presbyterian, and
besides appearing on the scene in the midst of the opposition
more than once, he also 'declared his resolution to swear twenty
new constables, and suppress the rioters by force of arms'.[19]
He was taking a risk personally by thus seeking fair treatment
for the Methodists and he was one of the few such officials Charles
met during these months of persecution.

But Charles did not want 'the force of arms' as his protection. In various towns one or two of his people struck back at

the antagonists, but he urged them all to bear the ill-treatment without the least retaliation. He 'advised the society' at St Ives, 'to possess their souls in patience, not threatening, or even mentioning the late uproar, but suffering all things for the sake of Jesus Christ'.[20]

Although the Methodist people, living as they did amidst their persecutors, must have often been provoked to retaliate, they largely followed Charles's counsel. In turn, they soon witnessed the results of their behaviour and Charles states, 'Some of our bitterest enemies were brought over by the meekness of the sufferers.'[21] He mentions instances of the conversion of men who had been leaders of the rioters, but who had been influenced by the Christian response of those they persecuted.

The Mayor of St Ives told Charles 'that the ministers were the principal authors of this evil...' and that they were 'continually representing us ... as popish emissaries and urging the enraged multitude to take all manner of ways to stop us'.[22] We may well understand that most ministers were bitter at the actions of Charles, a fellow clergyman, as he came into their parishes and drew numbers of their people away to hear him. Moreover, many of these men were themselves strangers to the gospel that Charles preached and therefore were so aroused that they did all they could to oppose him. And the ruffians were happy to comply with the suggestions urged by the ministers. To many of them the rioting was a sort of game, and they undoubtedly enjoyed molesting the Methodists, just as though they were engaging in a sporting match.

But above all, there was widespread fear that the Methodists might prove to be the agents of a foreign power. In the Reformation and the Puritan movement the church of Rome had been largely driven out of England. It was, however, constantly seeking to return and therefore the ministers had little difficulty in portraying these itinerant preachers as Jesuits, subtly seeking to bring in Romanism again.

Charles declared the gospel in several other Cornish towns. He met with both opposition and blessing, and says, for instance, as an example of the latter, 'I rode to Morva, and invited the whole nation of tinners to Christ. I took the names of several who were desirous of joining in a society ...we doubt not our seeing a glorious church in this place.

'...I believed a door would be opened this day, and, in the

strength of the Lord set out for St Just, a town of tinners, four miles from Morva, twelve from St Ives. My text was, ''The poor have the gospel preached unto them.'' ... The hearts of thousands seemed moved, as the trees of the forest, by the wind which bloweth where it listeth. The door stood wide open, and a multitude are just entering in. Here it is that I expect the largest harvest.'[23]

While Charles was in the midst of these labours in Cornwall and was witnessing a new measure of success in his ministry, he received word from John that he was wanted in London. A conference had been arranged to take place between the three branches of workers in the revival: the Arminian Methodists, the Calvinistic Methodists and the Moravians.

Concerning his last meeting in Cornwall, for the time being, Charles wrote, 'I rode on rejoicing to Gwennap. As soon as I went forth, I *saw* the end of my coming to Cornwall, and of Satan's opposition. Such a company assembled as I have not seen, excepting a few times at Kennington. By their looks I perceived they all heard, while I lifted up my voice like a trumpet ... The Convincing Spirit was in the midst, as I have seldom, if ever known. Most of the gentry from Redruth were just before me, and so hemmed in, that they could not escape. For an hour my voice was heard by all, and reached farther than their outward ears ... God hath now set before us an open door, and who shall be able to shut it?'[24]

Rejoicing therefore in the harvest he expected to see reaped in Cornwall in later days, Charles set out for London. He had 'near three hundred miles to ride in five days, but,' he says, 'I was willing to undertake this labour for peace, though our journey was too great for us and our weary beasts, which we have used almost every day for these three months.'[25]

He reached London in the time he had suggested, only to discover he had made the difficult trip in vain.

See how great a flame aspires,
    Kindled by a spark of grace!
Jesu's love the nations fires,
    Sets the kingdoms on a blaze;
To bring fire on earth he came;
    Kindled in some hearts it is;
Oh, that all might catch the flame,
    All partake the glorious bliss!

When he first the work begun,
    Small and feeble was his day;
Now the word doth swiftly run,
    Now it wins its widening way;
More and more it spreads and grows,
    Ever mighty to prevail;
Sin's strongholds it now o'erthrows,
    Shakes the trembling gates of hell.

Saw ye not the cloud arise,
    Little as a human hand?
Now it spreads along the skies,
    Hangs o'er all the thirsty land;
Lo! the promise of a shower
    Drops already from above;
But the Lord will shortly pour
    All the Spirit of his love!

                (Charles Wesley).

11.
Spreading the flame

Following his arduous ride from Cornwall, Charles had reason to feel disappointed. The conference was not held. A misunderstanding had taken place in the arranging of the meeting, for Spanenberg, the Moravian leader, had insisted that the archbishop be present and when this did not prove possible he refused to attend.

Before long, however, Charles was on his way to the Midlands again. He met John at Nottingham and wrote, 'October 21st, [1743]. My brother came, delivered out of the mouth of the lion. He *looked* like a soldier of Christ. His clothes were torn to tatters. The mob of Wednesbury, Darlaston, and Walsall, were permitted to take him by night out of the society-house, and carry him about several hours, with a full purpose to murder him. But his work is not finished; or he had now been with the souls under the altar.'[1]

John had suffered extremely vicious treatment and there can be no doubt several of the rioters fully intended to kill him. But in the midst of this fearful trial John had remained as calm as if he had been quietly at work in his study.

With similar courage Charles now went into the same area and preached, even 'in the heart of Darlaston'. Then he returned to the south and visited the societies and preached in the open air in London, Bristol and Wales.

A few months later Charles returned into the Midlands and visited the very towns in which John had been so viciously attacked. He spoke of Wednesbury as 'the field of battle' and reported, 'I cried, in the street, "Behold the Lamb of God, which taketh away the sin of the world." Several of our persecutors stood at a distance; but none offered to make the least disturbance.

'I walked through the blessings and curses of the people, (but the blessings exceeded)...Never have I observed such bitterness as in these opposers.'[2]

Charles reports that when he reached Darlaston he found that the town crier had been sent out with a proclamation ordering everyone to come to a certain public house and there sign a document certifying they would never hear the Methodist preachers again. 'About a hundred,' he says, 'they compelled by blows. Notwithstanding which, both then and at other times, they have broken into their houses, robbing and destroying. And still, if they hear any of them singing or reading the Scripture, they force open their doors by day and by night, and spoil and beat them with all impunity.'[3] He also states that at Walsall the mob had set up placards 'inviting all the *country to rise with them, and destroy the Methodists*'.[4]

But notwithstanding these threats Charles went again into these towns and preached. Several further passages could be quoted which manifest his courage and tireless zeal.

By this time, however, he recognized the possibility of walking needlessly into danger. 'I cannot help observing,' he stated, 'that we ought to wait upon God for direction when and where to preach, much more than we do: a false courage, which is fear of shame, may otherwise betray us into unnecessary dangers.'[5]

Charles moved on to other towns and continued to report the events in his *Journal*.

'*February 8th* [1744]... I called at brother Sants's, and found him just brought home for dead. The mob had knocked him down, and would probably have murdered him, but for a little child, who... alarmed the family by his cries.

'It was some time before he came to himself, having been struck on the temples by a large log of wood.'[6]

'*February 9th*. Our messenger returned from Lichfield... All the rabble of the county was gathered together yesterday, and laid waste all before them. A note I received from two of the sufferers whose loss amounts to about £200 ... Satan was not suffered to touch one of their lives. They have lost all beside...

'At nine we passed through Thorpe. I asked my companion, ''Where are the pretty wild creatures that were for braining me and my horse, the last time I came this way?'' He told me they had lost their spirit with their captain, a woman, the bitterest of them all, who died lately in horrible despair ...'[7]

'*March 4th*. The people of Newcastle were in an uproar... They got their candles ready, and gave thanks, that is, got drunk beforehand, and then came down to make a riot among us. Some of the brethren they struck, and threatened to pull down the desk ...Afterwards, news came that, at this very hour, they were pulling down the [society] house in St Ives.'[8]

Charles witnessed the growth and steadying of Methodism during his visit to the Midlands and the north of England, but larger blessing awaited him on his return to Cornwall. Little more than a year had passed since he had first gone to that part of England, and upon reaching Gwennap he was filled with delight by the enlargement of the work there.

'Here a little one is become a thousand,' he declared. 'What an amazing work hath God done in one year! The whole country is alarmed, and gone forth after the sound of the gospel. In vain do the pulpits ring of "popery, madness, enthusiasm". Our preachers are daily pressed to new places, and enabled to preach five and six times a day. Persecution is kept off till the seed takes root. Societies are springing up everywhere; and still the cry from all sides is, "Come and help us."'[9]

But in other parts of Cornwall persecution still raged. On one occasion, Charles reported of himself and a Church of England minister who was assisting him, 'We set our faces against the world, and rode to St Ives. Here the mob and ministers together have pulled down the preaching-house; and but a fortnight ago went round in the dead of night, and broke the windows of all that were suspected of Christianity ...

'Without were fightings, within fears; but my fears were all scattered by the sight of my dear children. I rejoiced over them with singing; but their joy and love exceeded. We all rejoiced in hope of meeting him in the air.'[10]

At St Just he found that 'Near two hundred are settled in classes,' and at Zunnor that 'Very few hold against the truth.' But at Penzance he reported the legal authority had declared to a Methodist, 'Thou shalt have no justice' and that the same was said to a woman at St Ives who complained that 'stones of many pounds' weight' had been thrown into her house and fell 'within a few inches of her sucking child'.

Upon returning to Gwennap he was given matchless evidence of the power of the gospel. The jail was empty!

'The whole country is sensible of the change,' he declared,

'for last Assizes there was a jail-delivery,—not one felon to be
found in their prisons, which has not been known before in the
memory of man. At their last revel they had not enough men
to make a wrestling-match, all the Gwennap men being struck off
the devil's list, and found wrestling against him, not for him.'[11]

Alongside of this work of the Wesleys (Arminian Methodism)
another work, that of Calvinistic Methodism, under the leadership of George Whitefield and Lady Huntingdon, was also growing. Unlike the Wesleys, Whitefield was devoting a large portion
of his time to America, and his ministry there witnessed tremendous success. He did not, however, attempt to organize his work
on that continent, for he enjoyed the co-operation of the
numerous evangelical pastors and to have built the results of his
labours into a separate body would have been a direct disloyalty
to that trust. But in England, where he met little but opposition
from the pastors, he formed several societies and erected them
into a well-planned organization.[12] In 1743 he held his first
conference and this step was followed some eighteen months later
by the Wesleys. By 1744 Calvinistic Methodism was as large
as Arminian Methodism and could have continued to make the
same progress had that remained Whitefield's intention.

Moravianism was also growing in England. Despite its errors
the lives of its adherents were zealous and warm, and many
people—among them several well-to-do persons—became its firm
followers. In Yorkshire Benjamin Ingham organized a number
of societies and in 1742 he took them all into the Moravian
movement.[13]

Notwithstanding their differences in doctrine, the three bodies
were having an effect upon England. They were causing a
multitude to recognize their responsibility to God and the change
that the gospel was making in numerous lives was having a
nation-wide influence.

Before the close of 1744 Charles was accused of immoral
behaviour. For some months a Thomas Williams had been
carrying false reports about both of the Wesleys and on account
of his actions Charles had refused to recommend him for ordination to the ministry of the Church of England.

Charles wrote, 'Disappointed of orders, he rages and rails on
us, as papists, tyrants, enemies of the church, etc., declares he
has found us out, and runs about, scattering firebrands, and vow-
ing revenge.'[14]

'Mr Larwood discovered to me W.'s real intention, ''to set up for himself''. Above five hundred of the Society [in Bristol], he told Larwood, would follow him.'[15]

This man, who was determined to enter holy orders, and was so proud that he was willing to divide the Wesleys' work in order to obtain a congregation for himself, took revenge by concocting a falsehood about Charles. He claimed Charles had acted immorally with some woman. The woman in turn signed an affidavit to this effect and placed it in the hands of the Rev. Thomas Broughton. Although Broughton had been a member of the Holy Club he had proved unfriendly towards the Wesleys following their conversion, and he now took the affidavit to the Bishop of London. The report spread around, many believed it and Howell Harris wrote in his *Diary*, 'Seeing how Bro. Charles Wesley's sins are come out even to the Bishop, and how it shocks Lady Huntingdon, and how if God won't interfere will prejudice all against us, and ruin him too.'[16]

But George Whitefield, who was then in America, wrote to Charles, 'Some have wrote me things to your disadvantage. I do not believe them. Love thinks no evil of a friend. Such are you to me. I love you dearly.'[17]

Charles became very anxious, not only concerning the tale itself, but also concerning the affidavit and the fact that it had been carried to the bishop. He refers to '... a message which the Bishop of London had sent to L.H. [Lady Huntingdon] ''that if I would come to him, and declare my innocency, touching the scandals and take the sacrament upon it, he would desire no further satisfaction, but himself clear me''. I immediately consented, and sent my brother advice of it.'[18]

In his letter to the bishop Charles declared, 'I therefore take this liberty, and do hereby solemnly declare that neither did I commit lewdness with her that person, neither did I ever solicit her thereunto, but am innocent in deed, word and thought as touching this thing.'[19]

It is manifest that Charles was entirely guiltless in the matter. Nevertheless the charge added to the burdens he already bore—the burdens of his homeless condition, his frequent facing of the mob, his constant travelling and the labour of his preaching and of his leading of the societies. He described his reporting to the bishop as merely the setting of a broken bone, and added, 'The halting will continue till I come to the land where all things are forgotten.'[20]

Difficulty, however, of a totally different nature now arose to confront the Methodists. France was about to invade England, with the particular intention of placing on the throne the grandson of the exiled King James II. This was Prince Charles, commonly known as 'the Young Pretender'. The plan was backed by the church of Rome and were it to succeed it would mean the restoring of that church to its former place of supremacy in the land.

In 1745 the Young Pretender sailed from France and landed on the north-west coast of Scotland. Numbers of Scots flocked to support him and before long Edinburgh was captured. He held court at Holyrood, the palace of his forebears, and won a grand victory at Prestonpans. But after marching in triumph towards London his forces were finally defeated at Culloden in Scotland, and therewith the threat to England's safety was ended.

The rebellion created difficulty for the Methodists because many Anglican clergymen and a number of other people asserted they were in league with the enemy. It was again declared that the Wesleys were actually Jesuits and their followers were members of the church of Rome. To offset these claims John Wesley published *An Address to the King*,[21] on behalf 'of the societies in England and Wales, in derision called Methodists'. He declared the Methodists were members of the Church of England and were fully loyal to His Majesty.

Nevertheless the rebellion occasioned real danger for Charles Wesley. A Yorkshire woman declared she had heard him swear allegiance to the Pretender and it was reported that the officials of the law had offered a reward of £100 for his arrest. He therefore rode to Birstall, the town in which the accusation was made, and presented himself to the justices. They said they did not intend to proceed with the matter and that he might leave, but he demanded that he meet his accusers and have the charges answered.

Charles was left waiting at the justices' door from eleven in the morning till seven in the evening and was then sent for. It turned out that the woman who made the accusation admitted she did not hear the words herself but she was told he had prayed 'that the Lord would bring home his banished'. One of the justices then stated he had been informed the Methodists constantly prayed for the Pretender. Charles thereupon explained that in the gospel God calls home to himself those who have been exiled from him by their sin and that this was what was meant by the phrase. The justices expressed their satisfaction and declared that his loyalty was unquestionable.

Undoubtedly, numerous people would have been happy to have seen Methodism charged with treason and its leaders imprisoned. Accordingly, Charles had acted with wisdom as well as courage in insisting that he be heard and in publicly declaring the loyalty of the Methodists, particularly that of his brother and himself.

During 1745 and 1746 Charles continued to travel the gigantic Methodist circuit. He went repeatedly from Cornwall to Yorkshire and returned, usually devoting time *en route*, to London and Bristol, the chief centres of the work.

When he visited a town in which he had already preached a few times he seldom experienced a repetition of the violence. By that time not only had the mobsters in these places largely satisfied their desire for riot, but a number of them had begun to respect Charles and the Methodist people, and some had been truly converted. For instance, during a visit to Wales Charles fell and sprained his leg, but he reported, 'Our greatest persecutor lent his chair to carry me to Wenvo. Indeed, the whole place seems turned at present towards us.'[22]

At Bath, which he called 'that Sodom of our land,' he stated, 'When I said, "Be drunk no more, swear no more etc.," they answered, "I will not swear: I will not be drunk again, as long as I live." The ale-house keepers and profligate young men are the most exemplary in their repentance.'[23]

And he was referring particularly to Cornwall when he said, 'The whole country finds the benefit of the gospel. Hundreds who follow not with us, have broken off their sins, and are outwardly reformed, and though persecutors once, will not now suffer a word to be spoken against this way.'[24]

Although he had formerly suffered such tremendous violence in St Ives, he now said concerning his visit there, 'At St Ives no one offered to make the least disturbance. Indeed, the whole place is outwardly changed in this respect. I walk the streets with astonishment, scarce believing it St Ives. It is the same throughout all the country. All opposition falls before us, or rather is fallen ... This also the Lord wrought.'[25]

Charles himself was changing, too. This was true particularly of his attitude towards those from whom he differed doctrinally. In his *Journals* and letters we no longer find his harsh thrusts against those he used to term the 'Predestinarians'; indeed, we find him fellowshipping freely with them. For instance, after preaching to a congregation adjacent to Plymouth—a work founded by Whitefield and which was led by a Calvinistic pastor—he says, 'We drank into one spirit, and were persuaded that neither life nor death, nor things present, nor things to come, shall be able to separate us.'[26]

Likewise concerning the doctrine of 'Christian perfection' Charles was manifesting a change. He no longer regarded this teaching as meaning a condition of utter sinlessness but merely one of spiritual maturity. These new convictions were to grow as the years passed and we shall notice this progress as we continue the study of his career.

But although the violence seldom now raged in towns where he had already preached two or three times on previous visits, when he went into a new area he still frequently met serious rioting. This took place, for instance, at Shoreham in Kent, where Charles made the acquaintance of a saintly, elderly clergyman, the Rev. Vincent Perronet. Perronet had two sons, Charles and Edward, who were men of earnestness and ability.

Describing his first visit to Shoreham Charles wrote, 'As soon as I began preaching, the wild beasts began roaring, stamping, blaspheming, ringing the bells, and turning the church into a bear-garden. I spoke on for half an hour, though only the nearest could hear. The rioters followed us to Mr Perronet's house, raging, threatening, and throwing stones. Charles Perronet hung over me, to intercept my blows. They continued their uproar after we were housed.'[27]

From this point onwards the Perronets played an important part in the lives of the Wesleys. Vincent frequently gave both Charles and John fatherly advice. His two sons became active assistants to John, and Edward is widely remembered for his hymn 'All hail the power of Jesu's name'.

It was, however, especially at the town of Devizes in Wiltshire that Charles faced further rioting—indeed, the worst of his entire career. He uses eight pages in his *Journal* to report the experience, including the following paragraphs.

'The curate's mob had been in quest of me at several places, particularly Mrs Philip's ... They broke open and ransacked her house; but not finding me, marched away to our brother Rogers's, where we were praying and exhorting one another to continue in the faith, and through much tribulation enter the kingdom.'[28]

'They continued raging and threatening for the first hour; and pressed hard upon us to break the door. The windows they did break to pieces, and tore down the shutters of the shop. The little flock were less afraid than I expected. Only one of our sisters fainted away: but underneath were the everlasting arms.

'Our besiegers had now blocked up the door with a wagon, and set up lights, lest I should escape ... They hurried away from us to the inn, where our horses were; broke open the stable door, and turned out the beasts, which were found some hours after in a pond, up to their chin in water.'[29]

Charles preached for three quarters of an hour the next morning. But the mob soon attacked, at first using a hand-operated pump to cover the Methodists with water. Then they resorted to a larger engine, 'which broke the windows, flooded the rooms and spoiled the goods. We were withdrawn to a small upper-room, in the back part of the house, *seeing* no way to escape their violence ... Our brother who keeps the society they laid hold on first, dragged him away, and threw him into the horse-pond, and broke his back, as was reported ... His wife fell into fits again.'[30]

'The Mayor's maid came ... and begged me to disguise myself in women's clothes, and try to make my escape ... The rioters without continued playing their engine ... but their number and fierceness increased, and the gentlemen plied them with pitchers of ale, as much as they would drink ...

'Our constable had applied to ... the only justice in town, who would not act. We found there was no help, in man, which drove us closer to the Lord, and we prayed by his Spirit, with little intermission, the whole day.'[31]

'Our enemies, at their return, made their main assault at the back door, swearing horribly they would have me, if it cost them their lives ...

'Now we stood in jeopardy every moment. Such threatenings, curses and blasphemies I have never heard. They seemed kept out by a continued miracle ...

'We were kept from all hurry and discomposure of spirit, by a divine power resting upon us ...

'They were now close to us, on every side, and over our heads, untiling the roof. I was diverted by a little girl, who called to me, ... "Mr Wesley! Mr Wesley! creep under the bed; they will kill you; they are pulling down the house." Our sister Taylor's faith was just failing, when a ruffian cried out, "Here they are, behind the curtain!" At this time we fully expected their appearance, and returned to the furthermost corner of the room...

'In about an hour after the last general assault the answer of faith came, and God made bare his arm. Soon after three, Mr Clark knocked at the door, and brought with him the persecuting constable. He said, "Sir, if you will promise never to preach here again, the gentlemen and I will engage to bring you safely out of town." My answer was, "I shall promise no such thing." '[32]

Two of the men who had been ringleaders in setting on the mob now began to 'quench the fire they themselves had kindled ...for the mob was wrought up to such a pitch of fury, that their masters dreaded the consequence, and therefore went about appeasing the multitude, and charging them not to touch us in our departure.'[33]

'While the constable was gathering his posse, we got our things ... and prepared to go forth. Now our constable's heart began to fail, he told us he much doubted if the mob *could* be restrained; for that thirty or more of the most desperate had gone down the street, and waited at the end of the town for our passing ... I went forth as easy as Luther to the Council ...

'We rode a slow pace up the street, the whole multitude pouring along on both sides ... Such fierceness and diabolical malice I have not seen in human faces. They ran up to our horses, as if they would swallow us; but did not know which was Wesley.'[34]

Charles had been accompanied throughout this experience by a fellow clergyman, the Rev. John Meriton. He had manifested true courage, and now, Charles reports, 'After riding two or three hundred yards, I looked back, and saw Mr Meriton on the ground in the midst of the mob, and two bulldogs upon him. One was first let loose, which leaped at his horse's nose; but the horse, with his foot, beat him down. The other fastened on his nose, and hung there, till Mr Meriton, with the butt-end of his whip, felled him to the ground. Then the first dog, recovering, flew at the horse's breast, and fastened there...The beast reared up, and Mr Meriton slid gently off. The dog kept his hold, till

the flesh tore off. Then some men took off the dogs ... I stopped
the horse ... He remounted with great composure, and we rode
off leisurely as before ...

'We joined in hearty praises to our Deliverer, singing the
hymn, "Worship, and thanks, and blessing," etc.'[35]

There was, however, a small company of Methodists in
Devizes and Charles felt a deep concern for them. They were
left in the midst of these brutal persecutors, and although he
prayed constantly for them, he also wrote a poem which largely
embodies his intercession on their behalf. He entitled it 'For The
Brethren at Devizes'. The following are some verses from it.

> Jesus of Nazareth look down
> On those thou call'st thy flesh and bone,
>   Thy suffering members here:
> Arise, in our defence arise,
> And now, in all the heathen's eyes,
>   On Israel's part appear.
>
> Let none forsake the fold, and fly,
> Let none through fear their Lord deny,
>   But stand the fiery hour;
> The greatness of thy mercy prove,
> The truth of thy redeeming love,
>   And all-sufficient power.
>
> Now, Saviour, now their fears remove;
> The sense of thy forgiving love
>   Abundantly impart
> To all whose sacred love we feel;
> The prayer of faith this moment seal
>   On every panting heart.[36]

Twenty-five years later John Wesley would say concerning
Devizes, 'The furious prejudice which has long reigned in this
town is now vanished away, the persecutors, almost to a man,
being gone to their account.'[37]

Rise, ye ransomed sinners, rise
Friends and neighbours to the skies;
Ye, by Jesu's blood bought near,
Ye to Jesu's Father dear;
Sing with me, give thanks, rejoice;
Make to God a cheerful noise;
I the wandering sheep have found,
Earth and heaven with praise resound!

I (yet, oh, not I, but he
Through my weakest ministry),
On the brink of the great deep,
Jesus found his wandering sheep;
Who their heavenly Owner was,
He hath marked them with his cross;
He who paid their price of old,
Now hath brought them to his fold.

Jesus, God o'er all supreme,
We ere long shall reign with him,
In celestial glory stand
With the sheep at his right hand;
Join the bright angelic throng,
Shout the new triumphant song,
Face to face our Shepherd see,
Gaze to all eternity.

(Charles Wesley,
'A thanksgiving for the success of the gospel in
Ireland during 1748.')

12.
Trials and triumphs in Ireland

On 21 August 1747, Charles Wesley wrote, 'I received a second summons from my brother, hastening me to Ireland.'[1]

Thomas Williams, whom the Wesleys had expelled from their movement because of his evil tongue, had professed to be repentant and, calling himself a Methodist, had started to preach in Dublin, the capital of Ireland.

At his request John Wesley had gone there and had recognized both Williams and the society he had begun. But not wanting to leave Williams in the work alone, John had written for Charles to come.

Charles arrived in Ireland on 9 September. He immediately faced difficulty, reporting, 'Here, the first news we heard was, that the little flock stands fast in the storm of persecution, which arose as soon as my brother left them ...

'God has called me to suffer affliction with his people. The popish mob, encouraged and assisted by the Protestant, are so insolent and outrageous, that, whatever street we pass through, it is up in arms ... The Grand Jury have had the plainest evidence of the riot laid before them; that mixed rabble of papist and Protestants broke open our [society] room, and four locks, and a warehouse, stealing or destroying the goods to a considerable value; beat and wounded several with clubs, etc., tore away the pulpit, benches, window-cases, etc., and burnt them openly before the gate, swearing they would murder us all. Yet it is much doubted whether the Grand Jury will find the bill. But doth not the Most High regard?

'I began my ministry with, "Comfort ye, comfort ye my people," etc. None made disturbance till I had ended. Then the rabble attended us with the usual compliments to our lodgings.'[2]

Realizing the need for a suitable building in which to conduct the Methodist work, Charles obtained a church that was
being used by John Cennick, who by now had become a Moravian evangelist. Cennick's people had done extensive repairs on
the building in expectation of being able to continue to rent it
at a low fee. With Charles's agreement, Williams offered to pay
the landlord double the rent, and the Moravians were
removed.[3] This action is so much out of character for Charles
Wesley, especially at this stage in his life, that we must assume
he did not fully understand Cennick's position.

In Dublin there lay an open area known as Oxmanton Green,
along one side of which there stood an army barracks. The green
was the scene of very frequent battles between the Ormon Mob
and the Liberty Mob and Charles says that in their engagements,
'They seldom part, till one or more are killed. A poor constable
was the last, whom they beat and dragged about, till they had
killed him, and then hung him up in triumph ... Last week a
woman was beaten to death by the rabble; but that was all fair,
for she was caught picking a pocket ... A poor, weakly man,
of Mr Cennick's society, was so abused by his neighbour, who
knocked him down, and stamped upon his stomach, that he died
soon after. The murderer was indeed brought to a trial; but
acquitted, as usual.'[4]

'They have threatened our lives. Mr Paterson they knocked
down, and cut in several places while on the ground; they threw
him into a cellar, and cast stones on him. Mrs Young and many
others were treated in the same manner. Half-hour past nine
the mayor came with his guard, and saw with his own eyes the
havoc the mob have made. He readily granted warrants to
apprehend them. Some of the poorest, papists mostly, were sent
to Newgate [prison]; but the better sort made a mock of his
authority, and walked about town, from alehouse to alehouse,
with the constables, whom, by drink and money, they had
secured for their party.'[5]

Of course, it required tremendous courage on Charles's part
to attempt to preach in so threatening a situation. But it also
required even greater courage to be a member of the Methodist
society and to live daily surrounded by this violent opposition.

Yet Charles preached in the open air and his people supported
him. He reports concerning his first Sunday in Dublin, 'After
commending our cause to God, I walked to the green. I believed

the Lord would make bare his arm in our defence. I called in his name, "Come unto me, all ye that are weary," etc. His power was upon the hearers, keeping down all opposition ... Returning, we were insulted by a gathering mob.'6

On the following Wednesday he wrote, 'I heard that, on Sunday last, after I was gone, the popish mob fell upon the women, but were beaten off by the soldiers. They threaten to come with all their forces next Sunday.'7 But on the Sunday he went forth again to the green and was able to say, 'Never have I seen a quieter congregation at the Foundery than we had at the green, both morning and afternoon. Many of the soldiers were within hearing, though behind the doors and walls, for fear of their officers. The papists stood like lambs. I quoted Kempis, which makes some of them confident I am a good Catholic.'8

In this open-air ministry Charles witnessed the blessing of God. He had not been in Dublin two weeks when he stated, 'I began examining the classes [at the society]; and met several who received the word last week. But, justified or unjustified, all are in earnest, and seem made without fear. I have not seen such soldiers before, so young, and yet so valiant.'9

Charles also tells of the triumphant death of a Christian woman. 'I heard,' he says, 'the best news of any since our coming hither—that our sister Baker is departed in full triumph. To one who asked her this morning how she did, she answered, "Bravely! bravely! never better." The pains of death had then got hold on her, but she smiled on the welcome messenger; took leave of her husband and children with calm joy; expressed great satisfaction at having chosen to suffer affliction with the people of God; confirmed those about her in the same happy choice; and soon after fell asleep, and awoke in paradise.

'I called at the house, as well to exhort the survivors, as to see the late temple of the Holy Ghost. The happy soul had left a smile upon the clay, to tell where she was gone. We were all comforted in prayer and thanksgiving.'10

At first Charles preached in four different buildings in Dublin, but none proved fully suitable. Then he purchased another—a warehouse 'near Dolphin's barn', and this, besides providing a place in which the society could gather, had rooms upstairs in which the preachers could live.

'I passed the day, he reported, at the house we have purchased near Dolphin's barn, writing and meditating. I could almost have set up my rest here; but must not look for rest on this side eternity.'[11]

His particular delight in these new quarters arose from the happy contrast between them and those in which he had been living. He had brought three helpers from England and the four men had been crowded in together amidst deplorable conditions. Just before he moved into the new rooms he said in a letter to John, 'I must go there, or to some other lodgings, or take my flight; for here I can stay no longer. A family of squalling children, a landlady just ready to lie in, a maid who has no time to do the least thing for us, are some of our inconveniences. Our two rooms for four persons (six when J. Healy and J. Haughton come) and I groan for elbow-room; our diet answerable to our lodgings; no one to mend our clothes; no money to buy more. I marvel that we have stood our ground so long in these lamentable circumstances. It is well I could not foresee while on your side of the water.'[12]

Charles also lets us see something of his financial needs at this time in a further letter to John.

Dolphin's Barn,
Oct. 13 [1747]

Dear Brother,

This is a dangerous place: so quiet and retired I could hide myself here of *my* time … 'Tis thousand pities to spoil this pretty house and garden. You shall *have it for your own, if Mr Clark does not choose it: but you must send me money to pay for it, if it be not sent already. The bill I have received, and spent before it came, upon* myself and companion. His money, and three guineas of Trembath's, and book money borrowed, and five guineas, and four given me for printing, are to be paid out of it—besides money for keeping our horses two months, and two persons' travelling expenses to Bristol with the horses. All which I must furnish out of my £20, so that I don't expect so many shillings surplus …

I do not care to tell you, lest it should not last, but I have more life of late than for a long time past.

Farewell[13]

By the time Charles had been in Dublin two months he was

more frequently receiving a welcome from the people in general.
The mayor declared he would imprison any man who as much
as called after the Methodists on the street, and a gentleman
offered them a large piece of land to build upon at a very
moderate price. At the opening service of the new meeting-house
near Dolphin's barn there were far too many hearers to gather
in the room. Charles therefore addressed 'between one and two
thousand', 'both within and without', who 'drank in the strange
glad tidings'. When the service was concluded he said, 'After
preaching five times today, I feel as fresh as in the morning.'[14]

Persecution, however, was far from ended.

'In our return from intercession,' he says, 'we were stoned
for the length of a street or two ... Here I received the first blow
since I came to Dublin.'[15]

'Hearing the minister had procured a mob to hinder our
preaching, I would not suffer any of our preachers or people
to expose themselves at Hanbury Lane. At night, our adversaries, who till then had expected us in vain, broke into the house,
and took possession.'[16]

Charles also leaves a note which manifests an incredible
heartlessness on the part of the public, in which he says, 'I visited
a poor wretch in Newgate, who is to be burnt next week for coin-
ing [counterfeiting]. The proof against her was not very full;
but her life and character cast her. She had lived in all manner
of wickedness, and narrowly escaped death before for killing her
son-in-law. Justice has now overtaken her, and she cries she is
lost for ever. I could not well discern whence her sorrow flowed;
but found hope for her in prayer.'[17]

When another three months had passed Charles felt the
Methodist cause at Dublin was sufficiently well established for
him to leave it for a time. He therefore penetrated inland, and
preached in such places as Tyril's Pass and Temple Macqueteer.
Some of the Methodist people lived in the former town and had
witnessed to their neighbours, and Charles wrote, 'God has
begun a great work here. The people of Tyril's Pass were wicked
to a proverb; swearers, drunkards, Sabbath-breakers, thieves,
etc., from time immemorial. But now the scene is entirely
changed. Not an oath is heard, or a drunkard seen among them.
They are turned from darkness to light. Near one hundred are
joined in society, and following hard after the pardoning
God.'[18]

But when Charles and his party moved on towards Athlone they found things very different. He reported, 'We were mounting a little hill when three or four men appeared at the top ... the stones flew. J. Healey was knocked off his horse with a stone, fell backward, and lay without sense or motion ... There were only five or six ruffians on the spot; but we saw many gathering to us from all sides.

'I observed the man who had knocked down J. Healey striking him on the face with his club; [I] cried to him to stop, which drew him upon me, and probably saved our brother's life ... They had gathered against our coming great heaps of stones, one of which was sufficient to beat out our brains ... 'One struck Mr Force on the head; at whom Mr Handy made a full blow. He turned and escaped part, yet it knocked him down, and for the present disabled him. As often as we returned we were driven off by showers of stones. Some were for returning home; but I asked if we should leave our brother in the hands of his murderers.

'We rode back to the field of battle, which our enemies had quitted, the Protestants beginning to rise upon them. It seems, the papists had laid their scheme at the instigation of their priest ... The man who wounded J. Healey was the priest's servant, and rode his master's horse. He was just going to finish the work with his knife, swearing desperately that he would cut him up, when a poor woman from her hut came to his assistance, and swore as stoutly that he should not cut him up. The man half killed her with a blow from J. Healey's whip, yet she hindered him till more help came ...

'We found J. Healey in his blood at the hut, whither the woman and her husband had carried him. He recovered his senses at the hearing of my voice. We got him to Athlone...

'I removed to a window in a ruined house, which commanded the market-place. The gentlemen, with the minister, and above two thousand hearers, gave diligent heed while I strongly invited them to buy wine and milk without money and price ...

'We marched very slowly for the sake of our patient, till we came to the field of battle. It was stained with blood abundantly. We halted, and sang of triumph and praise to God, who giveth us the victory through our Lord Jesus Christ.'[19]

'I returned to Dublin,' he states, 'half dead with the rain and snow.'

He was anxious, however, to get to Wales. Accordingly, shortly after John arrived to lead the work in Ireland, he took ship. The date was 20 March 1748.

Landing at Holyhead in the Isle of Anglesey he set out by horse. But in crossing to the mainland by ferry he found himself again in difficulty. 'The motion was so violent,' he says, 'that my young horse began prancing, and striving to take the water. I held him with the little strength I had; but an oar lying between us, I had no firm footing, and could not command him at arms' length. His unruliness frightened the other horse, who began kicking, and struck our brother down. I saw the danger, that, if my horse got his foot over the boat, it must overset, and had no strength to hinder it. It came into my mind, "Hath God brought me through the sea to be drowned here?" I looked up, and in that minute the horse stood still, and continued so till we reached the shore.'[20]

Charles's design in getting to Wales, was particularly that he might again see the young lady, Sally Gwynne, whom he had met just before going to Ireland. He had been in that land more than six months and had been subject to almost constant danger, had preached with great frequency, had been poorly fed and had suffered periods of intense tooth-ache. He was now far from well, the journey proved a severe trial and he longed to reach the Gwynne home, Garth, which lay some 140 miles to the south.

He wrote, '*Wed., March 23d.* I was overruled ... not to set out till past seven. The continual rain and sharp wind were full in my teeth. I rode all day in great misery, and had a restless, painful night at Tan-y-bwlch.'

'*Thur., March 24th.* I resolved to push for Garth, finding my strength would never hold out for three more days riding. At five [a.m.] I set out in hard rain, which continued all day. We went through perils of waters. I was quite gone when we came at night to a little village. There was no fire in the poor hut. A brother supplied us with some, nailed up our window, and helped us to bed. I had no more rest than the night before.'

'*Fri., March 25th.* I took horse again at five, the rain attending us still ... The weather grew more severe. The violent wind drove the hard rain full in our faces. I rode till I could ride no more; walked the last hour; and by five dropped down at Garth.'[21]

I look back with delight on every step, every circumstance, in that whole design of providential love. I rejoice with grateful joy at our blessed union, and feel my obligations to every person instrumental therein. Above all, I desire to thank my great Benefactor for giving you to my bosom, and to fulfil his gracious end by leading you to the marriage of the Lamb.

(Charles Wesley, in a letter to his wife, dated 1755).

13.
Miss Sally Gwynne becomes Mrs Charles Wesley

Garth was a large country mansion in Brecknockshire, South Wales. Its owner, Marmaduke Gwynne, was a man of substance and authority. He had nine children and some twenty servants and he maintained a domestic chaplain. There were seldom less than ten or fifteen guests residing in his house.

In 1736, when he first learned of Howell Harris's preaching, Marmaduke Gwynne had set out with the intention of apprehending him. But he had decided to hear the man first and upon doing so, was convinced that instead of being a wild fanatic, as he had been told, Harris was a true and powerful man of God. Gwynne heard Harris on many occasions after that, came into an experience of divine grace and became one of Harris's earnest followers.

Charles Wesley first met Marmaduke Gwynne at Bristol in 1745. But in 1747 he met Miss Sarah (Sally) Gwynne too. Charles was visiting a clergyman whose church was not far from the Gwynne home and he stated, 'Mr Gwynne came to see me at Mr Philips's, with two of his family. My soul seemed pleased to take acquaintance with them.' He had preached already three times that day, but he reported, 'I preached a fourth time at Garth ... the whole family received us as messengers of God.'[1] The following day he preached at a nearby village and then wrote, 'I returned to Garth rejoicing.' He was manifestly delighted in his new company, and two days later he again stated, 'I returned to Garth, and showed the end of Christ's mission, even to make all mankind happy.'[2]

Indeed, he experienced a particular joy in this initial meeting with Sally Gwynne. Although there was a wide difference in their ages—he was approaching forty and she was merely twenty-one—it was, as he later informed her, 'love at first sight'. 'You have heard me acknowledge,' he said in 1749, 'that at first sight "My soul seemed pleased to take acquaintance with thee." And never have I found such a nearness to any fellow-creature as to you. Oh, that it may bring us nearer and nearer to God, till we are both swallowed up in his love.'[3]

This relationship marked a new experience for Charles. He had had his period of flirtation with the young ladies in the Cotswolds during his first year at Oxford, and had become infatuated with one of them. But he had soon given up those friendships in order that he might devote himself solely to the things of God. During his days at the university he was also the object of the designs of an actress, and this also he soon over-came. In general, however, thus far he had held to the Holy Club's principle of ministerial celibacy and had not given any real attention to the opposite sex.

None the less, such an attitude was not natural to Charles Wesley. Although he possessed so highly sensitive and emotional a nature, he was also—as we have seen in his boldness before the mobs—a distinctively masculine person. He was characterized by qualities which could not but have rendered him attractive to women and which suited him to marriage, and it was undoubtedly this that James Hutton meant when he stated that both Charles and John were 'snares to women'. Likewise, while he was in Georgia Colonel Oglethorpe told him, 'On many accounts I should recommend to you marriage rather than celibacy. You are of a social temper, and would find in a married state the difficulties of working out your salvation exceedingly lessened, and your helps as much increased.'[4]

In 1739 Charles had learned that his friend George Stonehouse had just been married and he declared, 'It is a satisfaction to me that I had no hand in it ... G. Whitefield advised me (I thank him for his love) to follow Mr Stonehouse's example.'[5] Yet his tendency to view the married state with disinterest was somewhat lessened when, two days later, he reported, 'I had some conversation with Mrs Stonehouse; surely a gracious, lovely soul.'[6]

This first visit that Charles paid to Garth, however, lasted only six days. Following this brief but happy period he set out for Ireland on the mission there that we have just reviewed. In the midst of the deplorable living conditions that he then experienced, together with his constant preaching, the weight of persecution and frequent intense toothache, he brightened his days by corresponding with Sally.

Nevertheless, despite his immediate affection for her, he realized that there was one matter on which he must make certain: was she truly born again? She had been brought up in a staunch Church of England home and had undoubtedly attended the parish services regularly. She had also heard the resident chaplain read prayers before the assembled family and their guests morning and evening, and she had listened to the powerful ministry of Howell Harris on more than one occasion. But Charles wondered if she was merely 'almost persuaded', and he spoke of her as, like the man in the Scripture, at the edge of the pool and ready to step in. This concern is evident in the following letter that he wrote to her from Ireland.

> Dublin, Sept. 17.
> Why did eternal wisdom bring us together here, but that we might meet hereafter at his right hand, and sing salvation unto God who sitteth upon the throne, and to the Lamb for ever! Surely the will of God is our sanctification. Even now he waits to be gracious unto you; and before I see you (if ever I see you again upon earth) you will know your Redeemer liveth, and will feel his peace and power within your heart. This is my earnest expectation, and my constant prayer.'[7]

But although any likelihood of marriage seemed as yet far distant, Charles clearly had this prospect in mind. 'I had communicated my embryo intentions,' he wrote later, 'to my brother while in Ireland, which he neither opposed, nor much encouraged. It was then a distant first thought, not likely ever to come to a proposal; as I had not given the least hint to Miss Gwynne or the family.'[8]

Charles's mission to Ireland (his first) kept him there for more than six months. When he left he experienced, as we have seen, the difficult crossing of the straits and the long ride from the extreme north of Wales all the way through to the southern county. He had been manifestly poorly fed and overworked in Ireland, and when he reached Garth, having been forced by the extreme driving of the rain to walk the last half hour, he was utterly worn out.

'All ran to nurse me,' he wrote. 'I got a little refreshment, and at seven made a feeble attempt to preach. They quickly put me to bed. I had a terrible night, worse than ever.'

'*Sat., March 26th*, and the five following days I was exercised with strong pain, notwithstanding all the means used to remove it. My short intervals were filled up with conference, prayer, and singing.'

'*Sun., April 3d.* Through the divine blessing on the tender care of my friends, I recovered so much strength that I read prayers, and gave the sacrament to the family.'

'*Mon., April 4th.* Mrs Gwynne carried me out in her chair; and I found my strength sensibly return.'[9]

By this time Charles considered himself sufficiently improved to attempt starting out on his work again.

He continues, *Tues., April 5th.* She drove me to Builth. I took horse at three. Mr Gwynne and Miss Sally accompanied me the first hour. Then I rode on alone, weary, but supported. My accommodations at my inn were none of the best. I lay restless till midnight, expecting to return, as I had promised in case of a relapse.'[10]

Thus he had not only won the affection of Sally, but had gained also the goodwill of her father and mother.

Charles went on with his itinerant ministry, but Sally was on his mind. Within a week he made his way to Shoreham (south of London) and 'told Mr Perronet all my heart'. This was the Rev. Vincent Perronet to whom Charles referred as 'the Archbishop of the Methodists', and at least he did not oppose the idea of Charles's attraction to Sally Gwynne.

When Charles returned to Bristol, Mr Gwynne and Sally met him. Their friendship was growing stronger for he now began to let his use of her name pass from 'Miss Sally' to merely 'Sally'. The father and daughter then accompanied him to London, where he showed them Methodism at its headquarters, the Foundery, and also introduced them to Mr Blackwell the banker and to Mr Perronet at Shoreham. On the homeward journey he took them to Oxford and pointed out the various colleges. They went on together to Bristol, viewed the Methodist work there, and he also caused them to see God's goodness to the colliers at Kingswood. Finally they crossed into Wales and reached Garth, where he says, 'Mrs Gwynne received us with a cordial welcome.'

In this travelling in the company of Sally, Charles was

particularly happy. The element of confrontation appears largely
to have disappeared from his ministry and a new note has entered
into it. He speaks more than once of a 'supernatural strength'
given to him in his preaching and of a spiritual joy so intense that
both he and his hearers were overcome with tears of delight. 'I
began the sacrament' he reports of one such occasion, 'with fervent prayer and many tears, which almost hindered my reading
the service. I broke out into prayer again and again. Our hearts
were all as melting wax.'[11] There is a new exhilaration in his
actions and in his speech that suggests a man truly in love.

Almost a year after he had first met Sally Gwynne Charles
set out from Garth to undertake his second mission to Ireland.
After a difficult ride along unmarked trails he reached Holyhead,
the port from which he was to sail, and from there he wrote to
Sally. He actually refers only to spiritual love, but human love
is manifestly filling his mind. He says, 'This, this is the one thing
needful—not a friend—not health—not life itself, but the pure
perfect love of Christ Jesus. Oh give me love, or else I die! Oh
give me love, and *let* me die. I am weary of my want of love,
weary to death, and would fain throw off this body, that I may
love him who so loved me.

'If you do indeed love me for his sake (and I can as soon doubt
of my being alive), Oh wrestle with that Friend of sinners in
my behalf, and let him not go till he bless me with a sense of
his love. How shall I feed his lambs unless I love him? How shall
I give up all, even those friends who are dearer to me than my
own soul? How shall I suffer for One I do not love? O eternal
Spirit of love, come down into my heart and into my friend's
heart, and knit us together in the bond of perfectness. Lead us
by the waters of comfort. Swallow up our will in thine. Make
ready the bride, and then call us up to the marriage supper of
the Lamb!'[12]

It cannot be claimed that he met no opposition in Ireland this
time, but there was little of the violence he had formerly
experienced. Indeed, in many places he discovered his presence
was welcomed and his ministry desired. For instance, in reference
to Cork he stated, 'At present we pass through honour and good
report. The chief persons of the town favour us. No wonder then
that the common people are quiet. We pass and repass the streets,
pursued by their blessing only. The same favourable inclination
is all round the country.

'Many are turned from their outward sins ... But as yet the work is very superficial. Not one justified person have I found.'[13]

He preached at times to some large congregations. Although the figure is undoubtedly exaggerated, he reports a congregation of 10,000 at Cork. His hearers were from both Protestant and Catholic bodies, even though he said, 'Some of our clergy and all the Catholic priests take wretched pains to hinder their people from hearing us.'[14]

In typically feminine manner Sally had evidently advised him to take more care of himself physically. She had also warned him against rising, as was his habit, at four each morning, and urged that he do his best to sleep in a real bed at night and to take off his clothes before sleeping. In turn, he now wrote to her, 'You will allow me to commend myself. I have not lain on the boards since I left you, and have slept most immoderately till six every morning. This indulgence I impute to *a friend*, who constantly attends my slumbers, and hovers over me as my guardian angel ... I put off my clothes (remembering a friend's advice) every night, that I may make the most of my strength.'[15]

During his days in Ireland he seems to have felt as though she was there present with him. He says, for example, 'I got the whole morning to myself, and my beloved friends in Wales. I had sweet fellowship with them in reading their letters, and saw them, as it were, all about me at the throne of grace. I prayed a second time, [in spirit] with Sally Gwynne, a sincere mourner, just ready for the *consolation* ...'[16] 'I rode on alone, yet not alone ...My absent friends were never *less* absent.'[17]

Charles's stay in Ireland this time was shorter—it lasted only two months. On 8 October 1748 he sailed from Dublin, and after a very tempestuous crossing of the Irish sea and a difficult journey on horseback down through Wales, he once more reached Garth. 'I met our dearest friends there ...' he wrote, 'in the name of the Lord, and rejoiced and gave thanks for his innumerable mercies. At seven I preached with life and faith...'[18]

Charles remained at Garth for a week and apparently during that time he proposed marriage. As he expected, his proposal was accepted.

But he had another person besides Sally to consult. In 1738 he and John had agreed that neither of them would marry or take any step towards marriage without consulting the other. Therefore he now met John in Bristol and says, 'I fairly and fully communicated every thought of my heart. He had proposed three persons to me, S.P., M.W., and S.G.: and entirely approved my choice of the last. We consulted together about every particular, and were of one heart and mind in all things.'[19]

On his return to Garth Charles faced the task of informing Sally's parents of his intention and of securing their consent. There was certainly a large difference in the financial conditions of the Gwynne home and those that Charles could offer. But Sally's sister Becky introduced the subject to her mother and Mrs Gwynne replied that 'she would rather give her child to Mr Wesley than to any man in England'.[20]

Charles further reports, 'Mr Gwynne leaving the whole to his wife, I talked the matter fully over, and left it wholly with her to determine. She behaved in a most obliging manner, and promised her consent, if I could answer for £100 a year.'[21]

However, although Charles had won the approval of Sally's parents and of John, difficulty now arose from another direction. The Rev. Edward Philips, minister of the nearby church at Maesmynis, had regarded himself for some time as the one who undoubtedly would secure Sally Gwynne as his bride. He 'felt that he had a superior claim to the hand of his beautiful young neighbour, and bombarded her with letters to the effect, even going to the length of intercepting her correspondence.'[22]

Charles did not feel, however, that Philips posed any real competition. He merely reports, 'I was a little tried by the brutishness of my friend Philips, who got my advocate, M—n, over to his side. But their buffetings did me no great harm.'[23]

Moreover, Elizabeth Cart, a young lady in London, had set her affection on Charles. He says to Sally, 'Our poor dear S. Cart makes my heart ache to see her: she is so above measure dejected. *My* cheerfulness has murdered *hers* ... You will pity and pray for her, that she faint not in her evil day.'[24]

Charles had assured Mrs Gwynne he would raise £100 a year with which to support Sally, and he now began to arrange how to fulfil his pledge. He talked to John in London and the two of them went to Ebenezer Blackwell, a wealthy banker, and it was decided the money could come from the royalties on Charles's writings. John wrote to Mrs Gwynne to this effect, but Charles reported she was 'dissatisfied with my brother's proposal'. Charles had no regular income and no true home and she wanted some guarantee that he would be able to raise the £100 a year.

At this very time, however, Charles was making arrangements which would provide a more definite source of income. He was planning to publish in his own name two volumes, each entitled *Hymns and Sacred Poems*, the royalties from which would be forthcoming to him. Besides that income, he shared with John in the royalties from the several works they had already produced. Accordingly, he wrote to Mrs Gwynne, saying, 'Till now I neither knew nor cared what my writings and my brother's were worth. But I ordered my printer ... to make an exact estimate. His account of their value ... is £2500, exclusive of the book I am now publishing, which will bring in more than £200 clear, besides a new version of the Psalms worth as much or more, and my journals and sermons, which I am daily called upon to publish ...

'If after strictest scrutiny you are satisfied as to a provision, and Mr Gwynne and you see cause to give your consent, I would desire Miss Sally might secure her fortune in case of her own mortality, that it may return to her own family. I seek not hers but her ... I abhor the thought of being a gainer by her in temporals, and could not rest unless secured from this danger.'[25]

Vincent Perronet also wrote to Mrs Gwynne. He stated, 'The very writings of these two gentlemen are, *even at this time, a very valuable estate*; and when it shall please God to open the minds of people more, and prejudice is worn off, it will be still much more valuable. I have seen what an able bookseller has valued a great part of their works at, which is £2,500: but I will venture to say that *this is not half their value*. They are works which will last and sell while any sense of true religion and learning shall remain among us.'[26]

Undoubtedly, it was with a sense of relief and joy that Charles now wrote, 'I received letters from Garth, consenting to our proposals.'[27]

Charles had certain London lawyers draw up a document guaranteeing the £100 a year—'everything to Mrs Gwynne's wish'. But now further doubts arose. He says, 'Just as we were setting out for Wales, my brother appeared full of scruples, and refused to go to Garth at all. I kept my temper, and promised, if he could not be satisfied there, to desist ... I found my brother had appointed to preach in several places till Friday ... He seemed quite averse to signing his own agreement: yet at five we set out with a heavy heart ... [The next day] Before five I came, weary, faint, oppressed to Cardiff, and lay, being unable to stand.'[28]

Four days later they reached Garth. 'We talked over matters with Mrs Gwynne,' he said, 'and all my brother's fears were scattered. We read over the settlement. Mrs Gwynne proposed a bond till it could be signed. My brother signed the bond ...'[29]

Finally all was ready. There were no more hindrances. The following day, 8 April 1749, was the day planned for the wedding. Charles later reported the grand event: 'Not a cloud was to be seen from morning till night. I rose at four, spent three hours and a half in prayer, or singing, with my brother, with Sally, with Beck. At eight I led *my Sally* to church.

'Mr Gwynne gave her to me (under God): my brother joined our hands. It was a most solemn season of love! Never had I more of the divine presence at the sacrament.

'My brother gave out the following hymn:

Come, thou everlasting Lord,
By our trembling hearts adored;
Come, thou heaven-descended Guest,
Bidden to the marriage feast!

'He then prayed over us in strong faith. We walked back to the house, and joined again in prayer. Prayer and thanksgiving was our whole employment. We were cheerful without mirth, serious without sadness ... My brother seemed the happiest person among us.'[30]

Thus, in South Wales, on this beautiful spring day, did Miss Sally Gwynne, the daughter of prosperity and privilege, become the wife of a poor scholar, the poet, preacher and evangelist, Charles Wesley. And together they began a life of married joy and divine blessing which continued till death did them part some thirty-nine years later.

Charles Wesley intended that his marriage would not be allowed to hinder his ministry. In this respect he was like George Whitefield and Howell Harris, and he determined to preach not one sermon less because he was now a married man.

Indeed, he spent his honeymoon preaching. He and Sally stayed at Garth for ten days following the wedding and he

*Charles Wesley's house in Charles Street,
Stokes Croft, Bristol.*

ministered with his usual frequency throughout the area. Then he left for Bristol and London, but there was now a new exhilaration in his reports. 'Never, since I preached the gospel, have I been more owned and assisted of God...'[31] he declared three weeks after the marriage and in a letter to Ebenezer Blackwell, the London banker, he stated, 'I have not felt the least hurry or discomposure of mind before and ever since my marriage.'[32]

At about this time the Gwynne family moved their home from Garth in Wales to the town of Ludlow, near Hereford in England. Charles and Sally, however, sought a place of their own and Charles arranged to rent a modest home in Bristol.

Sally accompanied him on his next itinerant tour. She adapted well to the travelling and people everywhere rejoiced to see her. Their affection and interest are indicated in his words: 'All look upon my Sally with my eyes.'[33]

It is evident Charles had made an excellent choice. Sally had received a thorough education, not by attending school or college, but through tutors who came into the home. She had been particularly trained in music and played the harpsichord and sang beautifully. Although she had been brought up in a wealthy home, as she entered into her life as the wife of a poor evangelist she showed a calm willingness to share the sacrifices with him. She proved a warm, wholesome, capable and happy personality.

For although marriage in Charles' own case certainly seemed likely to be a spiritual aid and a blessing to the Methodist cause, for his brother it was different. For him marriage was unthinkable. It would certainly be a dereliction of duty, for the main burden of leadership, which entailed constant itinerancy, rested inevitably on John's shoulders. When in December 1748 George Whitefield had urged that both the Wesley brothers should marry, Charles had 'pleaded hard for his brother's exemption'.

(Frank Baker).

14.
Charles Wesley
and brother John's marriage

In October of this year, 1749, Charles Wesley became involved in one of the weirdest entanglements of his entire career.

John Wesley had founded at Newcastle in Yorkshire, not only a society but also a school and an orphanage. One of his chief workers in this establishment was a widow, Mrs Grace Murray. She was an earnest Christian and although there were rumours that she had found difficulty in getting along with some of the other women, the reports in general were highly commendatory. Sick people testified to her tenderness and her help and she was a woman of much prayer and ever busy seeking to win souls.

During 1748 John Bennet, one of Wesley's most capable and zealous young preachers, became ill and came under Grace Murray's care. Bennet had trained for a time in theology and then had turned to the study of law. He came from an excellent family, was well off and had founded several societies. He joined them in a circuit and on this he preached and visited continually. He spoke with conviction and the anointing of God was manifestly upon him.

Bennet remained under Grace Murray's care for five months. She was then thirty-three, was attractive physically and possessed an engaging personality. He was about the same age and a vital friendship sprang up between them. Indeed, before he left the institution they were engaged to be married.

But during the following year John Wesley also fell sick and came under Grace Murray's care at Newcastle. She had thought she was in love with John Bennet, but now that Wesley was near and had her attention for some weeks, an affection sprang up between them, and she felt she was in love with him. Nor was it one-sided, but Wesley was as fond of her as she was of him. In turn, as soon as he was better he had her accompany him, riding on his horse behind him, as he visited several societies in Yorkshire and Derbyshire.

She returned to Newcastle and for the following six months she corresponded with both men—with John Wesley and John Bennet. She evidently decided at one stage in favour of Bennet and, in keeping with Methodist practice, she and Bennet wrote to Wesley asking his permission that they be married.

Grace was not sure, however, as to which man she really wanted. She still manifested a deep affection for Wesley and, since she possessed such strong spiritual capabilities he asked her to accompany him on a visit of some weeks to Ireland. While they were there they entered into an arrangement known as a '*spousal de praesenti*,' which meant that they were virtually married, but without consummation.[1] Moreover, John had agreed to inform Charles before he finally entered into marriage and he was also responsible to inform the Methodist people. Accordingly the marriage was postponed and the ceremony was to be performed by a minister at a slightly later date.

When they returned to Bristol Wesley went about his labours as usual. But Grace then heard that people were using a very evil word about her in her relationships with Wesley and she also heard gossip about a friendship between Wesley and a Molly Francis. Feeling hurt by these developments, and probably because marriage with so outstanding a man as John Wesley seemed to her too good a possibility, she turned again to Bennet. Yet on meeting Wesley again she still declared she 'wanted to live and die with him'. Thereupon John wrote a long letter to Bennet. He charged him with 'unjust and treacherous behaviour', and he sent a copy of this letter to his brother Charles.

The thought of John's marrying Grace Murray immediately filled Charles with alarm. Charles had married into a family of possessions and position, whereas Grace Murray came from much poorer stock and had at one time worked as a domestic servant. These things were of high importance to Charles and although Grace was so earnest a Christian, he was certain she would not be accepted by the Methodist people as the wife of their great leader.

Moved by his native impetuosity, Charles was determined to prevent what, in his thinking, would be a terrible tragedy. He rode in haste from Bristol to the north of England and met John at Whitehaven. We can imagine his vehemence as he declared his opposition to the proposed marriage.

He then left for Hindley Hill, where Grace Murray was then staying. He told her that, since she had made a promise to marry John Bennet before she made one to John Wesley, she must marry Bennet. She was temporarily convinced and got on the horse behind Charles and rode with him to Newcastle. Bennet was there and in keeping with Charles's determination, on the following morning Grace Murray was married to John Bennet.

John Wesley was then at Leeds. There he met George Whitefield and learned the tragic news. John wrote, 'I was troubled. He [Whitefield] perceived it. He wept and prayed over me, but I could not shed a tear. He said all that was in his power to comfort me, but it was in vain. He told me, "It was his judge-ment that she was my wife, and that he had said so to J[ohn] B[ennet]; that he would fain have persuaded them to wait, and not to marry till they had seen me; but that my brother's impetuosity bore down all before it." '[2]

The following day Charles burst in upon his brother and Whitefield. He immediately accosted John, saying, 'I renounce all intercourse with you, but what I would have with a heathen man or a publican.'[3] Whitefield and John Nelson, one of Wesley's most valiant preachers, prayed with the two brothers and since Charles highly respected these two helpers, he gradually changed in his attitude towards his brother.

Charles undoubtedly felt that Grace Murray was not good enough to be married to a Wesley. But his anger was engendered especially by his belief that John had endeavoured to use his superior position to influence her to break her engagement to Bennet and to marry him. He soon, however, overcame his direct hostility, but for some months a coolness remained between him and his brother. Nevertheless, the influence exerted by Whitefield and Nelson undoubtedly prevented a serious division in Methodism that otherwise would have taken place.

John Wesley was heart-broken. He provides an account of the event in his *Journal*[4] but in the Library of the British Museum there is a manuscript, largely in his own handwriting, in which he describes the anguish he endured. There is every reason to believe that he loved Grace Murray and that she would have made him an excellent wife, and we cannot but deplore the impetuosity of Charles which prevented so desirable a circumstance from taking place.

The Grace Murray affair took place in October 1749 and, though heavy of heart, John went on with his work. He then spent four months in Ireland and one in Cornwall, and others in various parts of England.

In January 1751, however, he was called back to Oxford by the Rector of Lincoln College. He was there only long enough to cast his vote in an election, but we are told that, 'In the university ... he had been treated with unexpected respect and affection. A sentence in one of Charles Wesley's shorthand notes makes it extremely probable, if not certain, that once more the "Fellow of Lincoln" was tempted to escape from the strife of tongues, from vulgar misunderstanding and cruel slander, into the quietude of a cloistered life.'[5]

Nevertheless, on his return to London John wrote to the elderly Vincent Perronet, seeking his counsel as to whether he should return to the university or, remaining in his work, if he should marry. He received an answer and stated, 'I was clearly convinced that I should marry.'

A new name now comes into Charles Wesley's *Journal*. It is that of a Mrs Vazeille, a widow with four children and an estate of some £10,000. In February 1751 he reports, 'My brother ... told me he was resolved to marry! I was thunderstruck, and could only answer, he had given me the first blow, and his marriage would come like the *coup de grace*. Trusty Ned Perronet followed, and told me the person was Mrs Vazeille! one of whom I never had the least suspicion. I refused his company to the chapel, and retired to mourn with my faithful Sally. I groaned all the day, and several following ones, under my own and the people's burden. I could eat no pleasant food, nor preach, nor rest, either by night or by day.'[6]

Charles's opposition arose in part from the sudden realization that John actually intended to marry. It had been an accepted principle among the Holy Club men that a single life was better for a clergyman, and John had seemed the one who would carry it out. Moreover, in 1743 John had published a tract entitled *Thoughts on Marriage and Celibacy* in which he declared that 'Those who have power to abstain from marriage are free from a thousand nameless domestic trials,' and that 'These highly favoured celibates ought to prize the advantages they enjoy, and be careful to keep them.'⁷ Throughout the intervening years Charles had taken it for granted that John ought to remain single and it was partly this concept that had caused him to oppose John's marriage to Grace Murray.

Secondly, Charles strongly disapproved of Mrs Vazeille as the wife of his brother. On first meeting her he had referred to her as 'a woman of sorrowful spirit'. He and Sally had taken her to the Gwynnes' new home at Ludlow for a few days and in passing through Oxford he had pointed out and named the various colleges. But Charles knew that, like Grace Murray, she had been a domestic servant at one time, and he also felt she did not possess the spiritual qualities that would win the approval of the Methodist people.

None the less, John was in no way influenced by Charles's opinion. Charles had prevented him from marrying the woman he loved and he was determined not to allow him to interfere this time. He had fulfilled his obligation to Charles by merely informing him he intended to marry and nothing more was necessary.

The hastiness, however, with which John put his resolution into effect provided a further surprise to Charles and to hundreds of Methodists. He had mentioned his intention to Charles on Saturday, 2 February 1751 and on Sunday, 10 February, he fell on the ice and sprained his leg. He preached that morning with great difficulty, but following the service he had himself taken to Mrs Vazeille's home to recuperate. He remained there throughout the week, and on Sunday, 17 February he was carried to the Foundery and preached, although he still found it necessary to do so in a kneeling position. Then, on either the Monday or the Tuesday, he was married.

On the Tuesday evening and the Wednesday morning he preached again, despite being still unable to stand. Tyerman, one of his most important biographers, states, 'This was an odd beginning—the bridegroom crippled, and, instead of making a wedding tour, preaching on his knees in London chapels. A fortnight after his marriage, being, as he says, "tolerably able to ride, though not to walk," he set out for Bristol, leaving his newly married wife behind him.'⁸

Although Charles was severely disappointed, he began to show friendship to his sister-in-law, and to be reconciled to John. Ten days after the marriage he wrote, 'My brother came to the chapelhouse with his wife. I was glad to see him; saluted her; stayed to hear him preach.'[9] At their next meeting he kissed her, 'and was perfectly reconciled to her, and to my brother'. He then brought Sally and John's wife together and 'took all opportunities of showing [her] my sincere respect and love'.

Nevertheless, all was not well with the marriage. By the time four months had passed Charles wrote, 'I found my sister in tears; professed my love, pity, and desire to help her. I heard her complaints of my brother, carried her to my house, where, after supper, she resumed the subject, and went away comforted.'[10]

It soon became evident that John had made a very regrettable choice. His wife tried to travel with him but could not keep up the pace. The itinerant life bothered her, she disliked horse riding and complained about the inns, the poor food, the muddy roads and the rainy weather. Wesley said that to hear so much complaint about travelling was 'like tearing the flesh off his bones'.

Nevertheless, some blame for the differences must be attached to John. As the months came and went he maintained correspondence with several women, most of them young, and although spiritual matters were uppermost in his letters to them and in theirs to him, a personal and intimate element often intruded. One woman to whom he wrote was Sarah Ryan. She had been married three times and never legally separated from any of her husbands. But she professed to be converted and manifested many of the fruits of a new life. John installed her as housekeeper of his boys' school at Kingswood, and this circumstance particularly enraged Mrs Wesley, for John stayed at the school himself whenever he visited Bristol. Moreover, he confided in Mrs Ryan about his difficulties with his wife. She in turn seized some of his letters and read them before the congregation in the Foundery, and reportedly added certain details of her own imagining. She manifestly possessed a severe temper and one of Wesley's preachers, John Hampson senior, says that he once entered Wesley's house unexpectedly, found him on the floor and his wife standing over him, with some locks of his hair in her hands.

Finally, after twenty years she left him, 'purposing never to return'. 'I have not left her; I have not sent her away; I will not recall her,'[11] he declared. She apparently returned to him for one or two brief periods at later dates.

It is possible that at the time when he first learned that John was determined to marry, Charles's own marriage was undergoing some strain. We are told, 'Charles Wesley began the year 1751, harassed by family affairs and out of humour with John and the London Society. In marrying Sally Gwynne he had not detached her from "her two inseparable sisters, Betsy and Peggy". There were friends also coming and going …His shorthand notes … reveal a critical not to say querulous frame of mind. A Sunday spent at Hayes did not sweeten his spirit. He rode back to town the same day, but instead of taking refuge with "Sally" and her sisters, he looked in at the Foundery Society. In shorthand he writes: "Heard my brother exhort the society. I thought he misapplied his subject in trifles."… Ten days later he writes (in shorthand), "Heard my brother in the society. A poor society indeed! His words were quite trifling." '[12]

Charles was manifestly exasperated at the fact that John had married and he was utterly disappointed in the woman he had chosen. He was possibly out of patience at the time, but although he may sometimes have been displeased at having his sisters-in-law so often in his home, in general his relations with Sally were harmonious and gave evidence of true love.

Had Charles Wesley made a grave error in preventing John from marrying Grace Murray? Undoubtedly it was Charles's interference that moved John to his sudden decision to marry Mrs Vazeille and it seems probable that had John married Grace Murray, despite his being 'married to his work', his remaining life would have been happy and contented.

Epitaph of myself

Destined while living to sustain
An equal share of grief and pain:
All various ills of human race
Within this breast had once a place.
Without complaint she learned to bear
A living death, a long despair;
Till hard oppressed by adverse fate,
O'ercharged, she sunk beneath its weight;
And to this peaceful tomb retired,
So much esteemed, so long desired.
The painful mortal conflict o'er,
A broken heart can bleed no more!

(Mehetabel Wesley Wright, c.1740)

15.
Solemn events of 1750

During 1750—between the Grace Murray affair and John Wesley's marriage—two solemn events took place that are related to the life of Charles Wesley.

On 8 February London was shaken by a severe earthquake. 'It began in the south-east, went through Southwark, under the river, and then from one end of London to the other ... There were three distinct shakes, or wavings to and fro, attended with a hoarse rumbling noise, like thunder ... The inhabitants, struck with panic, rushed into the streets, fearing to be buried beneath the ruins of their tottering houses.'[1]

But in exactly a month's time, on 8 March, 'This morning, a quarter after five, we had another shock of an earthquake, far more violent than that of February 8. I was just repeating my text, when it shook the Foundery so violently that we all expected it to fall on our heads. A great cry followed from the women and children. I immediately cried out, "Therefore will we not fear, though the earth be moved, and the hills be carried into the midst of the sea: for the Lord of hosts is with us; the God of Jacob is our refuge." He filled my heart with faith, and my mouth with words, shaking their souls as well as their bodies.'[2]

Ten days later the south coast of England and the Isle of Wight were shaken, and in experiencing the three quakes the people were almost paralysed with fear.

Nevertheless, amidst this alarming situation a soldier, a supposed prophet, declared that in April there would be another earthquake and it would be so powerful that it would destroy half of London and Westminster. His statement was believed virtually everywhere and 'When the looked-for night arrived, Tower Hill, Moorfields, Hyde Park and other open places, were filled with men, women, and children, who had fled from houses

which they expected to become heaps of ruins; and there, filled
with direful apprehensions, they spent long hours of darkness,
beneath an inclement sky, in momentary expectation of seeing
the soldier's oracular utterance fulfilled. Multitudes ran about
the streets in frantic consternation, quite certain that final judgement was about to open; and that, before the dawn of another
day, all would hear the blast of the archangel's trumpet.

'Places of worship were packed, especially the chapels of the
Methodists, where crowds came during the whole of the dreary
night, knocking and begging for admission. At midnight, amid
dense darkness, and surrounded by affrighted multitudes,
Whitefield stood up in Hyde Park, and with his characteristic
pathos, and in tones majestically grand, called the attention of
listening multitudes to the coming judgement, the wreck of
nature, and the sealing of all men's destinies.'[3]

Horace Walpole, English man of letters and prominent politi-
cian, says that 'Within three days, seven hundred and thirty
coaches had been counted passing Hyde Park Corner, filled with
families, removing to the country.' And two weeks before the
expected shock was to have happened, Dr Sherlock, Bishop of
London, published an article, 'On the occasion of the late earthquakes,' in which he denounced the tremendous iniquity common among London's inhabitants and warned that it would be
judged by God.

Of course, the soldier's prophecy proved false. People waited
for the catastrophe and it failed to occur. The event should teach
us that any professed revelation that is not directly stated in the
Word of God is an evidence of deception, whether intentional
or otherwise.

Charles Wesley preached at least on four occasions on the fearful events, and one of his sermons, 'The Cause and Cure of
Earthquakes' was later published. He also wrote nineteen hymns
related to this subject. Here is part of one of them:

> How happy then are we,
> Who build, O Lord, on thee!
> What can our foundation shock?
> Though the shattered earth remove,
> Stands our city on a rock,
> On a rock of heavenly love.

> A house we call our own,
>   Which cannot be o'erthrown;
> In the general ruin sure
>   Storms and earthquakes it defies,
> Built immovably secure,
>   Built eternal in the skies.[4]

In the midst of the commotion caused by the earthquakes, Mehetabel Wesley Wright, a sister of Charles and John, passed away. Her life had been filled with sadness.

Born at South Ormsby in 1697, Mehetabel, known to the family as 'Hetty', early revealed an unusual animation in both mind and body. She received the same schooling as her sisters under the teaching of her mother, but her father gave her special care and when she was only eight or nine she copied for him in her own hand the notes he was making on the book of Job. He also gave her instruction in the classical languages and she learned Latin and some Greek. But above all she possessed an ability in the use of English and could express herself gracefully and forcefully in either prose or poetry.

Hetty shared the company of her five sisters, but for so lively a girl the life of the Epworth rectory must have seemed totally lacking in adventure. Following the fire, however, in which the house was destroyed, she and her sister Sukey were placed in the home of their uncle Matthew in London, and they were apparently there for two years. Matthew Wesley was an apothecary-surgeon and was well-to-do, and the girls—especially Hetty—must have noticed the difference between the freedom they found in his house and the tensions that so often characterized their home in Epworth. When they returned to Epworth they had new cause to find their existence dull. The house was only partly finished, the family's clothes, all lost in the fire, had been replaced with a few used garments, their father was in debt and there was constantly barely enough food.

Had Hetty been able to attend the university she would undoubtedly have succeeded as well as her brothers. But in those days the universities were open only to men. Girls of a poor class sought work as domestic servants, those of a better class looked for employment as teachers, but almost all waited to find a suitable man, preferably a very well-to-do one, whom to marry.

For the Wesley girls, however, the outlook was dark. The

young men of Epworth, in general, were of a standard much
below that of the Wesleys, and Hetty said of them,

> As asses dull, on dunghills born,
> Impervious as the stones their heads are found.

Moreover, Samuel was not in favour of any of the young men
she took up with. Writing in a Lincolnshire accent, she addressed,
somewhat playfully, the following lines to Susanna,

> Dear mother, you were once in the ew'n,[5]
> As by us cakes is plainly shewn,
>   Who else had ne'er come arter;
> Pray speak a word in time of need,
> And with my sour-faced father plead
>   For your distressèd darter!

Sir Arthur Quiller-Couch has told the story of Hetty's life.[6]
He writes in a fictionalized form but his book contains forty-
three pages of letters written by Hetty or members of the Wesley
family, and these provide the historic backbone of his account.

He pictures Hetty in the company of her five sisters when she
was in her twenties. He says, 'Hetty of the high spirits, the clear
eye, the springing gait; Hetty, the wittiest, cleverest, mirthfulest
of them all; Hetty, glorious to look upon... If the six sisters were
handsome, Hetty was glorious...add, too, her mother's height
and more than her mother's grace of movement, an outline
virginally severe yet flexuous...and you have Hetty Wesley...a
queen in a country frock and cobbled shoes; a scholar, a lady
amongst hinds; above all, a woman made for love, and growing towards love surely, though repressed and thwarted.'[7]

Undoubtedly Hetty Wesley abounded in animal spirits, was
full of mirth and possessed an intellect as rare as that of her
brother John and a poetic gift equal to that of Charles. But these
rich qualities and emotions found no opportunity for expression
in the rectory at Wroot, where the Wesleys were now living.[8]

When she reached the age of twenty-five Hetty appears to have
fallen in love. Her suitor was John Romley, who had served as
a school teacher but was now also curate to Samuel and was conducting the pastoral work at Epworth. He was a singer and
apparently, when visiting Hetty on a certain occasion he had

sung a song that annoyed her father. Samuel put him out of the house and told him never to enter it again.

Some time later, when Samuel was visiting in the town of Kelstern, he called on a well-off family named Grantham and offered them the services of Hetty as a companion for Mrs Grantham. Apparently she was not to be paid for her work. He returned home and informed his wife and daughters of the arrangement. Hetty was given no choice whatsoever; he trundled her off to Kelstern and, although the Granthams did not really want her, he left her there with them.

This action seems utterly heartless, but it must be borne in mind that in the eighteenth century the father was the head of his house. Samuel believed in this principle and carried it to an extreme. He probably felt that he was exercising a kindly father's prerogative in keeping his daughter away from temptation, by removing her from Romley and forbidding her to correspond with him.

Hetty's frustrations, however, were only increased. Fifteen months later—she was then twenty-seven—she revealed her plight in a letter to John. Writing from Kelstern, on 7 March 1725, she stated, 'I had answered your very obliging letter long before now, only your particular enquiry in Romley's affair put me upon so melancholy a task, that you can't wonder that I so long deferred the performance. You knew that my father forbad him his house on account of the old song...since which time I have never seen Romley. He writ to me several times since and we held a secret correspondence together, till a little while before I came to Kelstern. I desire you would not be insensitive how the intrigue broke off...

My father came to Kelstern... and proffered me to wait on Mrs Grantham. She accepted it and my father promised Mr Grantham that I should come hither, before I knew a word of it. When I did know, 'twas in vain for me to endeavour to persuade my parents not to send me. They were resolutely bent on my journey, so I came, very much against my consent, and had far rather have gone to my grave!...

'Tho I'm sensible of the great folly of complaining where the grievance admits of no remedy, yet I find that misery and complaint are almost inseparable in our sex, and I've often concealed my uneasiness to the hazard of sense and life, for want of some friend to console with and advise me.

'I am in a great measure careless what becomes of me. Home I would not go, were I reduced to beggary, and here I will never stay, where they tell me that they should never have desired my company, only my father proffered me, and they did not know well how to refuse me. And Mrs Grantham desires me to provide for myself against May Day.

'I intend to try my fortune in London, and am resolved not to marry till I can forget Romley, or see him again... But here I've no company but my fellow servants, and sometimes those that I care less of, viz. my lovers—a set of mortals who universally own me the most unaccountable woman that they ever knew. I'm condemned to constant solitude and have not been out of town since I came into it.'[9]

It is evident this poor woman had been driven to desperation. She was indeed 'careless what became of her' for despite her declaration, 'Home I would not go, were I reduced to beggary,' within seven months she did that very thing—she went home. And, her condition, in the minds of her parents, was worse than 'beggary', for although she was yet unmarried she was pregnant.[10]

Quiller-Couch represents the rector as locking her in a room and allowing her only bread and water. Whether that was so or not is not known, but it is clear he knew no mercy. Within a few days he forced her into marriage with a coarse, uneducated plumber, William Wright. Samuel even refused to perform the ceremony himself, but sent them to his neighbour, the Rev. Mr Hoole of Haxey.

The couple lived at first in the Lincolnshire town of Louth where Wright had his business. Within four months a baby girl was born, but before a year had passed she died.

Aided financially by Samuel's brother Matthew, the Wrights then moved to London and set up in business there. Charles was still attending Westminster School when they came to London. He rejoiced to learn that Hetty had moved to town, but at that time he had only seven days left before he was to leave for Oxford. He wrote, 'Little of that precious time... did I lose, being with her almost continually... In a neat little room she had hired did the good-natured, ingenuous creature... and I talk over a few short days we both wished had been longer.'[11]

A second child was born but it too died soon afterwards. When she lost a third child in the same way Hetty's spirit was completely crushed. Her husband was no help. Not only did he prove utterly incapable of recognizing her refined and poetic spirit, but he spent most evenings in the local public house and returned at a late hour, usually very drunk. Following the death of her third child she expressed her feelings in verse:

A Mother's address to her dying infant

Tender softness, infant mild,
Perfect, purest, brightest child!
Transient lustre, beauteous clay,
Smiling wonder of a day!
Ere the last convulsive start
Rend thy unresisting heart,
Ere the long-enduring swoon
Weigh thy precious eyelids down,
Ah, regard a mother's moan!
—Anguish deeper than thy own.

Ere thy gentle breast sustain
Latest, fiercest, mortal pain,
Hear a suppliant! Let me be
Partner in thy destiny:
That whene'er the fatal cloud
Must thy radiant temples shroud;
When deadly damps, impending now,
Shall hover round thy destined brow,
Diffusive may their influence be,
And with the blossom blast the tree![12]

Other selections from Hetty's poetry could be quoted but the above will suffice to manifest her skill and to portray her deep sorrow.

On one occasion Hetty returned to Wroot, but her father would not allow her in the house. Nevertheless, she had the idea that if she could win the forgiveness of the man of God, in the future the divine judgement manifest in the death of her infants might be averted. Accordingly, she wrote to her father, but her letter happened to contain the sentence, 'But as you planted my matrimonial bliss, so you cannot run away from my prayer when I beseech you to water it with a little kindness.' Samuel replied,

'In your next, if you would please me, I advise you to display less wit and more evidence of honest self-examination.'[13]

Hetty knew that she had the goodwill of her sisters and her brother Charles. And following her marriage John had offended his father by preaching at Epworth on 'Showing Charity to Repentant Sinners'. As the 1730s drew on she was beginning to stand up to her father, and the same became true of her attitude to her husband. She wrote a poem addressed to William in which she reminded him of her many efforts to make a home for him, of his increasing carelessness and his drunken companions. She ended by saying,

> Deprived of freedom, health and ease,
> And rivalled by such *things* as these,
> Soft as I am, I'll make thee see
> I will not brook contempt from thee!
> I'll give all thoughts of patience o'er
> (A gift I never lost before);
> Indulge at once my rage and grief,
> Mourn obstinate, disdain relief,
> Till life, on terms severe as these,
> Shall ebbing leave my heart at ease;
> To thee thy liberty restore
> To laugh when Hetty is no more.[14]

Life thus went on for Hetty, one monotonous month after another. Her father died in 1735 but he had never shown the slightest sign of mercy towards her. Had even one of her children lived she would have had someone on whom to shower her care and affection. Her mother and sisters now showed her respect, and John and Charles had from the first forgiven her. But William Wright, though he frequently boasted of her beauty when at the public house, was without any capacity to appreciate or love her.

There were, however, one or two brighter spots. From time to time she submitted a specimen of her poetry to some London literary journal and it was accepted. Also her uncle Matthew, fully recognizing her plight and knowing she was becoming increasingly unwell, sent her to Bristol and Bath, where she indulged in the hot springs and also enjoyed some intellectual company.

During the late 1740s Hetty began to attend the services of the Foundery. She must indeed have experienced the joy and peace of true conversion for John accepted her as a helper in his evangelistic efforts. At least, some years later he said to his sister Martha, 'I have often thought it strange that so few of my relations should be of any use to me in the work of God. My sister Wright was, of whom I should least have expected it; but it was only for a short season.'[15]

The shortness of Hetty's period of assisting John arose from physical causes. She laboured to bear up under her burden of loneliness and heart-break, till, by the time she reached fifty years of age she found her health failing her and she could continue no longer. Charles visited her during her last days, and on 5 March 1750 he reported, 'I prayed by my sister Wright, a gracious, tender, trembling soul; a bruised reed, which the Lord will not break.'[16]

We can but hope she was not left alone during these circumstances and that neighbours or sisters came in to help care for her. John was not in London at the time but Charles returned and his *Journal* states: '*March 14th*. I found my sister Wright very near the haven; and again on Sunday the 18th, yet still in darkness, doubts and fears, against hope believing in hope.'[17]

Within three days time, however, Hetty's weary life came to its close. Charles recorded, '*March 21st*. At four I called on my brother Wright, a few minutes after her spirit was set at liberty.'

Charles took charge of her funeral and said of the occasion, 'I had sweet fellowship with her in explaining in the chapel those solemn words, "Thy sun shall go no more down, neither shall the moon withdraw itself; for the Lord shall be thine everlasting light, and the days of thy mourning shall be ended." All present seemed partakers both of my sorrow and my joy.'

'*March 26th*. I followed her to a quiet grave, and wept with them that wept.'[18]

In his treatment of Hetty Samuel Wesley was undoubtedly basically acting as a man of his century. He declared to John, when the latter had preached on 'Showing Charity to Repentant Sinners', 'I bear no rivals in my kingdom!' Nevertheless, one cannot but feel that, despite his conviction that the guilty must be punished, he ought to have shown some kindness to his daughter, a woman of twenty-nine at that time, and to have felt some share of responsibility himself for having pushed her to the point of desperation.

How grand and useful a life Hetty Wesley might have known, had she not suffered her father's heartless domination! We must surely agree with Dr John Julian, who, in his *Dictionary of Hymnology,* stated the opinion, 'Mehetabel Wesley, if she did not write hymns, showed plainly that she could have done so with so much success which might have rivalled Charles' own... Mehetabel Wesley had an exquisite poetic genius.'

Well did her brother Charles say, as he followed her body to the grave, 'I wept with them that wept.'[19]

It has been affirmed, that none of our itinerant preachers are so much alive as they were seven years ago. I fear many are not. But if so, they are unfit for the work which requires much life...

Who of you is exemplarily alive unto God, so as to carry fire with him wherever he goes? Who of you is a pattern of self-denial even in little things? Who of you drinks water? Why not? Who has not four meals a day?... Who has every part of the plan at heart? always meets society, bands, leaders?... Who preaches the old thundering doctrine, no faith without light... Who is never idle?...

Do you see every preacher observe the rules? Do you reprove, and, if need be, send me word of the defaulters?... Is your whole heart in the work? Do not you give way to unconcern, indolence, and fear of man? Who will join heart and hand, according to the twelve rules?

(John Wesley, addressing his conference, 1755).

16.
Methodism's lay preachers

After the Wesleys had preached in a town two or three times they usually left behind them a company of men and women whom they had formed into a society. Each group in turn endeavoured to acquire a building—it might be a house, a barn or a hall—and this they used as their meeting-place. The society was part of a larger body which was termed a circuit.

By 1751 the Wesleys had thirteen of these circuits in England, Wales and Ireland, and they were ministered to by some sixty-eight preachers, all of whom were laymen. A few of these men had been well educated but the majority had experienced very little schooling and had been employed at manual tasks. But they had given up their labours as farmers, cobblers, miners, carpenters, and such like, and were now devoting themselves exclusively to their work as preachers. Most did not remain in one location but itinerated from one society to another in the circuit and they were supported from a fund administered by John Wesley.

The conditions characteristic of the lives of these men demand our attention. Most followed Wesley's pattern of getting up at four in the morning and spending the first hour with their Bible and in prayer and singing, and they often preached at five o'clock. During the 1740s, while preaching in the open air or in their meeting-houses, many were subject to frequent attacks by the mob, and they and their families lived continually in the midst of rioters and in constant danger. Nevertheless, they preached every day in the week and three or four times each Sunday, besides regularly visiting the homes of the Methodist people.

These men preached with tremendous fervour. Most of them had formerly been totally unconcerned about divine things, but upon hearing the gospel—from the lips of Charles or John Wesley, George Whitefield or one of the other evangelists—they had experienced an overwhelming conviction of sin. God had then drawn them to himself and brought them to believe on Jesus Christ for salvation and their lives had been transformed as a result. They were now filled with a zeal to declare the good news of salvation to everyone they could reach. They entered the pulpit with a burning desire to win men and women to Christ and they spoke with a powerful intensity of purpose. With an arresting authority they preached concerning the terrible nature of sin and a redemption offered to all mankind, about the dread sufferings of hell and the eternal joys of heaven. With a mighty passion they urged all their hearers then and there to receive the Saviour. These characteristics were not present in all, but were the chief features of most of them.

Again we must remind ourselves that these men did not have our comfortable means of travelling. They moved from society to society on horseback and were exposed to all forms of weather. They stayed in whatever homes were offered and sometimes these were little better than hovels, the food was scarce and there were frequently a number of troublesome children or crying babies.

Moreover, most of them were very poor. Over and above the few shillings they might be given when a society's funds accrued a surplus, each man received a grant of £12 a year. The entire income was undoubtedly less than a third of what they would have earned when they had worked at their trades. John Nelson, a Yorkshireman who had been a successful stonemason and had become a very capable preacher, stated in a letter to Charles Wesley, 'We have but ten shillings a week in all, and that is to keep a servant out of, and wages to pay her, which takes at least four shillings out of it, and we have coals and candles for the house, and soap to find, which will take two more, and all the goods in the house to keep in repair; and my meat when in the round [the circuit], and in my absence another preacher for it; so that my family hath not one shilling a week to find them both meat and clothes.'[1]

Nelson's wife was ill much of the time and yet so many Methodist preachers were welcomed into his home that on several occasions he found it necessary to sleep in his barn. Yet he continued in his ministry with untiring zeal. His labours were abundantly blessed of God and he must be considered as among the most useful of all the Methodist lay preachers.

In 1746—not long after the lay preaching had begun—Charles
Wesley had strongly recommended the practice. In those days
he recognized that since these men preached without ordination
they were breaking the rules of the Church of England. Yet notwithstanding this irregularity he declared, 'I conferred with
several who have tasted the love of Christ, mostly under the
preaching and prayers of our lay-helpers. How can anyone dare
deny that they are sent of God? Oh, that all who have the outward
call, were as inwardly called by the Holy Ghost to preach!'[2]

Or again, 'Both sheep and shepherds had been scattered in
the late cloudy day of persecution, but the Lord gathered them
again, and kept them together by their own brethren; who begin
to exhort their companions, one or more in every society. No
less than four have sprung up in Gwennap. I talked closely with
each, and find no reason to doubt their having been used of God
thus far.'[3]

'I...adored the miracle of grace, which has kept these sheep
in the midst of wolves. Well may the despisers behold and
wonder. Here is a bush in the fire, burning and yet not consumed! What have they not done to crush this rising sect? but,
lo! they prevail nothing!... For one preacher they cut off, twenty
spring up. Neither persuasions nor threatenings, flattery nor
violence, dungeons or sufferings of various kinds can conquer
them.'[4]

But although Charles Wesley had at first viewed the lay
ministry in this favourable light, by 1750 his attitude had altered.
He was unyielding in his allegiance to the Church of England
and he held that her clergymen stood in the apostolic succession.
This meant that only men who had been ordained by a bishop
had the right to preach. The one exception was for those who
licensed themselves as Dissenters—a status viewed with disdain
by any true Anglican. Charles then considered the lay ministry
a temporary practice which had served through some years of
crisis but which he hoped could soon be done away with.

Action in this matter was forced upon the Wesleys by the
behaviour of one of the lay preachers named James Wheatley.
Wheatley had been a cobbler, had professed conversion and had
been accepted by the Wesleys as one of their men. He ministered
in Wiltshire and was known for preaching with much style but
little substance. He appears to have been successful, not only
in drawing people to hear him but in winning their personal

admiration. But in 1751 Charles received a letter in which it was solemnly charged that Wheatley had repeatedly been guilty of adultery. Charles immediately sent for Wheatley to come to him, and dealt with him 'in tender love and pity'. But Wheatley proved 'stubborn and hard'. John then joined with Charles and they examined him in the presence of two of the accusing women.

'He pleaded guilty,' said Charles, 'yet justified himself. I walked with him apart. He threatened to expose *all* our preachers: who, *he said,* were like himself. I conferred with my brother, and drew up our resolution in writing, that he should not preach. Wheatley absolutely refused to submit.'[5]

Such statements put the Wesleys under a new responsibility. Of course, the accusation against '*all* their preachers' was untrue, but enquiry was needed to ascertain if it was true of any. Moreover, the assertion had been made by several people that some of the Methodist preachers were not sufficiently industrious and that many did not study to overcome their lack of knowledge. 'It put my brother and me,' wrote Charles, 'upon a resolution of strictly examining into the life and moral behaviour of every preacher in connexion with us...'[6] But Charles adds also the cryptic statement, 'The office fell upon me.'

Charles was chosen for the task by John, but we may be sure he also volunteered for it himself. This willingness arose, not only from his firm stand for the Church of England, but also from his belief that Methodism was moving in the wrong direction and that the entire practice of lay preaching needed to be reconsidered.

Accordingly, Charles immediately set out for the north of England. The date was June 1751. He called on several preachers in towns along the way and then did the same in and around Leeds. He interviewed them personally and whenever possible he heard them preach. Then he had them come together at Leeds and he addressed them on 'the qualifications, work and trials of the Methodist ministry'. It was apparently for this meeting that he composed a hymn which he intended should cause every preacher to examine his life. It includes the following verses:

> Arise, thou jealous God, arise,
>   Thy sifting power exert,
> Look through us with thy flaming eyes,
>   And search out every heart.

Our inward souls thy Spirit knows,
  And let him now display,
Whom thou hast for thy glory chose,
  And purge the rest away.

Do *I* presume to preach thy word
  By thee uncalled, unsent?
Am I the servant of the Lord,
  Or Satan's instrument?[7]

As he continued his special effort Charles was zealous in ordering men to return to their trades. He himself had experienced
the cultural preparation of Oxford University and he had also
known the definite call of God to the work of the ministry, and
he had little patience with men who manifested a lack both of
education and of the certainty of the divine call.

For instance, he heard from John Bennet about certain lay
preachers whom Bennet considered natively unequipped for their
work. Charles replied, 'Your last…supplied me with more abun-
dant proof of R.G.'s utter unworthiness to preach the gospel.
I have accordingly stopped him, and shall tomorrow send him
back to his proper business. A friend of ours (without God's help)
made a preacher of a tailor. I, with God's help, shall make a
tailor of him again… pray earnestly for me, that the Lord may
guide and direct me in my *most important* concern—to purge the
church, beginning with the labourers… I have silenced another
scandalous preacher, and sent a third back to his trade.'[8]

Charles was also disgusted at some of the preaching he heard.
He said of one of the men, Michael Fenwick, 'But such a
preacher I have never heard, and hope I never shall again. It
was beyond description. I cannot say he preached false doctrine,
or true, or any doctrine at all, but pure unmixed nonsense. Not
one sentence did he utter that could do the least good to any
one soul. Now and then a text of Scripture or a verse quotation
was dragged in by head and shoulders. I could scarce refrain
from stopping him.

'… I talked closely with him, utterly averse to working, and
told him plainly he should either labour with his hands, or preach
no more. He hardly complied, though he confessed it was his ruin,
his having been taken off his business. I answered I would repair
the supposed injury, by setting him up again in his shop.'[9]

Charles also tells of one of the preachers who had come to them from Scotland. He spoke with a very broad accent, and on hearing him Charles declared he would never do for preaching in England. 'I could not understand a word he said.'

Of another man he said, 'I heard J.J., the drummer again, and liked him worse than at first. He might perhaps have done good among the soldiers; but to leave his calling, and set up for an itinerant, was, in my judgement, a step contrary to the design of God, as well as his own and the church's interest.'[10]

He found a few men lacking in diligence and some who were critical of the Church of England. And concerning another, William Darney, who had recently published a small volume of his own hymns, although Charles consented to let him preach, he ordered him not to continue to rail at anyone and not to beg off the people. He also told him that he must 'not introduce the use of his doggerel hymns in any of our societies'.

When he learned that Charles was dismissing so many preachers John Wesley became concerned. Although he had agreed that an examination of the preachers was necessary he now thought that Charles might be going too far. He rejoiced in the large number of Methodist societies that had come into being and in the manner in which God had raised up preachers to fill their pulpits, but how could the work be maintained if so many of them were removed? He wanted to see more preachers rather than less and he told Charles that in dismissing some they already had and in choosing new ones, their criterion should be 'We must have grace before gifts.' But Charles replied, 'Are not both indispensably necessary? Has not the cause suffered, in Ireland especially, through the insufficiency of the preachers? Should we not first regulate, reform, and bring into discipline the preachers we have, before we look for more?'[11]

There was clearly a difference of opinion between Charles and John in this matter. There had never been full harmony since Charles had prevented John from marrying Grace Murray and the situation had been aggravated by John's marrying Mrs Vazeille.

Moreover, there was a growing degree of difference in doctrine. John now said to Charles in a letter, 'Some of our preachers have... openly affirmed, that you agree with Mr Whitefield touching perseverance at least, if not predestination too.'[12] This assertion was clearly an exaggeration but it is evidence that Charles no longer was as dogmatic against Calvinism as formerly he had been.

He had indeed already renewed fellowship with Whitefield. He soon declared his mind, in *An Epistle* which he addressed to Whitefield, saying,

> Come on, my Whitefield! (since the strife is past,
> And friends at first are friends again at last)
> Our hands, our hearts, and counsels let us join
> In mutual league, t'advance the work divine,
> Our one contention now, our single aim,
> To pluck poor souls as brands out of the flame;
> To spread the victory of that bloody cross,
> And gasp our latest breath in the Redeemer's cause.[13]

Charles now was similarly reconciled with Lady Huntingdon. He reported in 1751, 'In the fear of God, and by the advice of friends, I went once more to visit L.H. She expressed great kindness towards me, as did all the family ... My heart was turned back again, and forgot all that is past. The Spirit of love is a Spirit of prayer, and sealed the reconciliation.'[14]

In April 1751 Charles suffered a period of illness so severe that he felt he was near the end of life's journey. While upon his sick-bed he brooded about the lay preachers and the harm he foresaw them bringing to Methodism, and he determined to pour forth his thought to someone. He may well have considered writing to Whitefield but he was then out of England, visiting both Ireland and Scotland.

At any rate he wrote to Lady Huntingdon, and his letter reads, in part, 'I must leave you my mind in few words. Unless a sudden remedy be found, the preachers will destroy the work of God. What has wellnigh ruined many of them is their being taken from their trades ... The tinner, barber, thatcher, forgot himself and set up for a gentleman, and looked out for a fortune, having lost the only way of maintaining himself ... Some have fallen into grievous crimes and must therefore be put away. What will then become of them? Will they not cause the same confusion that is now in Wales? Will not each set up for himself, and make a party, sect, or religion? Or supposing we have authority enough to quash them while we live, or while my brother and I live,

who can stop them after our death? It does not satisfy my conscience to say, God look to that. We must look to that now
ourselves, or we tempt God.'[15]

Charles went on in this letter to complain about the need to
'reduce [John's] authority within due bounds'. It is difficult not
to assume that Charles was undergoing a period of depression
and we know that in such a mood he could exaggerate conditions.

But it is evident that John Wesley's attitude towards the lay
preachers was wiser than that of Charles. Here was a company
of men who, despite their lack of education and the noticeable
failings of a few, were being mightily used of God. A prominent Methodist historian makes the statement: 'Wesley's lay
preachers ... moved about from place to place, finding shelter
in the homes of their people, eating such things as were set before
them, lavishly rendering poorly-paid services on obscure villagers
... whose spiritual darkness they turned to marvellous light. Great
were their sufferings and sore their straits. Sometimes they
habitually lived on the verge of starvation ...

'Despite of suffering, however, the work was done, and an
example of self-sacrificing toil was set, which is a rebuke and
an inspiration to church workers throughout the world.'[16]

John Wesley was admittedly irregular in using these men, but
had Charles, with his Church of England principles, proved vic-
torious, Methodism would have been robbed of an important
means of spreading the gospel, not only in Britain but also in
America. Charles was in favour of seeing more and more men
enter the ministry of the Church of England and from this time
forth he devoted his labours more than ever to advancing the
welfare of that church.

Continue in the old ship. Jesus hath a favour for our church; and is wonderfully visiting and reviving his work in her. It shall be shortly said, 'Rejoice ye with Jerusalem, and be glad with her, all ye that love her: rejoice for joy with her, all ye that love her.'

(Charles Wesley, to the brethren at Leeds).

17.
Labouring to keep Methodism within the Church of England

During the early 1750s Charles Wesley's life took on a new purpose. Greatly fearing that the revival movement would yet be divided by the actions of several of the lay preachers, and also that they would force John to lead Methodism out of the Church of England, he gave himself over to the task of labouring to preserve unity in the work and to keep Methodism within the Anglican Church.

In 1752 he drew up a document with a view to furthering this aim. It read, 'We whose names are underwritten ... are absolutely determined, by the grace of God, (1) to abide in closest union with each other, and ... (2) never to leave the communion of the Church of England, without the consent of all whose names are subjoined.'[1] Charles signed first, and was followed by John and then by four of the lay preachers.

Nevertheless, the differences continued, and before the year had ended Charles considered separating from John. He broached the matter to Whitefield and although we do not have his letter we do have Whitefield's reply.

London,
Dec. 22, 1752

My dear Friend,

I have read and pondered over your kind letter with solemnity of spirit. In the same frame I would now sit down to answer it.

And what shall I say? Really, I can scarce tell. The connection between you and your brother hath been so close and continued, and your attachment to him so necessary to keep up his

interest, that I would not willingly for the world do or say
anything that may separate such friends ...

'God ... knows how I love and honour you, and your brother,
and how often I have preferred your interest to my own. This
by the grace of God, I shall continue to do ... More might be
said were we face to face.'[2]

Any thought, however, of separating from John was soon overcome. In the following year, 1753, John was taken so ill that
he felt his death was near. He wrote an epitaph that he intended
should be placed upon his tomb:

Here lieth the body of
John Wesley
A brand, not once only, plucked out of the fire.
Who died of a consumption in the fifty-first year
of his age,
Not leaving, after his debts are paid,
Ten pounds behind him:
praying
God be merciful to me, an unprofitable servant.[3]

During John's sickness both Charles and Whitefield rushed
to be with him. Charles reported, 'I told the society on Sunday
night, that I neither could nor would stand in my brother's place
(if God took him to himself;) for I had neither a body, nor a
mind, nor talents, nor grace for it.

'This morning I got the long-wished for opportunity of talking
fully to him of all which has passed since his marriage; and the
result of our conference was perfect harmony.'[4]

But amid John's illness, Charles learned that Sally also was
seriously ill. He says he received word from Lady Huntingdon
'that my wife was taken ill of the small pox ... that it was come
out, and the confluent kind'.[5] He rode with the greatest of
haste to Bristol and reported, 'I found my dearest friend on a
restless bed of pain, loaded with the worst kind of the worst
disease ... a most tender, skilful woman, was her nurse. Dr Mid-
dleton has been a father to her. Good Lady Huntingdon attends
her constantly twice a day...

'I came and rejoiced for the consolation. I saw her alive; but,
Oh, how changed! The whole head faint, and the whole heart

sick! From the crown of her head to the soles of her feet there
was no soundness ...

'I found the door of prayer wide open, and entirely acquiesced
in the divine will. I would not have it otherwise. God choose
for me and mine, in time and eternity.'[6]

After twenty-two days Mrs Wesley was brought back from
the edge of the grave. She was gradually restored to full health
but the disease had robbed her of her beauty and although she
was nearly twenty years younger than Charles, she now looked
almost as old. Yet despite the sad alteration in her appearance,
his love was unchanged and his letters continued to express his
undying affection.

John Wesley too was soon able to rise from his bed. He began
to ride a little every day and upon seeing some clear improvement in his health he spent a week at the hot wells in Bristol
and within two weeks was able to travel and preach again.

But in 1754 Charles's difference of opinion with John regarding Methodism's relation to the Church of England still continued. This is evident in a letter he wrote at that time to an
evangelical clergyman, the Rev. Walter Sellon.

'May I not desire it of you,' he wrote, 'as a debt you owe
the Methodists and me, and the church as well as him [John
Wesley] to write him a full, close, plain transcript of your heart
on the occasion. Charles Perronet, you know, has taken upon
him to administer the sacrament for a month together to the
preachers, and twice to some of the people. Walsh and three
others have followed his vile example. The consequence you see
with your own eyes ...

'Since the Melchisedechians have been taken in, I have been
excluded from his inner cabinet. They know me too well to trust
me with him ... They are indefatigable in urging him to go so
far that he cannot retreat ... The Methodist preachers must
quickly divide to the right or left, the church or meeting ...

'There is no danger of my countenancing them, but rather
of my opposing them too fiercely.' 'Tis a pity a good cause should
suffer by a warm advocate. If God gives me meekness, I shall,
at the conference, speak and not spare.'[7]

The discussion at the 1755 conference dealt almost solely with
one subject: 'The great question was the necessity or propriety of
the Methodists separating from the Established Church, and of
the Methodist itinerant preachers administering the sacraments.'[8]

John Wesley
(from Ward's mezzotint of the painting by Romney, 1790)

Of course, the matter of administering the sacraments was of supreme importance. Methodism considered itself as a movement within the Church of England, and in that church only men ordained by a bishop were allowed to administer the sacraments. But the Methodist lay preachers recognized that round about were various dissenting ministers—Presbyterians, Baptists and Congregationalists—who exercised this privilege among their people, and they desired the same right. Several of them urged John Wesley to lead Methodism out of the church, to make it into another dissenting denomination and ordain its lay preachers.

Yet after three days of conferring on this matter John declared that while the great step might be taken at some later point in Methodist history, this was not the time for it. His statement was that 'Separation is lawful, but it is not expedient.'

Meanwhile, John Wesley's personal convictions on the organization and government of the church were changing. In 1746 he had read a work on the *Constitution of the Primitive Church* by a bishop, Lord Peter King, and he had stated that 'In spite of the vehement prejudice of my education, I was ready to believe that ... bishops and presbyters are essentially of one order.'[9] And in 1756, concerning the government of the church by bishops he wrote, 'This opinion, which I once zealously espoused, I have been heartily ashamed of, ever since I read Bishop Stillingfleet's 'Irenicon'. I think he has unanswerably proved that neither Christ nor his apostles *prescribe* any particular form of church government; and, that the plea of *divine right* for diocesan episcopy was never heard in the primitive church.'[10] Accordingly, John now believed he possessed as much authority as any bishop to ordain men to the ministry.

Charles declared that John was weak because of his failure to take a firm stand over the retention of Methodism within the Church of England. The cause, however, was not vacillation on John's part but this alteration of his basic beliefs on the subject.

In turn, during 1755 Charles expressed his feelings on the matter in a poem, 271 lines in length, that he addressed to John. The publisher sent out 3000 copies and Charles ordered another 1000 to distribute himself.

Throughout the poem he pleads for,

> The church whose cause I serve, whose faith approve,
> Whose altars reverence, and whose name I love.

He goes on to declare that though Methodism should be free

> From ev'ry wilful crime, and moral blot,
> Yet still the Methodists *the church* are not.

And in reference to the coldness that he claims exists among the various groups of Dissenters, he says,

> See us, when from the papal fire we came,
> Ye frozen sects, and warm you at the flame.

Charles describes the revival in which he and John were playing such important parts and he prays that his vision of its effect, as cleansing and enlivening the church, may be entirely fulfilled. Yet he expresses his fear that John is more concerned about enlarging Methodism than the basic aim with which they had begun.

> When first sent forth to minister the Word,
> Say, did we preach ourselves, or Christ the Lord?
> Was it our aim disciples to collect,
> To raise a party, or to found a sect?
> No: but to spread the power of Jesus' name,
> Repair the walls of our Jerusalem,
> Revive the piety of ancient days,
> And fill the earth with our Redeemer's praise.[11]

In an effort to inform the people of his difference with John in regard to the Church of England, on the following two Sundays Charles read his entire *Epistle* before crowded audiences in Methodism's headquarters—the Foundery in London.

Certain authors have described Charles's attitude as 'bigoted in favour of the Church'. He was indeed severely strong in the opinion that none but a man ordained by a bishop has the right to administer the sacraments. He was dogmatically a churchman.

But many of the lay preachers held an opinion directly contrary to that of Charles. We have seen that Charles Perronet was said to have 'taken upon himself to administer the sacrament for a month together', and that 'Walsh and three others have followed his vile example'.

In turn, during 1756 Perronet's brother Edward—remembered today as the author of 'All hail the power of Jesu's name'—published a 279-page work in verse, *The Mitre*. In this he defiantly belittled the Church of England. We notice here three of its stanzas. Addressing the church directly he asserts,

> In short, thou'rt like a common shore
> Filling and emptying, never pure
>   From pride, or pomp, or sin:
> That (speak they truth who say they know,)
> With all thy scavengers can do,
>   They cannot keep thee clean.

Concerning the church's claim to have descended from Christ and his apostles he states,

> I think its source is easy traced,
> As are its claims in order placed,
>   Its furniture and crests;
> A blended spawn of church and state,
> Its father, *Constantine the Great*,
>   Its dam—the pride of priests.

Perronet then imagines a strong churchman's reaction to receiving the sacrament from the hands of lay preachers:

> What, take the ordinance from them!
> Oh, what a frenzy of a dream!
>   Nor deacon nor a priest!
> Sooner renounce our grace or friends,
> Than take it from their fingers' ends,
>   A lay, unhallowed beast.[12]

The Reverend Luke Tyerman, one of John Wesley's fullest biographers states, 'It certainly was strange that one of the fiercest attacks upon the Church of England, ever published, should be written by a Methodist itinerant preacher.'[13]

Of course, Charles Wesley was highly incensed over *The Mitre*. Both he and John endeavoured to have all copies seized but were not successful in their effort.

Charles continued to write to evangelical clergymen, and one who was his particular correspondent in this matter was the Reverend Samuel Walker of Truro. Concerning 'lay preaching' Walker declared, 'The thing is plainly inconsistent with the discipline of the Church of England, and so, in one essential point, setting up a church within her, which cannot be of her. When, therefore, it is asked, "Shall we separate from the Church of England?" it should rather be asked, "Shall we make the separation we have begun, a separation in all forms?" '[14]

To this Charles Wesley replied, 'Lay preaching, it is allowed, is a partial separation, and may, but *need* not end in one. The probability of it has made me tremble for years past, and kept me from leaving the Methodists. I stay, not so much to do good, as to prevent evil. I stand in the way of my brother's violent counsellors, the object of both their fear and hate.'[15]

Charles wrote several letters to John regarding this matter, one of which, written in 1756, includes the following paragraphs: 'Ought any new preacher to be received before we know that he is grounded, not only in the doctrine we teach, but in discipline also, and particularly in the communion of the Church of England?

' ...Is it not your duty to stop Joseph Cownley and (such like) from railing and laughing at the church? The short remains of my life are devoted to this very thing, to follow your sons ... with buckets of water, and quench the flame of strife and division which they have, or may kindle.'[16]

During this same year of 1756, Charles gave up his own itinerant ministry. As we have seen, for sixteen years he had travelled from town to town, preaching constantly, for much of that time without a settled home and frequently meeting mob violence. This journeying he now relinquished. He continued to make his home in Bristol, led the Methodist work there and alternated with John in conducting it in London.

Certain reasons for this change are evident. He undoubtedly recognized the responsibility he bore towards his wife; she had already lost two infants and we may be sure she felt the need of his company in such experiences. Moreover, although he was only forty-nine he was becoming worn out physically and could not keep up the pace that he had set for himself. The chief cause of the change, however, undoubtedly was that he feared the course that Methodism would take and he felt that by promoting its interests he would actually be working against the Church of England.

But in 1758 John Wesley sought to clarify his position as to Methodism's relation to the Church of England. He published a pamphlet, *Reasons Against a Separation from the Church of England.* Among other things he stated that God had raised up Methodism in order that it might exercise a purifying and reviving influence on that church and that separation would be a denial of the divine purpose.

The year 1760, however, witnessed an event that confirmed Charles Wesley's fears as to the future course of Methodism. Three lay preachers in Norwich took it upon themselves to administer the communion to their society. Charles wrote to John, charging him with failing to correct these men and declaring, 'Blame them as strongly as your conscience will let you. Otherwise you betray them and all the preachers. You betray your own authority and our children, and our church, and are the *author of separation.*

'...Can you find it in your heart to speak word tonight of continuing in the Church of England?'[17]

This last question drew from John 'a few words of exhortation to stay in the Church of England'. But he decided to do nothing for the time being about the three men in Norwich, stating he would let the matter rest till the next annual conference.

In 1762 Charles was forced by the action of two of John's men, Thomas Maxfield and George Bell, to rethink his belief in the doctrine of perfection.

As we have seen, during the early 1740s both the Wesleys had strongly declared 'Christian perfection', but had never been able to define their meaning. In one breath they spoke of it as meaning nothing more than a condition of Christian maturity, but in the next they declared it meant a state of sinlessness. They used of it the words, 'delivered from all sin', and said that 'the whole of the old nature was destroyed,' and they even went so far as to say that without this experience 'no man shall see God'. This teaching gave Wesley's position a special distinctiveness and provided a means whereby he could separate his people from other religious leaders and could bind them unto himself. Nevertheless, when pressed to defend this proposition he could easily resort to the other definition, that of Christian maturity.

But by 1760 Maxfield and Bell, who had been under Wesley's ministry for several years, began to deny Wesley's lesser definition of perfection. They declared it meant one thing only: complete destruction of the old sinful nature.

Bell further made a prophecy that the end of the world would arrive on 28 February 1763. His prognostication was believed by a great many, but of course the day came and the dread event did not take place. Bell's action brought bitter reproach on Methodism.

Both Bell and Maxfield then left Wesley and some 300 people also left the Foundery and attended Maxfield in his own place of worship. Wesley was deeply saddened.

Charles Wesley, however, faced the issue that Maxfield had brought to the fore. Recognizing that nothing human could ever be entirely perfect, he ceased all mention of Christian perfection as a state of 'sinlessness' and a Methodist writer declared that henceforth it was to him, 'the result of sincere discipline, comprehending affliction, temptation, long continued labour, and the persevering exercise of faith in seasons of spiritual darkness, when the heart is wrung with bitter anguish. By this painful and lingering process, he believed that ... a maturity is given to all the graces of the Christian character. Hence he condemned "the witnesses", as he called them; that is the persons who testified of the time and manner in which they were delivered from the root of sin, and made perfect in love, regarding them as self-deceived. In some of his "Short Hymns", he has given considerable importance to these peculiarities of opinion.'[18]

Returning to our consideration of Charles Wesley's endeavour to retain Methodism's relation to the Church of England we notice that in 1763 a further event took place which increased his apprehension that the future was not bright.

A man named Erasmus arrived in London. His person was in disarray and he seemed 'a stranger perishing for want and expecting daily to be thrown into prison'.[19] He had been for a time in Holland, but claimed to be a bishop of the Greek Orthodox Church. John Wesley showed him kindness but had one of his men write to the Patriarch of Smyrna enquiring about him. He received word that Erasmus was the Bishop of Arcadia on the Isle of Crete. Wesley also heard the same from Amsterdam, and accordingly accepted him as a link in the supposed chain of the apostolic succession.

Being much in need of a clergyman to assist him in administering the sacraments in London, Wesley had Bishop Erasmus ordain one of his men, John Jones. Jones was well educated, a medical doctor and was worthy of this distinction. The bishop also ordained two other lay preachers, Sampson Staniforth and Thomas Bryant.

Immediately several other lay preachers expressed fervent desires to be ordained too. Moreover, the rumour was circulated that John Wesley asked Erasmus to make him a bishop, but that Erasmus replied he could not perform this function by himself but that other bishops must also be present.

However, both Charles Wesley and a number of the Methodists refused to accept the bishop's ordinations. John Jones was embarrassed and before long he left Methodism. Staniforth was not allowed to exercise any ministerial functions and Bryant soon caused a schism in the society that he led. Moreover, Augustus Toplady declared the bishop was an impostor and the historian Dr Frank Baker states that he is 'almost certain' this declaration was true.

Thus, as the months came and went, the strong differences of opinion continued. Charles Wesley laboured to keep Methodism within the Church of England and John Wesley allowed it to follow the path on which, since its very inception, it had been moving—that of gradually leaving the church and of finally becoming another denomination of Dissenters.

Amongst Charles Wesley's writings are to be found some of the grandest hymns in the English language. For spontaneity of feeling, his hymns are pre-eminent. They are songs that soar. They have the rush and fervour which bear the soul aloft. They are a kind of cardiphonia, caught from the beating of his own heart, and the observation of hearts kindled by the great movement in which he bore so large a part.

(W. Garrett Horder,
The Hymn Lover, 1889).

When he was nearly eighty he rode a little horse, grey with age ... Even in the height of summer he was dressed in winter clothes. As he jogged leisurely along, he jotted down any thoughts that struck him. He kept a card in his pocket for this purpose, on which he wrote his hymn in shorthand. Not infrequently he has come to our house in City Road, and, having left the pony in the garden in front, he would enter, crying out, 'Pen and ink! Pen and ink!' These being supplied he wrote the hymn he had been composing.

(Henry Moore, an associate of the Wesleys and an early Methodist author).

18.
Charles Wesley, the poet

Charles Wesley came of a family that was especially gifted in the writing of poetry.

This faculty was manifest first in his father, Samuel, the Rector of Epworth. He left three lengthy works in verse, and we noticed one of his hymns that Charles sang as he stood beneath the gallows at Tyburn:

> Behold the Saviour of mankind,
>   Nailed to the shameful tree,
> How vast the love that him inclined
>   To bleed and die for thee!

Samuel, junior, also wrote with poetic skill and his works were published under the title *Poems on Several Occasions*. The *Methodist Hymn Book* included eight of his hymns but they lacked the power found in many of those by Charles.

We have already noticed the gift possessed by Hetty Wesley and regretted the circumstances that prevented her from exercising it more frequently. She had this gift in exquisite measure.

John Wesley also was characterized by a feeling for true poetry. In 1737, while he was in Georgia he published his first hymn book, *A Collection of Psalms and Hymns*.[1] This little volume contained seventy hymns that had been written during preceding years by various authors, but five are from his own pen, translations he made from the German. To put a translation into suitable form for the use of people of another language requires a skill as great as that of the original writer, and these and other translations that he made from the German are recognized as among the finest hymns in the English language.

John and Charles later published several hymn-books in their joint names,[2] and while it is not possible to ascertain which brother was the author of each composition, it is probable that John wrote some of them, over and above his translations. Moreover, John edited each of these books and to him we are frequently indebted for the wording in which Charles's hymns finally appeared.

The gift of writing poetry, however, thus evident in other members of the Wesley family, came to its grandest fulfilment in the life of Charles.

Although it has often been assumed that his gift began with his conversion at the age of thirty-one, the man who thereafter wrote poetry with such skill and such liberty had undoubtedly written it from his boyhood. Living as he did, the son of a father whose life was characterized by his bent for words of rhyme and sentences marked by metre, we may be sure that the lad who proved to possess the same gifts in still larger measure must have employed them from early days. We must imagine Charles as penning verses on all manner of activities while still a boy.

At the age of eight he left home to attend Westminster School in London, and there his gift for poetry was nourished and enhanced. In those days education was as yet little taken up with such subjects as science and mathematics. Its attention was chiefly turned back to the great days of Greece and Rome, and was devoted to a study of their artists, architects, prose writers and poets, and these historic considerations were the matters to which Charles necessarily gave himself during his years at Westminster.

'The classics still held the field, together with the arts of thinking, of writing, and of speaking, which went with them. Rhetoric, in particular, which we hardly consider a basic academic subject, was then a most important part of education both at grammar school and university level, and those strange "exercises" before graduation at Oxford and Cambridge were largely modelled on the practice of the Schools of Rhetoric organized in Athens by Marcus Aurelius. The study of rhetoric was essential to the matter, as well as to the manner, of the "acts" and "opponencies" at Oxford, and colleges offered prizes for "declamations".'[3]

Since he went directly from Westminster School to Oxford University, this was the atmosphere in which Charles Wesley lived from the time he was eight till he was thirty. He was so immersed in the writings of the great men of the bygone era that his thought was moulded after theirs and he subconsciously took on their habits of mind and their forms of expression. These classical personages are among the most capable teachers of all ages in the use of language, and during his highly formative years Charles Wesley became deeply learned in their art.

For its fullest employment, however, the gift of poetry requires a soul that overflows with rich emotion and which has a message that it feels it must declare to all mankind. Charles received both that emotion and that message in his conversion. In his new knowledge of divine truth and in the joy that now filled his heart, he immediately stated, 'I began an hymn upon my conversion,' and having thus begun, he continued, pouring forth his soul in song throughout the rest of his life.

We must not think of him as saying at any time, 'I am now going to write a hymn.' Rather, thoughts so flooded his mind and emotion so filled his soul that he spontaneously formed his thinking into metered lines and unconsciously gave the whole a unique emotional quality. Concerning many of his productions it is correct to say, 'They soar!' They leave the poor earthbound world of prose and are characterized by a power that lifts the soul of the hearer, and this is the essential quality of true poetry.

He later corrected his poems extensively, but the original writing arose from this spontaneous outburst of thought and feeling in a soul that was gifted and trained for their rich expression.

John Wesley emphasized the poetic qualities of his brother's hymns. In 1779 he published *A Collection of Hymns for the People Called Methodists,* a very large proportion of which had been written by Charles. In his preface John wrote, 'May I be permitted to add a few words with regard to the *poetry.* Then I will speak to those who are judges thereof, with all freedom and unreserve. To these I may say, without offence, (1). In these hymns there is no doggerel; no botches; nothing put in to patch up the rhyme; no feeble expletives. (2). Here is nothing turgid or bombast, on the one hand, or low and creeping on the other. (3). Here are no *cant* expressions; no words without meaning. Those who impute this to us know not what they say. We talk common sense, both in prose and verse, and use no word but in a fixed and determinate sense. (4). Here are, allow me to say, both the purity, the strength, and the elegance of the English language; and, at the same time, the utmost simplicity and plainness, suited

to every capacity. Lastly, I desire men of taste to judge (these
are the only competent judges), whether there be not in some
of the following hymns the true spirit of poetry, such as cannot
be acquired by art and labour, but must be the gift of nature.
By labour a man may become a tolerable imitator of Spencer,
Shakespeare, or Milton; and may heap together pretty compound
epithets, as *pale-eyed, meek-eyed,* and the like; but unless he is born
a poet, he will never attain the genuine spirit of poetry.'[4]

John manifested his own possession of the gift of poetry, not
only in the hymns he wrote and the translations he made but
also in the excellent manner in which he edited the hymn-books
put out in the joint names of himself and Charles. Although some
of his words quoted above may seem rather pretentious, we cannot fail to agree with his appreciation of the poetic and spiritual
worth of Charles's hymns.

Undoubtedly, a number of Charles Wesley's hymns which
possess the power to lift the soul will come to the reader's mind.
This quality is felt, for example, in such productions as 'Love
divine, all loves excelling,' 'Hark! the herald angels sing!'
'Leader of faithful souls and guide,' 'Oh, for a thousand
tongues,' 'Rejoice! the Lord is King,' 'Christ the Lord is risen
today,' and many others. It is particularly manifest throughout
'Jesus, lover of my soul,' and is magnificently present in its final
verse:

> Plenteous grace with thee is found,
>   Grace to cover all my sin;
> Let the healing streams abound;
>   Make and keep me pure within;
> Thou of life the Fountain art,
>   Freely let me take of thee;
> Spring thou up within my heart,
>   Rise to all eternity.

The question is frequently asked, 'How many hymns did
Charles Wesley write?'

Dr Frank Baker states, 'The figure of 8,990 of his poems which
I have read is near enough to nine thousand to proclaim that
'round' number as the total extent of his extant poems as he
left them.'[5]

Of course, these were not all hymns. Some compositions are

tributes to friends written following their death, or even during their life-times. Certain poems record historical events that occurred during the century in which Charles lived. A lyrical quality, however—a feeling that these lines could well be sung—characterizes virtually every poem he wrote. But by far the greatest part of his output is marked by a rich spiritual quality, and he intended these particular productions as 'hymns and spiritual songs' to be sung by the Methodist people.

Throughout this quantity of spiritual poetry Charles Wesley presents a vast aggregate of Christian truth. He deals with the great elements of theology, but as he expresses them they are not mere abstractions, but are the fundamental facets of his daily life. The living qualities of his hymns are manifest, for instance, in the table of contents of the 1779 *Hymns for the Use of the People called Methodists*.

Part I.

Section I. Exhorting sinners to return to God.

    II. Describing, 1. The pleasantness of religion

       "   2. The goodness of God.

       "   3. Death

       "   4. Judgement

       "   5. Heaven

       "   6. Hell

    III. Praying for a blessing

Part II.

Section I. Describing formal religion

    II.   "   inward religion

Part III.

Section I. Praying for repentance

    II. For mourners convinced of sin

    III. For persons convinced of backsliding

    IV. For backsliders recovered

Part IV.

Section I. For believers rejoicing

    II.   "   "   fighting

    III. "   "   praying

    IV. "   "   watching

    V.   "   "   working

    VI. "   "   suffering

    VII. "   "   seeking for full redemption

VIII. For believers saved
IX.   "   "   interceding for the world
Part V.
Section I. For the society meeting
II.   "   "   "   giving thanks
III.   "   "   "   praying
IV.   "   "   "   parting[6]

The book contained a total of 539 hymns and the very large majority of them came from the pen of Charles Wesley. Thus he presented, not the trivialities which characterize so much of our modern singing, but information on this extended range of doctrinal and practical aspects of the Christian life.

With new compositions arriving in such abundance the question arises as to the tunes to which they were sung.

Some people have assumed that the Wesleys set their hymns to the tunes the people had learned in the tavern. But this is far from correct, for the idea of singing the praises of God to strains to which they had formerly sung worldly[7] and even obscene songs was impossible to them. They were men of culture and they deeply appreciated the music of the Church of England. Their hymns possessed a true literary merit and they looked for tunes of a similar quality to which to sing them.

Charles and John turned first to certain of the music used in the church for the singing of the metrical Psalms. These were simple melodies which had long been associated with divine subjects and several of them proved suitable for various of Charles's hymns. They used also some of the music which had been composed by Luther and others during the Reformation.

Secondly, they turned to the works of the masters. They used certain of the compositions of Henry Purcell and other men of similar merit from preceding years. Haydn's compositions were then coming before the public, as were also the works of Handel, and these too they laid under tribute. Indeed, after Charles's death his son Samuel discovered in the library at Cambridge University six tunes in Handel's writing which were set to certain of Charles's hymns—a circumstance which reveals the composer's interest in Charles Wesley and his poetic works.

Music from a third source also proved of value to the Wesleys. These were the tunes used by the Moravians—magnificent chorales of the fatherland—and after translating the German hymns John often also adopted their tunes.

In 1740 a former actress, Mrs Rich, wife of the proprietor of the Covent Garden Theatre, was converted under the ministry of Charles Wesley. Through Mrs Rich Charles became acquainted with several men of musical talent, among whom was a converted Deist, J.F.Lampe. Mr Rich, who remained strongly opposed to the gospel, tauntingly asked John Wesley, 'What can you do with him, now that he's converted?' to which John replied, 'Why, we'll let him make tunes for the Methodists!' Lampe proved an earnest Christian and till his death was often busily employed in setting Charles Wesley's hymns to music.

The Methodist singing provided not only a means of lifting the souls of believers, but it was also an educating force, especially among the poor of Britain.

Large numbers of men and women heard Charles and John, George Whitefield and many other men preach out of doors, but they also heard the congregations sing Charles Wesley's hymns. Here were lines that spoke of God the Father, of Jesus Christ and of the Holy Spirit, of sin and judgement, of salvation by faith, of a new and higher life, of the joyful release awaiting in death and of the glory of heaven for evermore. Many a man, many a woman and many a child went from the meeting, not only deeply affected by the truths heard in the preaching, but also singing over in the mind some phrase or even an entire stanza picked up from one of the hymns. When the hymn was heard at a subsequent meeting something more of it was lodged in the memory, it was repeated as the days went by, and little by little the entire hymn was learned by heart.

Nor was this happy process limited to one hymn, but having thus learned some favoured selection many a person went on to learn another and another. Many began also to attend the society meetings and there they were instructed further in Christian truth and were regulated as to the practice of the Christian life. But the meetings of the societies, like those of the great outdoor throngs, were characterized by their singing—magnificent, hearty singing, not of doggerel rhymes set to some cheap jingle, but Charles Wesley's mighty hymns, sung to music that was simple but was also suited to its high task.

Many an illiterate person, upon being converted, learned to read and write. Almost every one of the early Methodists possessed two books; a Bible and a hymn-book. These volumes proved bosom companions, and the Methodist was daily reading his Bible and daily singing from his book of hymns. On the Lord's Day he carried the two volumes to the society and on certain evenings of the week he did the same again. In a multitude of instances, whereas a person had formerly known only a life of ignorance characterized by drunkenness and the sins of the flesh, now, because he was converted, he was not only sober and clean of life, but was reading his Bible and perhaps one or two spiritual books. and was singing and memorizing hymns.

How many of Britain's poor were thus raised to new standards of life cannot be estimated, but it must be recognized that the singing and memorizing of Charles Wesley's hymns was as much used of God in this glorious process as was the preaching of the many men who took part in it.

Charles Wesley's poetic nature undoubtedly influenced his preaching. This is not to say that he necessarily quoted verse in his sermons. He probably made use of certain of his compositions at times but the poetic influence was manifest in his very speech. We remember that he usually preached without definite preparation, yet as he spoke there was often a beauty about his words and a rhythm in his sentences. The soaring quality was frequently present as he declared the same truths as those that fill his hymns and the emotions that made him a poet also gave force and feeling to his utterance.

Among the English writers of religious verse the names of such men as John Donne, George Herbert, John Milton, Isaac Watts and William Cowper must ever be held in the highest esteem. Yet because of the vast quantity of his compositions and the lyric fire that characterizes so many of them the work of Charles Wesley merits the lasting remembrance it has received.

Indeed, Isaac Watts, although he left us something approaching six hundred hymns, said about one of Charles's compositions, 'That single poem, *Wrestling Jacob*, is worth all the verses which I have ever written.' Charles built this production on the Old Testament passage, 'There wrestled a man with him until the breaking of the day... And he said, I will not let thee go, except thou bless me... What is thy name?' (Gen. 32:24-27). Here is a part of the poem:

Come, O thou Traveller unknown,
  Whom still I hold, but cannot see;
My company before is gone,
  And I am left alone with thee;
With thee all night I mean to stay,
And wrestle till the break of day.

I need not tell thee who I am;
  My misery or sin declare;
Thyself hast called me by my name,
  Look on thy hands, and read it there.
But who, I ask thee, who art thou?
Tell me thy name, and tell me now.

Wilt thou not yet to me reveal
  Thy new, unutterable name?
Tell me, I still beseech thee, tell;
  To know it now resolved I am;
Wrestling, I will not let thee go,
Till I thy name, thy nature know.

Yield to me now, for I am weak,
  But confident in self-despair;
Speak to my heart, in blessings speak,
  Be conquered by my instant prayer;
Speak, or thou never hence shalt move,
And tell me if thy name is Love.

'Tis Love! 'tis Love! Thou diedst for me!
  I hear thy whisper in my heart;
The morning breaks, the shadows flee;
  Pure universal love thou art;
To me, to all, thy mercies move;
Thy nature and thy name is Love.

My prayer hath power with God; the grace
  Unspeakable I now receive;
Through faith I see thee face to face,
  I see thee face to face, and live;
In vain I have not wept and strove;
Thy nature and thy name is Love.

I know thee, Saviour, who thou art,
  Jesus, the feeble sinner's Friend;
Nor wilt thou with this night depart,
  But stay and love me to the end.
Thy mercies never shall remove;
Thy nature and thy name is Love.

I always designed my son for a clergyman.
Nature has marked him for a musician: which
appeared from his earliest infancy. My friends
advised me not to cross his inclination. Indeed
I could not if I would. There is no way of hinder-
ing his being a musician but cutting off his
fingers. As he is particularly fond of church
music, I suppose if he lives he will be an organist.
(Charles Wesley, Letter, 1770 (?))

19.
Husband and father

We have seen that at the time of their marriage Charles and his Sally were truly in love. And we have also noticed that when in 1753 she suffered the smallpox the disease robbed her of her beauty, but the change in her appearance caused not the least lessening of his affection. And this love is evident throughout their lives.

Their affection is particularly manifest in their correspondence. It is apparent even in his salutations, for he begins his letters with such phrases as 'My best beloved Sally,' 'My dearest of dear ones,' and 'My ever dearest Sally'. At times he begins without any salutation and launches in with a statement, such as 'My prayer for my dearest partner is...' and 'Blessed be the day my dearest Sally was born.'

He frequently declares his yearning for her company. 'I long to have you with me,' comes into many a letter. Following a particularly delightful experience he declares, 'Only your presence could make it any pleasanter,' and in another letter he is praying, 'On Friday next, grant my heart's desire—see her I love next himself.' At a time when she wrote to say she was coming to London and would be at a certain friend's house at a stated date, although he was then in Norwich he responded, 'I shall lose no time, but take horse on Monday morning, and, with the blessing of God, seize you on Tuesday at your lodgings.'[1] Declarations of this nature occur throughout his correspondence.

This affection was unabated despite a frequent shortage of money. Charles received no regular salary but earned a royalty on the sale of his hymn-books. On rare occasions individuals gave him money and we must assume that at times the societies to which he ministered remunerated him to some slight extent.

John had guaranteed that he would receive £100 a year and it is possible the income from the above sources provided this amount.

Several of Charles's statements, however, indicate a lack of ready cash. 'Money we must get by any lawful means,' he told Sally, on one occasion, 'or debt will stare us in the face.' 'Our first temporal,' he said at another time, 'is to get out of debt...'And in still another letter he asked, 'How does your money hang out? As for me, I spend none and have none to spend.'[2]

It appears, however, that, possibly after they had been married a few years, Sally came into an inheritance. He speaks in one letter about 'our rents from Wales', and in another about the expected 'money from Brecon'. He likewise reports that a '...broker informs me, that I must add £40 to your £1000 to buy £1000 stock...'[3]

Later in life Charles appears to have overcome the financial shortages of his earlier years. He never owned a house of his own, but we do find him wanting the first opportunity to bid on an organ that he expected would be offered for sale, and he apparently had the money on hand.

Charles and Sally Wesley became the parents of eight children. But they underwent the sorrow of seeing five of these little ones die, either in infancy or in very early childhood. Three, however, were spared to them; Charles junior, born 1757; Sarah (whom they also called Sally) in 1759, and Samuel in 1766.

As his three little ones began to grow up other matters beside his ministry demanded a share in Charles Wesley's attention. For instance, we find him writing to his wife about the children and their common diseases—such things as measles and whooping cough—and he wants to be informed when Charley has his first tooth. Likewise, the dread possibility that any of the children might contract smallpox is frequently on the mind of both mother and father.

Furthermore, Charles was much concerned about the education of his children. Charley attended a school for a few years but his education was accomplished largely through tutors who were brought into the home. Their efforts were supplemented by Sally who taught the children in music and English literature. And whenever he was at home Charles instructed them in the classics—the subject in which he was himself so well-informed.

It appears, however, that Charles proved somewhat awkward in trying to establish a close rapport with his children. He held something of the same philosophy as his mother. For instance, we find him telling Sally, 'Make it your invariable rule to *cross his will,* in some one instance every day of your life.'[4] Moreover, just as at Epworth he and his brothers and sisters had not been allowed to mingle with the children of the village, so now he expected the same of his youngsters. He said to his wife, 'I cannot help cautioning you about Charles (and Sally too), to take care he contracts no acquaintance with other boys. Children are corrupters of each other.'[5] And at a time when Samuel was seven his father began a letter to him with the words, 'Come now, my good friend Samuel, and let us reason together.'[6] When Sarah was in her teens, like her mother she lost her beauty through suffering the smallpox and her father commented that the loss would save her from temptations![7]

Charles's failure to communicate at the level of his children was not occasioned in the least by a lack of affection. His love is constantly manifest but the cause probably lay in his age. Charles was fifty at the time of the birth of young Charles, fifty-two by the birth of Sarah and fifty-nine by that of Samuel. He seemed more like a grandfather than a father from the standpoint of his years. Moreover, he viewed life with an exceptional earnestness, which, although it did not make him severe, largely robbed him of any childish playfulness.

From their earliest childhood the children of Charles and Sally Wesley were accustomed to the sound of classical music. Sally had inherited a musical gift and had been taught by qualified teachers. During her married life she played the harpsichord and sang, and although her voice was not particularly strong it had an excellent range and was remarkably sweet. In turn, when her children cried she sang to quieten them and when some amusement was wanted by the little ones she provided it by singing. The works of the great composer Handel were then enjoying a rich popularity in England and she especially delighted in singing certain of his oratorios. It seemed almost a matter of course, then, for the young Charles and Samuel each to give evidence of a natural musical genius.

Charles himself tells us that before Charles junior had reached the age of three he played 'a tune on the harpsichord readily, and in just time. Soon after he played several, whatever his mother sung, or whatever he heard in the streets.' [8] When he was four his father took him to London and certain of England's great music masters declared their amazement at his ability. One man, 'a singer, for whom Handel wrote the tenor parts in his Messiah...gave the boy Purcell's songs, with Scarlatti's lessons. Mrs Rich gave him Handel's [lessons] and afterwards promised to supply him with tickets for all the oratorios, if his father would bring him up to town.'[9]

On his return to Bristol the lad was placed to study under one of the city's most prominent organists. And on a second visit to London Sir Charles Hotham 'promised him an organ, and that he should never want any means or encouragement in the pursuit of his art'.[10]

Samuel proved to be equally as gifted as his older brother. His father tells us, 'Before he could write, he composed much music. His custom was to lay the words of an oratorio before him, and sing them all over. Thus he set (extempore for the most part) Ruth, Gideon, Manasses, and the Death of Abel. We observed, when he repeated the same words, it was always to the same tunes. The airs of Ruth, in particular, he made before he was six years old; laid them up in his memory till he was eight; and then wrote them down.

'He was full eight years old, when Dr Boyce came to see us, and accosted me with, "Sir, I hear you have got an English Mozart in your house... This boy writes by nature as true a bass as I can do by rule and study. There is no man in England has two such sons." '[11]

The Wesleys' daughter Sarah, whom they also called Sally, did not possess her brothers' gift for music. She appears, however, to have had something of her father's feeling for poetry and was especially fond of prose literature.

In 1771 Charles and his family moved from Bristol to London. This action was taken at the urging of John Wesley, who desired his brother's help in ministering at the Foundery, and wanted him to live close by. But a Mrs Gumley, a wealthy woman who had been won to Christ under the preaching of Charles, offered him a fine, large home, fully furnished and without charge. It was situated in the suburb of Marylebone and therefore was too distant to be fully satisfactory to John.

The move to London, however, provided increased opportunities for furthering the boys' musical careers. Of course, their father desired above all things that they should receive Christ as their Saviour and he would also have been happy to have seen them enter the ministry. They showed, however, little interest in things spiritual and seemed deaf to his entreaties.

Charles could not afford the great music masters as teachers for his sons. But two of the best musicians then in London were so taken by their talent that they offered to teach them without charge and this they did for at least two years. Even so, their father later stated that he paid 'several hundred pounds' for their training during the period that followed.

As the boys grew up they increasingly kept company with prominent people in the musical world. They attended concerts and played before distinguished audiences and it was evident that they would both make music the chief pursuit of their lives.

As Charles and Samuel grew into young men they regularly gave concerts in their home, Charles playing the organ and Samuel either the violin or harpsichord. We are told, 'A large room, which would hold about eighty persons, was generally crowded. The ticket for each course was three guineas; profits were, however, small, owing to the expenses for performers and refreshments. The Bishop of London, Lord Dartmouth, Lord Barrington, Lord and Lady De Spencer, the Danish and Saxon ambassadors, and many other distinguished persons were regular subscribers.

'John Wesley, in gown and bands, attended one of the concerts with his wife, to show that he did not consider that there was any sin in such entertainments, as some of the Methodists were inclined to think. General Oglethorpe, now more than eighty years old, came on February 25th, 1781, to hear the sons of his old secretary. Here he met John Wesley, and kissed his hands in token of respect. Wesley says, "I spent an agreeable hour at a concert at my nephews'; but I was a little out of my element among lords and ladies." '[12]

Lord Mornington, the father of the Duke of Wellington, became a particular friend of the young Wesleys. He was himself a musician and frequently visited the home, bringing his violin and playing with them. While Samuel was still a boy Lord Mornington ordered a suit of scarlet for him and this he usually wore while performing at the concerts.

The development of the boys in the world of music had its effect upon their own lives and upon the life of their father.

Readers will readily recognize the difference brought about in the life of Charles Wesley by the musical careers of his sons.

We have seen him as he went forth during the 1740s, bold for God and fearless of any man. On entering a town he would take his stand in some prominent spot, lift up his voice and with unquestionable earnestness plead with men and women to receive Jesus Christ. He met the violence of the mob, was ridiculed in the press and became, like the apostle Paul, 'the offscouring of all things'.

Charles's relations with people of the world of music were very different from what they had been with the people of Methodism. Methodists everywhere became critical and the Reverend John Fletcher expressed the feelings of many when he wrote to Charles, asserting, 'You have your enemies as well as your brother. They complain of your love for music, company and fine clothes, great folks, and the want of your former zeal and frugality. I do not need to put you in mind to cut off sinful appearances... Only see you abound more and more, to stop the mouths of your adversaries.'[13]

However, Charles Wesley believed he was only being a kind father in recognizing the one true ability possessed by his sons and giving them opportunity to exercise it. He still lived before them his life of prayer and self-denial and witnessed to them of the gospel and the saving power of Jesus Christ. But they gave no evidence of ever coming to a realization of their need of the Saviour. He talked to them about 'the new birth', but there is no record of their ever seeking during his lifetime the salvation that had meant so much in the lives of their father and their Uncle John.

Nevertheless there is evidence that after the death of their father both Charles and Sarah experienced the new birth and both died as members of a Methodist society. But while Charles was alive he had reason to feel that at best they were only seekers. Charles Wesley knew at first hand the sorrow experienced by so many Christian parents.

He wills us in our partner's steps to tread;
And, called and quickened by the speaking dead,
We trace our shining pattern from afar,
His old associates in the glorious war,
Resolved to use the utmost strength bestowed,
Like him to spend and to be spent for God,
By holy violence seize the crown so nigh,
Fight the good fight, our threefold foe defy,
And more than conquerors in the harness die.

(Charles Wesley, 'An elegy on the Late Rev.
George Whitefield, M.A.' 1770).

20.
Fellowship renewed

As we saw earlier, not long after he was married Charles Wesley
renewed fellowship with George Whitefield and with Lady Huntingdon. Later on in life he endeavoured to do the same with
friends in the Moravian movement.

During his early manhood he had had close ties with
Whitefield. While at Oxford the two men became acquainted
and Charles wrote of the event,

> Can I the memorable day forget,
> When first we by divine appointment met?
> Where undisturbed the thoughtful student roves,
> In search of truth, through academic groves;
> A modest, pensive youth, who mused alone,
> Industrious the frequented path to shun,
> An Israelite, without disguise or art,
> I saw, I loved, and clasped him to my heart,
> A stranger as my bosom-friend caressed,
> And unawares received an angel-guest.[1]

In 1739 Whitefield began to preach in the open air and, again
as we have seen, he thrust John and Charles out into the same
great task. Charles wrote,

> Nor did I linger, at my friend's desire,
> To tempt the furnace, and abide the fire:
> When suddenly sent forth, from the highways
> I called poor sinners to the feast of grace;
> Urged to pursue the work by thee begun
> Through good and ill report I still rushed on,

Nor felt the fire of popular applause,
Nor feared the torturing flame in such a glorious cause.[2]

During the same year, despite Whitefield's pleading with him
not to do so, John Wesley had preached and printed a most
vehement sermon 'Against Predestination'. Whitefield had
published a gently worded answer in 1741, yet would not continue to pursue any controversy with the Wesleys. But Charles
at this time stood firmly with John and spoke severely against
his former friend.[3] And this had remained Charles's attitude
largely throughout the 1740s.

By 1752, however, Charles was ready to separate from John.
He wrote to Whitefield, telling him of his problem and apparently
suggesting that they join forces. But Whitefield replied, saying,
'The connection between you and your brother hath been so
close ... and your attachment to him so necessary to keep up
his interest, that I would not willingly for the world do or say
anything that may separate such friends.'[4]

Moved by an attitude such as this and by Whitefield's long-
standing unselfish actions, in 1755 Charles addressed to him an
'Epistle' in which he declared there was no longer any barrier
between them. We quoted earlier his opening words,

Come on, my Whitefield! (since the strife is past,
And friends at first are friends again at last).

In reference to the division that had occurred between them
in 1741 and subsequent years, he stated,

Ah! wherefore did we ever seem to part,
Or clash in sentiment, while one in heart?
What dire device did the old serpent find,
To put asunder those whom God had joined?
From folly and self-love opinion rose,
To sever friends who never yet were foes;
To baffle and divert our noblest aim,
Confound our pride, and cover us with shame;
To make us blush beneath her short-lived pow'r,
And glad the world with one triumphant hour.

But lo! the snare is broke, the captive's freed,
By faith on all the hostile powers we tread,
And crush through Jesus' strength the serpent's head,

One in his hand, oh, may we still remain,
Fast bound with love's indissoluble chain;
His love the tie that binds us to his throne,
His love the bond that perfects us in one;
His love (let all the ground of friendship see)
His only love constrains our hearts t' agree,
And gives the rivet for eternity.[5]

Charles had also renewed close ties with Lady Huntingdon. In eighteenth-century England the aristocracy were of high importance and were accorded a position much above the rank and file of mankind. But Lady Huntingdon had experienced the miracle of the new birth and she lived a strongly Christian life. Moreover, like Whitefield she held to the theological system usually known as 'Calvinism', but which Whitefield termed 'the doctrines of grace'. She made Whitefield one of her chaplains and large companies of titled people—men and women of learning, of artistic and literary ability and of great wealth—gathered in her home twice a week for some years to hear him.

We have already seen that, in 1751, Charles stated, 'I went once more to visit L.[ady] H.[untingdon]. She expressed great kindness toward me ... My heart was turned back again, and forgot all that is past.'[6] During a period of sickness a few months later, fearing that Methodism was about to separate from the Church of England and, needing someone to whom to pour out his soul, he had written to her at length.

Lady Huntingdon was expending her wealth in the construction of chapels in various parts of England. In their pulpits she used several preachers who were thoroughly evangelical in doctrine and were in holy orders in the Church of England.

From 1751 onwards Charles had warm fellowship with Whitefield and Lady Huntingdon. Whitefield assisted the Wesleys' work by preaching for them when opportunity allowed and we find Charles saying, for instance, of his efforts at Leeds, 'The door has continued open ever since Mr Whitefield preached here, and quite removed the prejudices of our first opposers. Some of them were convinced by him, some converted and added

The Countess of Huntingdon

to the church: "he that escapes the sword of Jehu shall Elisha slay".[7]

Although Charles gave up his life of itinerant preaching in 1757, this was not, as has been claimed, so that he might spend his days in laziness. He alternately conducted the Methodist work in Bristol and in London. At Bristol there were the New Room and the chapel at Kingswood, one or two societies in outlying towns and one at Bath, the resort of the wealthy. And when he was in London, besides the large congregation at the Foundery, there were five other Methodist chapels—some in London and others in the suburbs. Accordingly, even without the labour of itinerating throughout England Charles Wesley had work that kept him constantly busy.

Besides Charles by now had a wife to help and support and children for whose instruction and upbringing he was responsible. But, above all, his grand undertaking, over and above his preaching, was his poetry. As well as writing poetry he edited and revised poems he had previously written, and throughout the rest of his life he devoted himself unsparingly to this occupation. It is to this period of his life that we owe a great many of the nearly 9,000 poetical works which constitute his chief memorial.

During these years Methodism existed in two forms. Methodism, as a popular movement, had been founded by Whitefield and throughout his lifetime he was known as 'the Leader and Founder of Methodism'.[8] During the 1750s his wooden 'Tabernacle' in Moorfields, London, was replaced by a fine, large new structure of brick. He also built a new church in Penn Street, Bristol and a new chapel in Tottenham Court Road, London. Wesley had acquired four or five small chapels in or around London but his headquarters was still the former cannon factory, the Foundery, the poor appearance of which contrasted with that of Whitefield's Tabernacle just a block or so away. A number of people of aristocratic rank attended the Tabernacle, while the Tottenham Court Road Chapel, besides being the largest non-establishment church in Britain, had among its membership several men of prominence in art, literature and politics.

During the early 1740s a movement had sprung up around Whitefield and he had established for it a very practical form of organization. He had societies and preachers in several parts

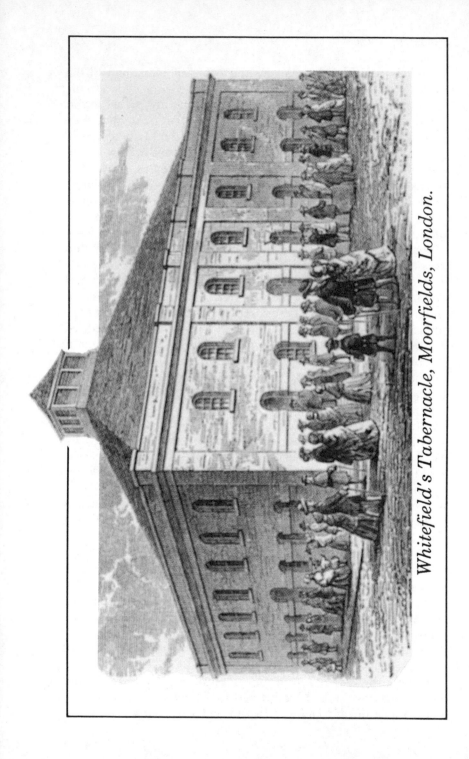

Whitefield's Tabernacle, Moorfields, London.

of England, and in 1744 had as many followers as Wesley. But
he spent the next four years in America and upon his return
to England, knowing that for the rest of his life he would be
spending much of his time overseas, and also disliking any sense
of rivalry with Wesley, he gave up all leadership of his movement. 'Let the name of Whitefield perish, and let me be the servant of all!' was repeatedly his statement. Thereafter he worked
with any men, so long as they were sound in the evangelical faith,
and he frequently proved of assistance to Wesley.

But although the strife between John Wesley and Whitefield
had been brought to an end by Whitefield's yielding up his
prominence and allowing his movement to die away, differences
remained between Wesley and Lady Huntingdon. She
recognized his hard work but said he was self-centred and cunning, while he asserted that she was an excellent woman, but
proud and imperious, And, since Wesley possessed an autocratic
nature, while Lady Huntingdon as an aristocrat was used to giving orders, they were sometimes referred to as 'Pope John and
Pope Joan'.

In 1766, however, Lady Huntingdon made an effort to effect
greater harmony in the work. She suggested there should frequently be a meeting between the representatives of the two doctrinal positions—that is, herself and Whitefield for the Calvinists
and John and Charles Wesley for the Arminians. To this they
all agreed and accepted also the idea of playing down the points
of doctrinal difference and emphasizing the great elements of
the gospel that they all held in common. Charles Wesley spoke
of the agreement as 'a sort of quadruple alliance', and Howell
Harris referred to it as 'the Public Peace Union'.

This agreement immediately began to be put into practice.
Charles wrote on 21 August 1766, 'Last night my brother came.
This morning we spent two blessed hours with George
Whitefield. The threefold cord, we trust, will never more be
broken. On Tuesday next my brother is to preach in Lady Huntingdon's chapel at Bath. That and all her chapels (not to say,
as I might, herself also) are now put into the hands of us
three.'[9]

Lady Huntingdon also commenced a ministerial training college at Trevecca in Wales and she gave practical evidence of
her trust in this recently-accomplished alliance by placing two
of Wesley's men, William Fletcher and Joseph Benson, in the

Whitefield's Tottenham Court Road Chapel, at the time, the largest dissenting church in Britain and probably in the world.

chief positions in the management and teaching of the college. Undoubtedly many of the common people throughout Methodism felt a sense of relief to know the wall of division was so largely broken down.

In the summer of 1769 Whitefield left on his seventh and final trip to America. And when he sailed Methodism was in this seemingly harmonious condition. On 30 September of the following year he died. But he was loved and his memory was respected among Wesley's people as well as among his own. The same was true of Lady Huntingdon and it was evident that both of them would continue to be revered by historians for their labours during the first century of Methodism.

Before long, however, the wall of division was raised again. John Wesley published the minutes of his 1770 conference. He said he feared the spread of Antinomianism[10] and therefore he spoke in a manner which certainly seemed to deny 'justification by faith' and to assert the doctrine of 'salvation by works'. He stated, for instance, 'We have taken it for a maxim, that "A man is to do nothing in order to justification". Nothing can be more false. Whoever desires to find favour with God should "cease from evil, and learn to do well". Whoever repents should "do works meet for repentance". And if this is not in order to find favour, then why does he do them for?'[11]

The other propositions that Wesley made in these minutes were similar in style and sentiment. John Wesley, who in other matters could speak with utter clarity, on this doctrinal subject at this important point in the history of Methodism, spoke with this misleading ambiguity.

As Wesley undoubtedly expected, severe discord followed. Charles Wesley took no open part in the strife, although on the basis of his earlier statements we must assume that he did not agree with his brother's action. There is no published word from him in this second controversy.

Calvinistic Methodists (and there were probably as many of them as of Wesleyan Methodists in England, Wales, Ireland and Scotland) were highly aroused. The chief doctrine, they supposed, of the Christian faith, was here denied by the one who long had been foremost in defending it. Lady Huntingdon, feeling she must disassociate herself from all suggestion of 'salvation by works', required anyone who agreed with Wesley's propositions to leave Trevecca College. And a relative of hers, the

Honourable Rev. Walter Shirley, urged several pastors to attend Wesley's next conference with him and ask what he actually meant by his statement.

Other men were now aroused to defend the Calvinistic side of the strife. In the controversy of 1741 Wesley had faced only Whitefield and Cennick—men who acted towards him in kindness and forbearance—but now he met men of a different order. These were chiefly Sir Richard Hill, his brother Rowland Hill and Augustus Toplady. These three asserted that Wesley had stirred up the strife in order, firstly, to break off fellowship with Lady Huntingdon and to lessen her influence among the people; secondly, to lessen the esteem in which Whitefield was held, and thirdly to portray himself as the originator of the revival work and to charge that Whitefield had made the first break in the movement.

Wesley had two of his men, Walter Sellon and Thomas Olivers, take over his part in the battle. Sad to say, the men on both sides went far beyond the bounds of Christian decorum in their severity against their opponents, but although the actions of the Hills and Toplady have been widely made known, the statements of Sellon and Olivers and their associates, which were equally shameful, have remained hidden.[12]

Lady Huntingdon, though unyielding in her stand on the doctrinal matter, took no part personally in this conflict. Charles Wesley also remained aloof from such disgraceful proceedings. But the affair estranged him still further from his brother. He blamed John for breaking up the agreement and in a letter to Lady Huntingdon, written just after Whitefield's funeral, he stated, 'You remember a sort of quadruple alliance entered into three or four years ago, which *one of the parties never thought of from that day to this*. How soon is that alliance come to nothing! One [Whitefield] is safely landed—another is *removed to an immeasurable distance*—while *we* yet live, scarce one short year perhaps, between *us two* let there be peace.'[13]

In response to a request that had been made by Whitefield, John Wesley preached his funeral sermon. He extolled his preaching ability, remarked on the unparalleled extent of his winning of souls and also praised him for the friendliness and warmth that characterized his life.

Charles, who knew Whitefield so well, acclaimed him in what may be termed a biographical sketch in verse, 536 lines in length.[14] This is not to assert that Charles had come into full agreement with him, but in it he manifested the affection he bore towards Whitefield, praised the unselfishness of his actions and declared his sorrow at Whitefield's death.

They had parted nearly thirty years earlier, but when ten years had passed they had come into fellowship again and within another five years these two kindred spirits had found their hearts bound together in ties of inseparable Christian love.

Besides his efforts to keep Methodism within the Church of England, Charles also endeavoured to bring about a reunion of the Moravians with the Methodists. As we have seen, there had been strong differences between the two bodies in 1741 and during the following four or five years Charles had frequently denounced what he considered their apostasy. But in 1771 he sought to renew fellowship with them. He again corresponded with James Hutton, the London book dealer and the man who had been the founder of the work that became the Fetter Lane Society. Throughout the intervening thirty years Hutton had been a leading figure among the Moravians and more than once had indicated his strong feelings against the Methodists. But despite Charles's attempts to bring about a reunion, nothing came of his efforts.

In his concern, however, about the threatened separation from the Church of England, in 1786 Charles wrote to another important Moravian personality, the Rev. Benjamin Latrobe, 'The friendly intercourse of your society and ours might be another likely means of preserving our children in their calling. My brother is very well inclined to such a correspondence ... If our Lord is pleased to use us as peacemakers under him, we may yet do something towards preventing any separation at all ... The great evil which I have dreaded for near fifty years is a schism. If I live to see that prevented, and also to see the two sticks, the Moravian and English church, become one in our Saviour's hand, I shall then say, "Lord, now lettest thou thy servant depart in peace." '[15]

Charles's daughter Sarah said that during his latter years her father repented of his strong words against the Moravians uttered in his earlier life and that he more than once made statements to this effect in his correspondence with James Hutton.

We may well rejoice in the strength with which Charles Wesley stood against what he was certain was false doctrine, but we may rejoice even more in this recognition that his earlier attitude had been wrong and in the efforts he made to renew a broken fellowship.

While the evil days come not, nor the years draw nigh, when thou shalt say, I have no pleasure in them ... in the day when the keepers of the house shall tremble, and the strong men shall bow themselves, and the grinders cease because they are few, and those that look out of the windows he darkened ... and the grasshopper shall be a burden, and desire shall fail: because man goeth to his long home, and the mourners go about the streets.

(Ecclesiastes 12: 1-5).

For I am persuaded, that neither death, nor life, nor angels, nor principalities, nor powers, nor things present, nor things to come, nor height, nor depth, nor any other creature, shall be able to separate us from the love of God, which is in Christ Jesus our Lord.

(The apostle Paul, *Romans* 8: 38-39).

21.
The joys and sorrows of old age

From the time of his conversion onwards one of the chief features
of Charles Wesley's life had been his spiritual happiness. Admittedly, he had his hours of depression and there were occasions
on which he wanted to go to heaven immediately. But beneath
it all there was an abiding peace and joy.

His happiness is manifest especially in his hymns. The section of the *Methodist Hymn Book* entitled 'Hymns for believers
rejoicing' contains seventy-eight compositions, mostly from his
pen, and they all tell forth the Christian's triumph. The following hymn, written about 1749, is redolent with spiritual delight:

> Oh, how happy are they
> Who the Saviour obey
> And have laid up their treasures above!
> Tongue can never express
> The sweet comfort and peace
> Of a soul in its earliest love.
>
> That sweet comfort was mine,
> When the favour divine
> I received through the blood of the Lamb;
> When my heart first believed,
> What a joy I received,
> What a heaven in Jesus's name!
>
> 'Twas a heaven below
> My Redeemer to know;
> And the angels could do nothing more
> Than to fall at his feet,
> And the story repeat,
> And the lover of sinners adore.

> Jesus all the day long
> Was my joy and my song;
> Oh, that all his salvation might see!
> 'He hath loved me,' I cried,
> 'He hath suffered and died
> To redeem even rebels like me.'
>
> Oh, the rapturous height
> Of that holy delight
> Which I felt in the life-giving blood!
> Of my Saviour possessed,
> I was perfectly blessed,
> As if filled with the fulness of God.[1]

This basic contentment and joy glows throughout almost all of Charles Wesley's writings. It is present in one entry after another in his *Journal* and is the chief feature of most of his letters. He experienced it even during his times of sickness and when he wrote his hymns his soul was often in a state of ecstasy.

Even in his advancing years Charles remained busy in witnessing for the Lord. This is manifest in a letter he wrote in 1776 to a musician, Joseph Kelway, a man who had been an associate of Handel. In those days the human life span was somewhat shorter than it is today and Charles, who was then sixty-nine and worn out from his labour, believed he had not long to live. He said to Kelway, who was in his seventies, 'The joy I felt at seeing you... somewhat resembled the joy we shall feel when we meet again without our bodies. Most heartily do I thank God that he has given you a longer continuance among us; and, I trust, a resolution to improve your few last precious moments. *We* must confess, at *our* time of life, that "one thing is needful", even to *get ready for our unchangeable eternal state.* But what is that readiness or meetness?

'You are convinced of my sincere love for your soul, and therefore allow me the liberty of a friend. As such I write, not to teach you what you do not know, but to stir up your mind, by way of remembrance, and exhort both you and myself,

> Of little life the most to make,
> And manage wisely your last stake.

'…The true repentance is better felt than described. It surely implies a troubled and wounded spirit, a broken and contrite heart…

'By this brokenness of heart our Saviour prepares us for divine faith, and present pardon, sealed upon the heart which passes all understanding, in joy unspeakable and full of glory, and in love which casts out the love of sin…'[2]

Thus to the elderly musician Kelway, Charles presented the gospel and in doing so he testified to the joy experienced in truly being a Christian.

Nevertheless, although this happiness remained a basic element of Charles Wesley's life, during his latter years he also experienced much sorrow.

He was disappointed first in that none of his children gave evidence of being born again.

We must remind ourselves of the large difference in age between the children and their father. We can form some idea of this by calculating his age at the time when each of them reached the age of twenty: in the case of Charles junior he was seventy, in Sarah's case seventy-two and in that of Samuel nearly eighty. He constantly manifested his concern for their welfare but he failed in his efforts to influence them for God. His relationships with them are therefore to a large extent marked by a lack of joy.

The younger Charles's one ability lay in his music. He was indeed a genius, but apparently of an eccentric type. Thomas Jackson, who knew the Wesleys personally, states, 'It is doubtful whether, throughout the entire course of his life, he was able to dress himself without assistance.'[3] He never married and was cared for by his mother and sister. He earned his livelihood by teaching music and as an organist, first at the Lock Chapel and later at the Marylebone parish church. When the position of organist at St Paul's was open he applied for it, but was turned down merely because he was 'a Wesley'. His musical abilities won him several invitations to play before the royal family, and the Prince of Wales (later King George IV) engaged him to teach his daughter, Princess Charlotte. Charles junior remained a member of the Church of England, but until he was middle-aged he showed no realization of his need to be born again, and his father told him, 'You do not sufficiently take God into your counsel.'

Sarah's experience, in relation to her father was, for some

time, similar to that of her brother Charles. Although she did
not manifest a talent for music she apparently had inherited
something of her father's feeling for poetry. She also possessed
an appreciation of good literature and certain letters she wrote
later in life reveal a true ability in expressing her thoughts with
meaning and clarity. When she was in her teens, like many an
adolescent, she did not agree with her father's wish that she
refrain from attending balls and such like affairs and she did
not get up early enough in the mornings to please him.

On an occasion when she was temporarily out of London he
wrote to her, saying, 'I think you may avail yourself of my small
knowledge of books and poetry. I am not yet too old to assist
you a little in your reading, and perhaps improve your taste in
versifying. You need not dread my severity. I have a laudable
partiality for my own children. Witness your brothers, whom
I do not love a jot better than you; only be you as ready to show
me your verses as they their music.'⁴

The father's spiritual concern for his daughter is evident in
another letter, in which he said, '[This] you gained by the
despised Methodists, if nothing more—the knowledge of what
true religion consists in; namely, in happiness and holiness; in
peace and love; in the favour and image of God restored; in
paradise regained; in a birth from above, a kingdom within you;
a participation in the divine nature. The principal means or
instrument of this is faith; which faith is the gift of God, given
to every one that asks.'⁵

It looks as though all the children adhered to the Church of
England and for a time at least, regarded the Methodists as a
'despised' body. Later in life—probably after her father's
death—Sarah attended the Methodist meetings in London, and
in her letters to her uncle John she gave evidence not only of
her appreciation of him personally but also an acceptance of the
gospel he preached.

Charles Wesley's deepest sorrow came through his son Samuel.
Besides being a genius in the realm of music Samuel had abilities
which could have raised him to prominence in several other
activities. Yet despite his talents he seemed to find it difficult
to make a living and was always short of money. He became
closely friendly with a man who was a Roman Catholic and,
apparently assuming he could become a well-paid organist in
the Catholic Church, Samuel became a member of that body.

He marked his transfer of allegiance by composing a mass, and while Catholics rejoiced and the pope sent greetings, Charles Wesley was broken-hearted.

In his distress he sought relief by expressing his sorrow in verse. The poem he wrote on Samuel's action runs to twenty-five stanzas, three of which read,

> Farewell, my all of earthly hope,
> My nature's stay, my age's prop,
> Irrevocably gone!
> Submissive to the will divine,
> I acquiesce, and make it mine;
> I offer up my son.
>
> Shocked at the hypocrites profane,
> My son, when undeceived, restrain,
> From worse, if worse can be;
> Nor let him all religion cast
> Behind, and shelter take at last
> In infidelity.
>
> But while an exile here I live,
> I live for a lost son to grieve,
> And in thy Spirit groan,
> Thy blessings on his soul to claim,
> Through Jesu's all-prevailing name
> Presented at thy throne.

Before many years had passed, however, Samuel disputed with a priest. He claimed his right to think for himself in matters of religion and asserted, 'The crackers of the Vatican are no longer taken for the thunderbolts of heaven: for excommunication I care not three straws.'[6] Some time after his father died he withdrew completely from the Roman church.

Two other elements besides the difference in age appear to have affected Charles Wesley's relationship with his children. One was that his wife, who was of a kind and gentle nature, seems to have failed to reprove them sufficiently. The other was the tendency on the part of Charles to expect his youngsters to conform, to some extent, to his own high standards of Christian behaviour —something of the Holy Club's manner of self-discipline.

Charles Wesley was also grieved by the actions of his brother, which he thought would bring about Methodism's separation from the Church of England.

During the 1770s John began to make preparations for the orderly continuance of Methodism following his death.

First, in 1776 he opened a large new chapel in City Road, London. This replaced the Foundery and became the head-quarters of Methodism.

Secondly, he had a *Deed of Declaration* drawn up. This document legally defined 'the conference of the people called Methodists,' and authorized this body to appoint preachers for all the Methodist societies following his own death and that of Charles.

Thirdly, he took upon himself the right to confer ordination. This action was brought about especially by the need in America. Following the War of Independence the political and ecclesiastical ties between England and the colonies were severed. Yet there were 15,000 Methodists in America, but since none of their preachers had been ordained, these people were denied the sacraments. Wesley appealed to an English bishop to ordain three men who were to sail for America but his request was refused. Accordingly, in keeping with his belief that 'bishops' and 'presbyters' were one office he claimed that he was a bishop as much as any man and therefore that he had a right to ordain.

John Wesley also had become acquainted with a Dr Thomas Coke, and this man was influencing him to take this step. Coke was educated at Oxford, was well-to-do and was an ordained clergyman of the Church of England, but he urged Wesley to set him apart to lead the Methodist work in America. Accordingly, despite Coke's previous episcopal ordination, on 1 September 1784, at five in the morning, Wesley ordained him 'superintendent' of Methodism in America. He also ordained two other men as ministers who were to accompany Coke to the New World. A little later he ordained another three men to serve Methodism in Scotland.

When he learned what John had done Charles was over-whelmed. 'I am thunderstruck. I cannot believe it,' he wrote. John published a statement justifying his action and Charles asserted in a letter, 'I can scarcely yet believe it, that in his eighty-second year my brother, my old intimate friend and companion, should have assumed the *episcopal character*, ordained elders, consecrated a bishop, and sent him to ordain the lay preachers in America! I was then in Bristol, at his elbow, but he never gave me the least hint of his intention.'[7]

John said he was still a member of the Church of England and declared he would never leave it. But more than once Charles reminded him of the statement of the Chief Justice, Lord Mansfield: 'Ordination is separation!'

Throughout these years Charles continued his ministry. He frequently visited the jail in London and manifested the same concern for the inmates that we have seen him express during his earlier years. He also preached in the City Road Chapel, but as the 1780s came on he was often hindered by his age. We are told, 'The poet was becoming feeble. When thoughts did not flow freely he would make long pauses, as if waiting for divine help. At such times he closed his eyes, fumbled with his hands about his breast, leaned with his elbows on the Bible... Sometimes he had to ask the congregation to sing once or twice in the course of the sermon.

'When he felt stronger, and was under some happy influence, he expressed himself with fluency and force. His short and pointed sentences, rich in Scripture phraseology, and full of evangelical truth, made a great impression on the people. His prayers were still marked by special power.'[8]

His feebleness, however, provoked complaints among his hearers. Several of them asserted that the work at City Road was dying and they refused to attend. In turn certain of the younger laymen, among whom were some exceptionally capable preachers, indicated their wish to be allowed to preach. His heart was in the work as much as ever but he no longer possessed the physical strength to minister in the manner he desired.

During 1787 Charles remained at home a great deal of the time. John assured him frequently that this practice would hasten his death. 'Dear brother,' John wrote, 'you must go out every day, or die. Do not die to save charges. You certainly need not want anything as long as I live.'

John himself was four years older than Charles, but despite his age, while Charles became weaker, John went about his ministry with renewed strength. 'My youthful brother sets out for Cornwall,' says Charles in one letter, and 'My brother is here in perfect health,' in another. Repeatedly, during his lifetime John had been thought to be dying from consumption, but he persisted in his ministry, riding four thousand miles a year and he claimed that the outdoor exercise restored his health.

Charles's family were a constant concern to him. Some authors have suggested that he felt he had done wrong in allowing his sons to devote their lives so completely to music. Be that as it may, he was constantly wounded by their lack of desire for the things of God. John was of the same mind, and in 1788 he said to Charles, 'Never was there before so loud a call to all that are under your roof. If they have not hitherto sufficiently regarded either you, or the God of their fathers, what is more calculated to convince them, than to see you so long hovering upon the borders of the grave?'[9]

As January 1788 advanced, however, Charles found himself too weak to take even the shortest ride. He remained in his house and by February was confined to his bed. He had no actual disease and suffered no pain, but he was worn out physically. One of the Methodist preachers stated, 'He had no transports of joy, but solid hope, unshaken confidence in Christ, and perfect peace.'

Late in the month of March, being too feeble to use a pen, Charles requested his wife to write down the lines he now dictated:

> In age and feebleness extreme,
> Who shall a sinful worm redeem?
> Jesus, my only hope thou art,
> Strength of my failing flesh and heart;
> Oh, could I catch a smile from thee,
> And drop into eternity!

This was the last effort in composing poetry by the man whose production of verse throughout life had been so large. He was now unconscious much of the time and it was evident the end was near.

On Saturday, 29 March 1788, his family came into his room. For some moments his hand lay in that of his daughter Sarah, and then his breath gently ceased. His spirit quit its tenement of clay and soared to take its place in the paradise of God.

John had intended that Charles's body should be interred,

as his would be, in the burial-ground at the City Road Chapel. But Charles had indicated he did not want to be buried there because it was unconsecrated ground. He was laid to rest, according to his wishes, in the graveyard of the Marylebone parish church. Samuel Bradburn, one of the ablest of the Methodist preachers, gave the address at the funeral service from the Scripture, 'A prince and a great man is fallen this day in Israel.'

Charles Wesley was a man of unquestioned integrity and unfailing sincerity. His chief failure was his impulsiveness and a tendency to be hasty in his temper. He was a most fervent and forceful preacher and in this capacity he played a large part in the eighteenth-century revival. His courage was manifest in the face of violence and in the way he would return to confront the same mob time after time till hearts were subdued and sometimes his chief opponents even became his staunch defenders. He was a man of independent mind, strong in his opinions and firm in his convictions.

Charles Wesley was learned in the classics and, more importantly, in the Scriptures, and he was a man of prayer and faith. Above all, he was a gifted poet and for the lyric quality of his hymns we must surely claim for him the first position among the writers of English religious verse.

The Minutes of the 1788 Methodist Conference carried this report: 'Mr Charles Wesley, who after spending four score years with much sorrow and pain, quietly retired into Abraham's bosom. He had no disease, but after a gradual decay of some months "The weary wheels of life stood still at last." '

His tombstone bears the words he had written about another minister:

> With poverty of spirit blest,
> Rest happy saint, in Jesus rest;
> A sinner saved, through grace forgiven,
> Redeemed from earth to reign in heaven.
>
> Thy labours of unwearied love,
> By thee forgot, are crowned above;
> Crowned, through the mercy of the Lord,
> With a free, full, immense reward.

Epilogue

Charles Wesley's widow, Sally, was given an annual grant of £50 from the Methodist Book Room—virtually royalties from the sale of her husband's hymn-books. She moved from Mrs Gumley's large home to a smaller house and her daughter Sarah and her son Charles lived with her. She attended the Methodist society, either at West Street or City Road, but took no public part in the activities. She died in 1822 at the age of ninety-six.

References

Chapter 1

1. Dr Annesley is said to have had twenty-five children, several of whom died in infancy.
2. John Kirk, *The Mother of the Wesleys*, Jarrold, London (1864), p.12.
3. The original hand-written manuscript is in the Bodleian Library, Oxford (*Ms. Rawl. C. 406*). It was published in 1703 under the title *The Education of the Dissenters' Academies*.
4. *Ms. Rawl.*, p.3.
5. The average salary for a clergyman was then about £60.
6. *Ms. Rawl.*, p.3. The wedding took place in the parish church of St Mary le Bone. (Telford, ed., *The Letters of John Wesley*, Epworth Press, London (1931), vol.1. p.44).
7. L. Tyerman, *The Life and Times of the Rev. Samuel Wesley, M.A.*, London (1866), pp.208-9.
8. *Ms. Rawl.*, p.3.
9. It has long been assumed that it was the queen who appointed Samuel to Epworth, but Dr Frank Baker has provided evidence that it was the king who conferred this favour. See Maldwyn Edwards, *Family Circle*, Epworth, London (1949), p.12.
10. Several Methodist authors have assumed that Samuel's income at Epworth was wretchedly small. The nearly £200 per annum may be compared with the £28 received in his first curacy and the £50-£60 received by the average clergyman at the time.
11. George J. Stevenson, *Memorials of the Wesley Family*, Partridge, London (1876), p.79.
12. Kirk, *Mother of the Wesleys*, p.117.
13. Tyerman, *Samuel Wesley*, p.303.
14. *Ibid.*, p.304.
15. During the nineteenth century several writers asserted that Samuel could never have been guilty of such a deed. But in 1953 a series

of letters written by Susanna at the time of his absence were found in an antiquary's shop in Manchester. They were published in the *Manchester Guardian* on 2 July of that year and were later published in the *Proceedings of the Wesley Historical Society*,   XXIX, pp.50-57.

16. This was not the fire from which John was rescued—that came later.

17. Tyerman, *Samuel Wesley*, p.127.

Chapter 2

1. Stevenson, *Wesley Family*, p. 385.
2. Tyerman, *Samuel Wesley*, p.203.
3. Stevenson, *Wesley Family*, p.163.
4. *Ibid.*, p.165.
5. *Ibid.*, p.164.
6. For its finances the average Anglican church is not solely dependent on the giving of its congregation but largely on the income from inherited sources. Although Samuel says that at times he received £200 a year, in some years his income was £170 or even less. Yet when we remember that in his first curacy his income was £28, while he was a chaplain it was £70 and during his time at South Ormsby £50, it is evident he was now well beneficed. Several authors have made the mistake of making it appear that his income at Epworth was wretchedly small.
7. John Wesley says that upon his next visit to Epworth he took down the statement of each member of the family concerning the ghost. His account of the affair was published in 1784 in the *Arminian Magazine*, pp.548, 606, 654.
8. John Telford, *The Life of the Rev. Charles Wesley, M.A.*, Wesleyan Methodist Bookroom, London (1900), pp.24-25.
9. *Ibid.*, p.25.
10. *Ibid.*, p.24.

Chapter 3

1. Charles Wesley, *Journal*, Thomas Jackson, London (1849), reprinted Baker Book House, Grand Rapids, Michigan (1908), vol.2. p.432.
   (Hereafter referred to as *Journal*).
2. John Whitehead, *The Lives of John and Charles Wesley*, Worthington, New York, p.66.
3. John Wesley states that he read these two works by William Law in 1727 or 1728, but Frank Baker, writing in the *Proceedings of the Wesley Historical Society*, vol.XXXVII, part 3, pp.78-82, asserts that Wesley is manifestly wrong in his dating. 'Not even Wesley's

diaries and letters may be regarded as sacrosanct; they contain numerous errors in detail, such as incorrect days of the week, as well as inaccurate naming of places and people...' (p.80).

4. *Ibid.*, p.79.

5. Ordination in the Church of England is in two stages. The first is that of deacon, after which, in general practice, a period of time elapses in which the ordinand proves himself worthy. He then enters upon the second stage, that of ordination as a priest.

6. Frank Baker, *Charles Wesley as Revealed in his Letters*, Epworth Press, London (1948), p.10.

7. *Ibid.*, p.10.

8. *Ibid.*, p.14.

9. In his article 'The Oxford Diaries and the First Rise of Methodism' (*Methodist History*, XII, no. 4, July 1974, pp.110-135), Dr Richard Heitzenrater states that the often-reproduced picture *The Holy Club in Session* gives a false concept of the club. He says, 'It was not an organized body with elected officers, but was rather a spontaneous fellowship of men who sought the assistance of one another as an aid to personal discipline and religious growth.' He points out that the men portrayed in the picture were never all at Oxford at the same time.

10. *George Whitefield's Journals*, Banner of Truth Trust, London (1960), p.48.

11. Stevenson, *Wesley Family*, p.131. The 'castle' was one of Oxford's two prisons.

12. *Ibid.*, p.30. Telford, *Charles Wesley*, p.28, says that having been a King's Scholar at Westminster Charles had received a studentship valued at £100 a year during his course at Oxford, but there is no evidence that this was so.

13. Several authors have failed to recognize that John applied to succeed his father in the living at Epworth. But Broughton's letter, reporting the refusal, is given in Luke Tyerman's *The Life and Times of John Wesley*, Hodder & Stoughton, London (1880), vol. 1, pp.102-104. John Telford (editor of John's *Letters*) says, 'Wesley evidently yielded to family pressure, and afterwards was willing to take the living; but it was given to another' (John Wesley, *Letters*, vol.1, p.166). V. H. H. Green states, 'It seems ultimately that John Wesley intimated he would be willing to take the living...but by that time it had been offered to and accepted by Samuel Hurst' (Green, *Young Mr Wesley*, Edward Arnold, London (1961) p.246).

14. Baker, *Charles Wesley Revealed in his Letters*, p.19.

15. *Ibid.*

16. Stevenson, *Wesley Family*, p.150.

17. Telford, *Charles Wesley*, p.41.
18. While visiting Samuel and his wife Charles wrote, 'I reproved my sister-in-law...for evil speaking... Quite wearied out by her incessant slanders, today I had a downright quarrel with her about it. My brother, on these occasions, is either silent, or on my side' (*Journal*, vol.1, p.80).
19. Stevenson, *Wesley Family*, p.367.

Chapter 4
1. Baker, *Charles Wesley Revealed in his Letters*, p.20.
2. Kirk, *Mother of the Wesleys*, p.218.
3. John Wesley, *Journal*, Epworth Press, London (1938), vol.1, pp.135-6.
4. L.Tyerman, *The Oxford Methodists*, Hodder & Stoughton, London (1876), p.74.
5. John Wesley, *Journal*, vol.1, pp.142-3.
6. The portion of Charles Wesley's *Journal* that has been published begins at this point.
7. *Journal*, vol.1, pp.1-2.
8. *Journal*, vol.1, p.4.
9. *Journal*, vol.1, p.9.
10. *Journal*, vol.1, p.9.
11. *Journal*, vol.1, p.3.
12. *Journal*, vol.1, p.6.
13. *Journal*, vol.1, p.5.
14. *Journal*, vol.1, p.15.
15. *Journal*, vol.1, p.17.
16. *Journal*, (special edition by Colley, London 1909), p.36.
17. *Journal*, vol.1, p.20.
18. *Journal*, vol.1, p.21.
19. *Journal*, vol.1, p.22.
20. *Journal*, vol.1, p.4.
21. *Journal*, vol.1, p.27.
22. *Journal*, vol.1, pp.35-6.
23. *Journal*, vol.1, p.46.
24. *Journal*, vol.1, p.49.

Chapter 5
1. *Journal*, vol.1, p.58.
2. *Journal*, vol.1, p.68.
3. *Journal*, vol.1, p.72.
4. *Journal*, vol.1, p.73.
5. *Journal*, vol.1, p.74.
6. *Journal*, vol.1, p.74.

7. *Journal*, vol.1, p.75.
8. *Journal*, vol.1, p.76.
9. Whitefield was converted in the very month that Samuel Wesley, on his deathbed, had assured Charles that 'The Christian faith shall surely revive in this kingdom. You will see it, though I shall not.'
10. *Journal*, vol.1, p.79.
11. John Wesley, *Journal* vol.1, p.422.
12. When Whitefield reached Georgia he knew of Wesley's failure there and that reports of his faulty behaviour were being circulated in England. Wesley needed commendation and this he gave in an exaggerated form, saying, 'The good Mr Wesley has done, under God, in America is inexpressible. His name is very precious among the people' (*Whitefield's Journals*, p.157). In republishing the *Journal* later, knowing the statement was an exaggeration, he deleted it, not out of any desire to disparage Wesley, but to make his record more reliable.
13. *Journal*, vol.1, p.82.
14. John Wesley, *Journal*, vol. 1, p.440.
15. *Ibid.*, p.442.
16. *Journal*, vol.1, pp.84-85.
17. *Journal*, vol.1, p.85.
18. *Journal*, vol.1, p.86.
19. *Journal*, vol.1, p.87.
20. *Journal*, vol.1, p.88.
21. William Holland, *A Narrative of the Work of the Lord in England*. Manuscript in the possession of the Moravian Church Library, Muswell Hill, London.
22. *Journal*, vol.1, p.89.
23. *Journal*, vol.1, p.89.
24. *Journal*, vol.1, p.90.
25. *Journal*, vol.1, p.91.
26. *Journal*, vol.1, p.92.
27. John Wesley, *Journal*, vol.1, p.476. John here emphasizes the personal pronouns. Martin Luther had expended some lines in doing the same in his *Commentary*.
28. *Journal*, vol.1, p.95.

Chapter 6
1. Stevenson, *Wesley Family*, p.217.
2. *Journal*, vol.1, p.96.
3. *Journal*, vol.1, p.96.
4. *Journal*, vol.1, pp.98-9.
5. *Journal*, vol.1, p.99.

6. *Journal*, vol.1, p.125.
7. *Journal*, vol.1, pp.96, 100-101.
8. *Journal*, vol.1, p.102.
9. *Journal*, vol.1, p.112.
10. *Journal*, vol.1, p.100.
11. *Journal*, vol.1, p.102.
12. John Wesley, *Journal*, vol.1, p.482.
13. *Ibid.*
14. *Journal*, vol.1, p.129.
15. *Journal*, vol.1, p.109.
16. *Journal*, vol.1, p.130.
17. *Journal*, vol.1, p.133.
18. *Journal*, vol.1, p.117.
19. *Journal*, vol.1, p.120.
20. *Journal*, vol.1, p.121.
21. *Journal*, vol.1, p.123.
22. *Journal*, vol.1, p.123.
23. J.E. Hutton, *A History of the Moravian Church*, London (1909), p.274.
24. John Wesley, *Letters*, vol.1, p.261.
25. *Journal*, vol.1, p.139.
26. John Gillies, *Memoirs of the Life of George Whitefield, M.A.*, Dilly, London (1772), p.34, footnote.
27. John Wesley, *Journal*, vol.2, p.121.

Chapter 7

1. Richard Bennett, *The Early Life of Howell Harris*, (Welsh ed. 1909, English edition, Banner of Truth Trust 1962, pp.41-42).
2. Gillies, *George Whitefield*, pp.37-8.
3. *Journal*, vol.1, p.146.
4. *Journal*, vol.1, p.151.
5. *Journal*, vol.1, p.150.
6. *Journal*, vol.1, p.155.
7. *Journal*, vol.1, p.155.
8. *Journal*, vol.1, p.157.
9. *Journal*, vol.1, p.157.
10. *Journal*, vol.1, p.158.
11. *Journal*, vol.1, pp 158-9. 'J. Hutchins' was really John Hutchings, a member of the Holy Club. Both Whitefield and the Wesleys had hopes of his becoming an evangelist. But he was apparently not strong physically and, marrying into one of the wealthy Moravian families, was not heard of afterwards in evangelistic circles.
12. *Journal*, vol.1, p.135. Charles first met Seward on 13 November 1738.

13. *Journal*, vol.1, p.161.
14. *Journal*, vol.1, p.163.
15. *Journal*, vol.1, pp.163-4.
16. *Journal*, voľ.1, pp.164-5.
17. *Journal*, vol.1, pp.169-70.
18. *Journal*, vol.1, p.170.
19. *Journal*, vol.1, p.171.
20. *Journal*, vol.1, p.170.
21. *Journal*, vol.1, p.171.
22. *Journal*, vol.1, p.173.
23. *Journal*, vol.1, p.174.
24. Quoted from an article by the Rev. Dr Geoffrey F. Nuttall in the *Proceedings of the Wesley Historical Society*, vol.XLII, part 6, pp.183-5. The 'bills' were personal notes from hearers, telling of their spiritual need and asking Charles to pray for them.
25. *Journal*, vol.1, pp.173-4.

Chapter 8

1. Hutton, *History of Moravian Church*, p.206.
2. *Journal*, vol.1, p.206.
3. *Journal*, vol.1, p.206.
4. The Rev. George Stonehouse was the rector of St Mary's, Islington, and Charles had frequently assisted him, but was not officially his curate. Stonehouse was independently wealthy. He now resigned his position and joined the Moravians.
5. *Journal*, vol.1, p.207.
6. *Journal*, vol.1, p.212.
7. *Journal*, vol.1, p.213.
8. *Journal*, vol.1, p.223.
9. *Journal*, vol.1, p.228.
10. *Journal*, vol.1, p.237.
11. John Wesley, *Journal*, vol.2, pp.221-2.
12. *Ibid.*, p.226.
13. They also took place for a time under the ministry of John Cennick, who was then working with Wesley at Kingswood. But Cennick disliked them and they soon ceased.
14. John Wesley, *Journal*, vol.1, p.307.
15. John Wesley, *Sermons on Several Occasions*, p.366.
16. *Ibid.*, p.367.
17. *The Journal of the Welsh Presbyterian Historical Society*, XXXVLL, no.2, p.80.
18. *The Moravian Messenger*, vol.XVL.
19. This matter is reported more fully in A. Dallimore, *Life of George Whitefield*, Banner of Truth Trust, vol.2, pp.71-2.

20. 'A Letter to the Rev. Mr John Wesley in Answer to his Sermon Entitled "Free Grace" ', published in America in December 1740 and in London in March 1741, republished in the 1834 edition of Gillies' *George Whitefield*, pp.626-642.

Among the several mistakes in the addition made to this work by Aaron Seymour a serious one is the inclusion of a letter Whitefield wrote to some unknown young man and the assumption (following Robert Southey) that this letter was written to Wesley (p.61). This error has been copied by numerous authors.
21. Tyerman, *George Whitefield*, vol.1, p.482.
22. *Journal*, vol.1, p.275.
23. *Journal*, vol.1, p.291.
24. *Journal*, vol.1, p.294.
25. Whitefield, *Works*, Dilly Edinburgh (1771) vol.2, p.77.

Chapter 9

1. *Journal*, vol.1, p.260.
2. An officer charged with the collection of revenues and the administration of justice.
3. *Journal*, vol.1, p.260.
4. *Journal*, vol.1, p.261.
5. *Journal*, vol.1, p.261.
6. *Journal*, vol.1, under the dates indicated for 1741.
7. *Journal*, vol.1, p.287.
8. *Journal*, vol.1, p.289.

Chapter 10

1. Stevenson, *Wesley Family*, p.222.
2. *Ibid.*
3. *Ibid.*, p.223.
4. *Ibid.*, p.225.
5. Susanna Wesley is buried in the Bunhill Fields Cemetery, across the road from Wesley's Chapel in City Road, London.
6. Stevenson, *Wesley Family*, p.217.
7. *Journal*, vol.1, p.307.
8. *Journal*, vol.1, p.308.
9. *Journal*, vol.1, pp.309-10.
10. *Journal*, vol.1, pp 310-11.
11. *Journal*, vol.1, p.312.
12. *Journal*, vol.1, p.313.
13. *Journal*, vol.1, p.315.
14. *Journal*, vol.1, p.315.
15. *Journal*, vol.1, p.317.
16. *Journal*, vol.1, pp.324-5.

17. *Journal*, vol.1, pp.325-6.
18. *Journal*, vol.1, p.326.
19. *Journal*, vol.1, p.328.
20. *Journal*, vol.1, p.326.
21. *Journal*, vol.1, p.325.
22. *Journal*, vol.1, p.327.
23. *Journal*, vol.1, p.329.
24. *Journal*, vol.1, p.332.
25. *Journal*, vol.1, p.333.

Chapter 11
1. *Journal*, vol.1, pp.337-8.
2. *Journal*, vol.1, p.345.
3. *Journal*, vol.1, p.346.
4. *Journal*, vol.1, p.347.
5. *Journal*, vol.1, p.349.
6. *Journal*, vol.1, p.350.
7. *Journal*, vol.1, p.350.
8. *Journal*, vol.1, p.354.
9. *Journal*, vol.1, p.367.
10. *Journal*, vol.1, p.370.
11. *Journal*, vol.1, p.375.
12. See Dallimore, *George Whitefield*, vol.2, pp. 149-159.
13. In 1753 Ingham and his followers withdrew from Moravianism.
14. *Journal*, vol.1, p.365.
15. *Journal*, vol.1, p.366.
16. T. Beynon ed., *Howell Harris's Visits to London*, Cambrian News Press, Aberystwyth (1960), p.65.
17. Whitefield, *Works*, pp.128-9.
18. *Journal*, vol.1., p.393.
19. Baker, *Charles Wesley Revealed in his Letters*, p.54.
20. *Journal*, vol.1., p.390.
21. John Wesley, *Journal*, vol.3., p.123.
22. *Journal*, vol.1, p.403.
23. *Journal*, vol.1, p.406.
24. *Journal*, vol.1, p.420.
25. *Journal*, vol.1, p.420.
26. *Journal*, vol.1, p.427.
27. *Journal*, vol.1, p.428.
28. *Journal*, vol.1, p.442.
29. *Journal*, vol.1, p.443.
30. *Journal*, vol.1, p.444.
31. *Journal*, vol.1, p.445.
32. *Journal*, vol.1, pp.446-7.

33. *Journal*, vol.1, p.448.
34. *Journal*, vol.1, p.448.
35. *Journal*, vol.1, p.449.
36. *Journal*, vol.1, pp.459-60.
37. John Wesley, *Journal*, vol.5., p.448.

Chapter 12
1. *Journal*, vol.1, p.454.
2. *Journal*, vol.1, p.457.
3. 'Heard from Ireland how cunning, narrow and bigoted I think Bro. Charles acts against the Moravians' (*Howell Harris's Visits to London*, p.174).
4. *Journal*, vol.1, pp.458-9.
5. *Journal*, vol.1, p.459.
6. *Journal*, vol.1, p.460.
7. *Journal*, vol.1, p.460.
8. *Journal*, vol.1, p.461.
9. *Journal*, vol.1, p.460.
10. *Journal*, vol.1, pp.463-4.
11. *Journal*, vol.1, pp.462-3.
12. Baker, *Charles Wesley Revealed in his Letters*, p.46.
13. *Ibid.* Dr Baker states that the italicized words are in cipher in the original letter.
14. *Journal*, vol.1, p.463.
15. *Journal*, vol.1, p.463.
16. *Journal*, vol.1, p.465.
17. *Journal*, vol.2, p.6.
18. *Journal*, vol.2, p.2.
19. *Journal*, vol.2, pp.3-5.
20. *Journal*, vol.2, pp.10-11.
21. *Journal*, vol.2, p.11.

Chapter 13
1. *Journal*, vol.1, p.455.
2. *Ibid.*
3. Baker, *Charles Wesley Revealed in his Letters*, p.55
4. *Journal*, vol.1, p.35.
5. *Journal*, vol.1, p.151.
6. *Journal*, vol.1, p.151.
7. Baker, *Charles Wesley Revealed in his Letters*, p.56
8. *Journal*, vol.2, p.12.
9. *Journal*, vol.2, p.11.
10. *Journal*, vol.2, pp.11-12.
11. *Journal*, vol.2, p.15.

12. Baker, *Charles Wesley Revealed in his Letters,* p.57
13. *Journal,* vol.1, p.20.
14. *Journal,* vol.1, p.19.
15. Baker, *Charles Wesley Revealed in his Letters,* pp.58-9
16. *Journal,* vol.2, p.31.
17. *Journal,* vol.2, p.37.
18. *Journal,* vol.2, p.41.
19. *Journal,* vol.2, p.44.
20. *Journal,* vol.2, p.45.
21. *Journal,* vol.2, p.45.
22. Baker, *Charles Wesley Revealed in his Letters,* p.62
23. *Journal,* vol.2, p.45.
24. Baker, *Charles Wesley Revealed in his Letters,* p.62
25. *Ibid.,* p.63.
26. *Journal,* vol.2, p.51.
27. *Journal,* vol.2, p.51.
28. *Journal,* vol.2, p.54.
29. *Journal,* vol.2, p.55.
30. *Journal,* vol.2, p.56.
31. *Journal,* vol.2, p.58.
32. Baker, *Charles Wesley Revealed in his Letters,* p.69
33. *Journal,* vol.2, p.61.

Chapter 14
1. The matter of *'spousals de futuro'* and *'spousals de praesenti'* is fully examined in articles by two Methodist scholars. The first is 'John Wesley's First Marriage', by Frank Baker in the *London Quarterly and Holborn Review,* vol. 192, no. 3, October 1967, p. 305. The second is 'John Wesley's Only Marriage' by Frederick E. Maser in *Methodist History,* October 1977.
2. John Wesley, *Journal,* vol.3, p.439.
3. *Ibid.*
4. *Ibid.* pp.438-440.
5. *Ibid.* p.514, footnote.
6. *Journal,* vol.2, p.78.
7. L. Tyerman, *John Wesley,* vol.1, p.432.
8. *Ibid.,* vol.2, p.105. Before the marriage John drew up a statement to the effect that his wife's money would remain within her own hands, and declaring he wanted none of it for himself.
9. *Journal,* vol.2, p.79.
10. *Journal,* vol.2, p.83.
11. John Wesley, *Journal,* vol.3, p.400.
12. *Ibid.* p. 513.

Chapter 15
1. John Wesley, *Journal,* vol.3, p.453.
2. *Ibid.,* pp.456-7.
3. Tyerman, *John Wesley,* vol.2, pp. 71-72.
4. *Ibid.,* p.74.
5. 'Ew'n' in the Lincolnshire dialect means 'oven'.
6. Sir Arthur Quiller-Couch, *Hetty Wesley*, Harper, London (1903). Published frequently in subsequent years and finally by J.M. Dent & Sons (1931).
7. *Ibid.* pp.34-6.
8. Samuel had accepted the parish of Wroot, though he still held that of Epworth.
9. Original letter in the *Methodist Archives,* John Rylands University, Manchester. Quiller-Couch and certain other authors assumed this letter was written by Martha Wesley, but it is now known to have been written by Hetty.
10. Andrew Lang, after enquiring from Canon Overton, suggests that the father of Hetty's child was a man named 'Hilyard' (British Museum Add. Ms. 42711), but there is probably more truth in the suggestion of V.H.H. Green, (*Young Mr Wesley,* p.109) that it was 'a young lawyer, Will Attkins'.
11. Quiller-Couch, *Hetty Wesley,* p.235.
12. *Ibid.* pp.253-4.
13. *Ibid.* p.257.
14. *Ibid.* p.266.
15. John Wesley, *Journal,* vol.3, p.457.
16. *Journal,* vol.2, p.68.
17. *Journal,* vol.2, p.69.
18. *Journal,* vol.2, p.69.
19. The author expresses his particular thanks to Dr Frank Baker for his assistance concerning facts and dates in relation to Hetty Wesley's life.

Chapter 16
1. J. W. Laycock, *Methodist Heroes in the Great Haworth Round,* Wadsworth, Keighley (1909), pp. 184-5.
2. *Journal,* vol.1, p.413.
3. *Journal,* vol.1, p.419.
4. *Journal,* vol.1, p.428.
5. *Journal,* vol.2, p.83. Wheatley then began an independent work in Norwich.
6. *Journal,* vol.2, p.84.
7. Tyerman, *John Wesley,* vol.2, p.128.
8. Baker, *Charles Wesley Revealed in his Letters,* p.86
9. *Journal,* vol.2, pp.90-91.

10. *Journal,* vol.2, pp.90-91.
11. Baker, *Charles Wesley Revealed in his Letters,* p.83.
12. Tyerman, *John Wesley,* vol.2, pp.143-4.
13. George Osborne, ed., *The Poetical Works of John and Charles Wesley,* vol.VI, pp.67-72.
14. *Journal,* vol.2., p.81.
15. Baker, *Charles Wesley Revealed in his Letters,* p.83.
16. John S. Simon, *The Revival of Religion in England in the Eighteenth Century,* Culley, London, pp.292-3.

Chapter 17
1. Tyerman, *John Wesley,* vol.2, p.138.
2. Whitefield, *Works,* vol 3. p. 76.
3. *Journal,* vol.2, p.97.
4. *Journal,* vol.2, p.99.
5. *Journal,* vol.2, p.100.
6. *Journal,* vol.2, p.100.
7. Tyerman, *John Wesley,* vol.2, pp. 201-3. Charles uses the word 'Melchisedechians' in reference to the biblical Melchisedech, who was 'without father, without mother, without descent, having neither beginning of days...' He is belittling the lack of ordination on the part of the itinerants in so describing them.
8. *Ibid.* p.200.
9. *Ibid.* vol.1, p.508.
10. *Ibid.* vol.2, p.244.
11. Charles Wesley, 'An Epistle to the Reverend Mr John Wesley', London (1755).
12. Tyerman, *John Wesley,* vol. 2, pp.242-3.
13. *Ibid.* p.255.
14. *Ibid.* p.246.
15. *Ibid.* p.247.
16. Baker *Charles Wesley Revealed in his Letters,* p.97.
17. *Ibid.* p.98.
18. Tyerman, *John Wesley,* vol.2, p.442.
19. Frank Baker, *John Wesley and the Church of England,* Abingdon Press, Nashville, (1970), p.200.

Chapter 18
1. Printed by Lewis Timothy, Charlestown, 1737.
2. *Hymns and Sacred Poems,* 1739, 1742 (three separate books); 1749 (2 vols).
3. Frank Baker, *Charles Wesley's Verse,* Epworth Press, London (1963), p.10.
4. John Wesley, *A Collection of Hymns for the People Called Methodists,* Mason, London (1779), p.4.

5. Frank Baker, *Charles Wesley's Verse*, pp.5-6.
6. John Wesley, *Collection of Hymns for Methodists*, p.6.
7. It is said that Charles wrote one of his hymns so that it might be sung to a then common tune similar to the well-known 'Here we go round the mulberry bush...'

Chapter 19

1. *Journal*, vol.2, p.195.
2. *Journal*, vol.2, p.219.
3. *Journal*, vol.2, p.262.
4. Baker, *Charles Wesley Revealed in his Letters*, p.109.
5. *Ibid.*
6. *Ibid.*, p.111.
7. Telford, *Charles Wesley*, p.266.
8. *Journal*, vol.2, p.151.
9. Telford, *Charles Wesley*, p.261.
10. *Journal*, vol.2, p.152.
11. *Journal*, vol.2, pp.154-5.
12. Telford, *Charles Wesley*, pp.264-5. On this occasion John Wesley wore his gown and bands and his wife came in rich silks and ruffles.
13. Original letter in *Methodist Archives*, John Rylands University, Manchester.

Chapter 20

1. Journal, vol.1, p.419
2. 'An Epistle to the Rev. George Whitefield,' *The Wesleys' Poetical Works*, vol.VI, pp.67-72.
3. See pp.93-94.
4. Whitefield, *Works*, vol.2, p. 464.
5. 'Epistle to Whitefield', p.287.
6. *Journal*, vol.2, p.81.
7. *Journal*, vol.2, p.87.
8. See Dallimore, *George Whitefield*, vol.1., pp.381-3.
9. *Journal*, vol.2, p.247.
10. An attitude in which it is assumed that because a person is 'justified by faith', he is thereafter under no obligation to live righteously or to perform good works.
11. Tyerman, *John Wesley*, vol.3, p.73.
12. Wesley's men used the following titles to refer to the Hill brothers and Toplady: 'devil factors', 'Satan's synagogue', 'children of the old roaring hellish murderer who believed his lie', 'advocates for sin', 'witnesses for the father of lies', 'blasphemers', 'Satan-sent preachers', 'devils', 'liars' and 'fiends' (Seymour, *The Life*

and Times of Selina, Countess of Huntingdon, vol.1, p.475). Certain
authors have mistakenly attributed these words to the Hills and
Toplady, but they too were guilty of equally bad attitudes and
statements.

13. *Ibid.*
14. *Journal,* vol.2, pp.418-31.
15. Baker, *Charles Wesley Revealed in his Letters,* p.131.

Chapter 21
 1. *Sacred Songs and Solos,* Marshall, Morgan & Scott, London, no.889.
 2. *Journal,* vol.2, pp.285-6.
 3. Telford, *Charles Wesley,* p.269.
 4. *Journal,* vol.2, p.276.
 5. *Journal,* vol.2, p.277.
 6. Stevenson, *Wesley Family,* p.509.
 7. Baker, *Charles Wesley Revealed in his Letters,* p.137.
 8. Telford, *Charles Wesley,* pp.275-6.
 9. Tyerman, *John Wesley,* vol.3, p.525.

Select bibliography

Wesley, Charles. *The Journal of, to which are appended selections from his correspondence and poetry,* ed. Thomas Jackson, London, 1849, 2 vols, reprinted 1980 by Baker Book House, Grand Rapids, Michigan.

Baker, Frank. *Charles Wesley as revealed by his letters,* Epworth Press, London, c. 1948.

Baker, Frank. *Charles Wesley's verse,* Epworth Press, London, 1964.

Bird, Frederick Mayer. *Charles Wesley and Methodist hymns,* Warren F. Draper, Andover, 1864.

Edwards, Maldyn. *Family circle: a study of the Epworth household in relation to John and Charles Wesley,* Epworth Press, London, 1949.

Flint, Charles Wesley. *Charles Wesley and his colleagues,* Public Affairs Press, Washington, D.C. 1957.

Gill, Frederick. C. *Charles Wesley the first Methodist,* Abingdon Press, New York, 1964.

Jackson, Thomas. *Memoirs of the Rev. Charles Wesley,* John Mason, London, 1848.

Kirk, John. *The mother of the Wesleys,* Jarrold and Sons, London, 1868.

Laycock, J. W. *Methodist heroes in the great Haworth round,* Wadsworth, Keighley, 1909.

Rattenbury, John Ernest. *The evangelical doctrines of Charles Wesley's hymns,* Epworth Press, London, 1954.

Simon, John S. *The revival of religion in the eighteenth century,* Robert Culley, London.

Stevenson, George J. *Memorials of the Wesley family,* Partridge & Co., London, 1876.

Whitehead, John. *Lives of John and Charles Wesley,* Worthington, New York.

Wood, A. Skevington. *The inextinguishable blaze,* Paternoster Press, London, 1960.